11. Freydís Eiríksdóttir
12. Ilona Zrínyi
13. Mother Lü
14. Sor Juana Inés de la Cruz
15. Sojourner Truth

16. Naziq al-Abid
17. Zelia Nuttall
18. Susan La Flesche Picotte
19. Molly Craig
20. Sister Rosetta Tharpe

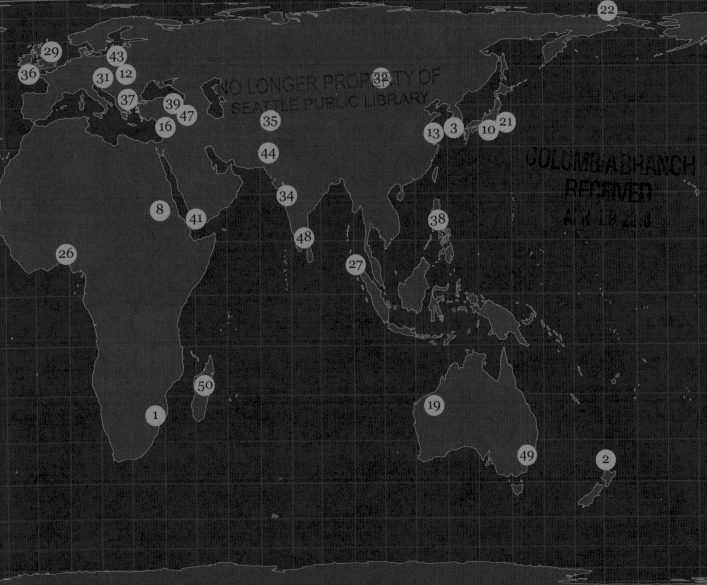

36. Jeanne de Clisson
37. Olympias of Macedon
38. Trinidad Tecson
39. Tamar of Georgia
40. Marsha P. Johnson

41. Arwa al-Sulayhi
42. Fannie Lou Hamer
43. Irena Sendler
44. Benazir Bhutto
45. Carolina Maria de Jesus

46. Juana Azurduy de Padilla
47. Pailadzo Captanian
48. Velu Nachiyar
49. Kate Leigh & Tilly Devine
50. Ranavalona I

# Tough Mothers

A REJECTED PRINCESSES BOOK

# Tough Mothers

## Amazing Stories of History's Mightiest Matriarchs

# JASON PORATH

DEY ST.

*An Imprint of* WILLIAM MORROW

**DEY ST.**

HarperCollins books may be purchased for educational, business, or sales promotional use. For information, please email the Special Markets Department at SPsales@harpercollins.com.

FIRST EDITION

Library of Congress Cataloging-in-Publication Data has been applied for.

ISBN 978-0-06-279609-7

18 19 20 21 22    QG    10 9 8 7 6 5 4 3 2 1

To my mom, toughest of all.

May I one day be as capable as you.

And to Jeremy, who hates the spotlight.

May I one day be as generous as you.

# Contents

INTRODUCTION ix

HOLD UP A SECOND! xi

Labotsibeni Gwamile LaMdluli (C. 1858–1925, SWAZILAND) .................................................. 1

Te Ao-Kapurangi (19TH CENTURY, NEW ZEALAND) ..................................................... 5

Man-deok Kim (1739–1812, KOREA) ...................................................................... 7

Vera Peters (1911–1993, CANADA) ....................................................................... 11

Jigonhsaseh (12TH CENTURY, UNITED STATES [HAUDENOSAUNEE CONFEDERACY]) ................... 15

Rebecca Lukens (1794–1854, UNITED STATES) ......................................................... 19

Bella Abzug (1920–1998, UNITED STATES) .............................................................. 23

Amanirenas (C. 60 BCE–C. 10 BCE, SUDAN [KINGDOM OF KUSH]) .................................... 29

Madam C. J. Walker (Sarah Breedlove) (1867–1919, UNITED STATES) ............................ 33

Masako Hōjō (1157–1225, JAPAN) ........................................................................ 39

Freydís Eiríksdóttir (10TH CENTURY, NORWAY/CANADA [VINLAND]) ............................... 43

Ilona Zrínyi (1643–1703, HUNGARY/CROATIA) .......................................................... 45

Mother Lü (1ST CENTURY, CHINA) ....................................................................... 49

Sor Juana Inés de la Cruz (1651–1695, MEXICO) ..................................................... 51

Sojourner Truth (1797–1883, UNITED STATES) ......................................................... 57

Naziq al-Abid (1898–1959, SYRIA) ........................................................................ 63

Zelia Nuttall (1857–1933, MEXICO) ....................................................................... 67

Susan La Flesche Picotte (1865–1915, OMAHA NATION/UNITED STATES) ........................... 71

Molly Craig (C. 1917–2004, AUSTRALIA) .................................................................. 77

Sister Rosetta Tharpe (1915–1973, UNITED STATES) ............................................. 81

Sutematsu Ōyama (1860–1919, JAPAN/UNITED STATES) ..................................... 85

Ada Blackjack (1898–1983, SIBERIA/ALASKA/UNITED STATES) ............................ 89

The Mirabal Sisters (1924/27/35–1960, DOMINICAN REPUBLIC) ....................... 97

Angela Jiménez (1896–1982, MEXICO/UNITED STATES) ..................................... 101

Marie Equi (1872–1952, UNITED STATES) ............................................................. 107

Funmilayo Ransome-Kuti (1900–1978, NIGERIA) .............................................. 113

Cut Nyak Dhien (1848–1908, INDONESIA [ACEH]) ............................................... 119

Isabel Godin des Odonais (1728–1792, ECUADOR [VICEROYALTY OF PERU]) ........ 123

Isabella of France (C. 1295–1358, FRANCE/ENGLAND) ...................................... 127

Sacajawea (1788–1812, UNITED STATES) .............................................................. 131

Mandukhai Khatun (1448–1510, MONGOLIA) ................................................... 137

Ida Laura Pfeiffer (1797–1857, AUSTRIA) .......................................................... 141

Mother Jones (Mary Harris Jones) (1837–1930, UNITED STATES) ..................... 145

Savitribai Phule (1831–1897, INDIA) .................................................................. 151

Soraya Tarzi (1899–1968, AFGHANISTAN) ........................................................... 155

Jeanne de Clisson (1300–1359, FRANCE) ........................................................... 159

Olympias of Macedon (C. 375–316 BCE, GREECE) ............................................. 163

Trinidad Tecson (1848–1928, PHILIPPINES) ....................................................... 167

Tamar of Georgia (1160–1213, GEORGIA) .................................................... 171

Marsha P. Johnson (1944–1992, UNITED STATES) ......................................... 175

Arwa al-Sulayhi (C. 1048–1138, YEMEN) ..................................................... 179

Fannie Lou Hamer (1917–1977, UNITED STATES) .......................................... 183

Irena Sendler (1910–2008, POLAND) ........................................................... 189

Benazir Bhutto (1953–2007, PAKISTAN) ...................................................... 193

Carolina Maria de Jesus (1914–1977, BRAZIL) ............................................. 199

Juana Azurduy de Padilla (1780–1862, BOLIVIA/ARGENTINA) ....................... 203

Pailadzo Captanian (1882–1968, ARMENIA/UNITED STATES) ......................... 207

Velu Nachiyar (1730–1796, INDIA) ............................................................... 211

Kate Leigh (1881–1964, AUSTRALIA) and Tilly Devine (1900–1970, AUSTRALIA) .................... 215

Ranavalona I (1778–1861, MADAGASCAR) ................................................... 219

OTHER NOTABLES 226

IT DOESN'T HAVE TO STOP HERE! 229

ACKNOWLEDGMENTS 230

BIBLIOGRAPHY 231

INDEX 241

# Introduction

There are two origin stories for this project. The short version is a lunchtime conversation between coworkers at DreamWorks, spitballing the worst ideas possible for an animated princess movie. One of them leaves the studio and develops the idea; it goes viral and there's a series of books. Short, simple, easy.

The longer origin story is about my mother.

Here are some things you need to know about my mom. Her anniversary presents from my stepdad early in their marriage included a flamethrower, a chainsaw, and a power scythe.* In her fifties, she reshingled the roof to our house by herself, refusing to let me or any of my legion of brothers† help, because we wouldn't do as good a job (she was probably right). When she decided to make a website for her jewelry business (after she taught herself to make jewelry), she made it by herself, in secret, teaching herself how to code too. She did so knowing full well that half of the family are software engineers. She didn't want help. And she made a great website.

---

\* I didn't know they were a thing either.

† I have seven brothers, no sisters. Yes, my mother is a very patient woman.

Despite all that, when she was growing up my mother was a pariah.

My mom was born in Kentucky in the 1940s. It was not a world with a place for women like her. She spent years trying to fit in—she was a cheerleader!—all the while suspecting that there was something different about her, that she was some sort of aberration. It wasn't until she was in her thirties that she began to flourish. She eschewed the expectations put on her and started doing what *she* wanted to do. Before long, she had her own job; she was a published author; her art was gaining notice; she had become that intensely capable person I've described to you. Faced with a world with no place for her, she *carved her own place out of granite*. And at that moment, as all doors opened to her, she asked herself: What do I really want out of life? Who do I choose to be?

And she chose to be my mom.

She never looked back on that choice. *But I did.* I remember catching glimpses of the life she'd had before, of all that she'd put down to raise me and my brothers. I continually meditated on the magnitude of that choice, unable to hold it in my head. Had she been only half herself all this time? Had she pushed her own personality, her likes and dislikes, dreams and goals, to the side, just to give me the best life possible? Is that the sacrifice all mothers make? Is it worth it? Was I worth it?

In part, I began Rejected Princesses to pay my mother back, to prove that her choice had been worth it. Of course, I was proving this to myself more than to her—she never questioned her choice even once. She knew that she didn't stop being herself just because she had her sons. If anything, she became more herself, because she'd walked down the path she wanted, of her own volition. The trade-offs she'd made, she'd make again, if she could.

But another large part of this work was to reach out to every girl who has ever been in my mom's situation, who felt they were someone for whom the world had no place. This is a book full of extreme personalities, of lives lived fully, brashly, boldly (if not always wisely). These are your mothers, your grandmothers, your birthright. You are not alone.

To the weirdos, pariahs, and aberrations: Glory in your edges and never let them dull. Don't file yourself down for anybody.

And to the mothers—mine and all others out there, giving selflessly—no words will ever be able to fully recognize all that you put aside. "Thank you" is too meager, too small, too inadequate, but it's all we have.

Thank you.

## A Note on the Scholarship

I'm not a professional historian—my background is in film criticism and animation. However, I do my damndest to make sure everything here is right (there are more than 200 citations in the back), but I'm only human. This is a book meant to inspire, illustrate, and intrigue—not to be the end point of your inquiry. My work sits on the shoulders of giants: historians who've worked tirelessly to bring these stories to light. If you are interested in learning more, I urge you to do so, using the bibliography as a starting point.

# Hold Up a Second!

## YOU SHOULD KNOW WHAT YOU'RE ABOUT TO READ

Unlike what you may be used to reading, **this book doesn't pull punches**. It's not censored. Sometimes there's rough content.

Not every entry is suitable for every reader (despite the cartoony demeanor). To accommodate readers of all ages, this book is arranged by maturity level, not alphabetically by name. (For an alphabetical list, check the index.)

The following guide markers can help you decide what's a good fit for you.

As the book goes on, the icons change from green to yellow to red. The way to think about these divisions is, how much evil are you comfortable with in the world?

- Green is simple. Good beats evil, the world is moral. Think PG.

- Yellow is more complex. No black and white, just shades of gray. Think PG-13.

- Red requires maturity. You must be your own moral guide. Think R.

Additionally, look out for these icons that tell you what's in an entry.

Lastly, to highlight the continuity of history, this book points out where people in this volume and those in Volume One (*Rejected Princesses*) interact. Names in **purple** indicate figures covered in Volume One, and names in **blue** indicate figures covered in this book. Keep an eye out for them!

## On to the stories!

# Labotsibeni Gwamile LaMdluli

## (C. 1858–1925, SWAZILAND)

## *The Mother Who Bought Back Her Country*

Labotsibeni Gwamile LaMdluli was a woman of many names, the most colorful of which was likely her adopted royal name, Gwamile. The name was both a verb and adjective, meaning "to stand firm and unshakable; to be indomitable, adamant."

It was a fitting name, as Europe would come to learn.

This Swazi ruler was a shrewd negotiator even in her youth. When she was being courted by the crown prince Mbandzeni, she turned him down, teasing that she could not marry a person from a common village. Undeterred by this hard-to-get play, he went back to her after being crowned king, his new bona fides on display. This time she said yes, and within a year they had a son, Bhunu.

Gwamile's negotiation skills would prove vital, as her country was threatened by one of the dirtier tricks of the European colonizer* handbook. It went like this: they approached the king asking for land grants for mineral rights and the like. The king, not understanding the concept of private land ownership (the idea didn't exist in Swazi society, and the foreigners weren't in a hurry to explain it in depth), agreed. He viewed the money paid as tribute.

In short, Mbandzeni sold the country without realizing it. Making matters worse, he repeatedly sold the same rights to multiple people—again, not really understanding the underlying concepts—which resulted in years of skirmishes and confounding litigation.

This became Gwamile's problem in 1889, when her husband died. Her son, the newly crowned Bhunu, was no help. A petulant teen more interested in drinking and fighting than the nuances of policy, he quarreled with Gwamile and ignored her advice.† His lowest moment came when he was brought before a foreigner court for his involvement in a murder,

---

\* The who's who of all this is confusing, and changed throughout the story, but in a nutshell: initially they were dealing primarily with the South African Republic (aka Transvaal), a proto–South African state run by Dutch settlers (Boers). However, the British muscled in around 1902 and ran the show afterward. It's more complicated than that (isn't everything), so if you're looking for nuance, racism, horrific violence, and/or to have your day ruined, look into the Boer Wars!

† This wasn't a small thing. Queen Mother is an official title in Swazi society, and kings can be subject to fines for defying their mothers. For a fun thought exercise, imagine replicating this in contemporary Western society.

and had his rank downgraded from king to paramount chief. When he died suddenly five years into his reign, few regarded it as a great loss.

Suddenly, Gwamile was running the entire country. Because Bhunu's successor was his five-month-old son, Mona (later Sobhuza II), Gwamile had to run affairs until her grandson came of age. While she initially suffered some political blowback—some thought she might have assassinated her reckless son—in a testament to her political savvy, she quickly consolidated power by showing wisdom and forethought.

Part of her brilliance was to realize this was to be a long-term struggle, and to strategize when and how to fight. Having witnessed other nations destroyed and swallowed wholesale by the colonial forces, Gwamile knew Swaziland was in very real danger of the same. She brought in European-educated advisors and began fighting British schemes by British means. She sent official petitions and inquiries directly to London, asking for clarification as to the exact legal status of Swaziland and in effect gummed up the bureaucracy with paperwork. She knew the local administrators were flying by the seat of their pants, without consulting the crown. Her legal challenges sparked internal debate and bought her time.

Simultaneously, Gwamile organized a scheme to repurchase her country's lands. In this too, she was shrewd—flattering and outwardly cooperating with the British, never directly opposing the idea of carving up her country. But it was a ruse to get them to assume she was on their side. Once she had done so, she pointed out that the lands the Europeans had ostensibly bought still had Swazi people living on them. She magnanimously offered to settle the thorny matter by paying to cancel the leases. In the same way that the Europeans had sidled up with promises of friendship, she was offering to make their lives easier to achieve her own goals.

Gwamile had a deep well of money to draw from, due to a well-organized tax system she'd set up among her chiefs. Not only was this used to buy back lands, but also to open a school system—one that she made sure was free of Christian missionaries and was strictly secular. One of the first beneficiaries of this focus on education was her grandson, Sobhuza II, whom she trained to follow in her footsteps in soft opposition to the British.

Once the British realized her schemes, they flew into a rage. They called her autocratic, intemperate, and selfish. They spread lies about her embezzling the funds and tried to turn her people against her—another classic colonizer move.* The Swazis fired back, describing her as *mzimba kawudabuki ngenblamba yamadoda*: "a body that does not crack from the insults of important men." Indeed, she did not crack. Gwamile ruled until 1921, when she ceded

---

* The British did the same thing in Ghana, breaking up the Asante Confederacy with infighting, as covered in Volume One (*Rejected Princesses*) with the tale of Queen Mother **Yaa Asantewaa**.

the throne to her grandson Sobhuza II, whom she had trained well. He continued her work and by the time the nation declared independence in 1968, he'd regained over 63 percent of Swazi territory. He went on to become the longest-reigning monarch of any nation in verified history, ruling for almost 83 years straight. Under his rule, the nation's economy prospered and many of the country's older traditions were brought back. In so doing, Sobhuza II and the rest of the country made sure to recognize Gwamile as one of the nation's greatest heroes.

## · ART NOTES AND TRIVIA ·

Gwamile is pictured here inside one of the traditional huts of Swazi culture. She's guiding her young grandson's education over a map of Swazi territory. His feet are dyed red from the soil, as were Gwamile's, due to her tendency to walk across her territories.

In the background, a European man is running away from a flash flood. The man is modeled on Robert Coryndon, Resident Commissioner of Swaziland, who was one of Gwamile's most ardent opponents in her legal wrangling.

The flash flood is a reference to Gwamile's famed powers as a rainmaker. One story goes that upon being shown water pipes in Johannesburg, Gwamile replied, "When I want water, I make the rain myself." She was said to have made the rain overflow against places that she held grudges, even destroying some European mining equipment at one point.

# Te Ao-Kapurangi

## (19TH CENTURY, NEW ZEALAND)

## *The Mother Who Stuffed Her House*

The sight of Te Ao-Kapurangi was bewildering. Here was a woman who'd been kidnapped by an enemy tribe years ago, now suddenly back home, standing on a rooftop, in the middle of a war zone. But as it turned out, her homecoming was as heroic as it was confusing. For Te Ao-Kapurangi may be the only person in human history to save her people and end a war, merely by standing on a roof.*

She'd been kidnapped in 1818 by a chief of the Ngā Puhi, an aggressive Māori tribe who'd been expanding their borders through force (and guns). Being a woman of high rank, Te Ao-Kapurangi was quickly married off to the chief, even though she was already married and had two children.

According to one account, her new husband treated her well and she was well respected, so take that for what it's worth. The chief was at the least very affected by the loss of a child she bore him to accidental exposure to fire: in mourning, he took the name Te Wera ("the burning").

In 1822, it became evident that the Ngā Puhi were going to go to war against Te Ao-Kapurangi's birth tribe, the Te Arawa. She knew this would be a massacre: not only were the Te Arawa hopelessly outgunned (literally—they had one musket, the Ngā Puhi had many more), but they weren't taking the threat seriously. They'd holed up on an island, and were convinced the Ngā Puhi couldn't move a fleet of war canoes overland to attack them.

They were wrong: the Ngā Puhi were so motivated, they hacked a path through the jungle and dragged their canoes uphill.

Te Ao-Kapurangi begged the Ngā Puhi chiefs to spare her people, for they weren't involved in the revenge that motivated the war. The war chief grudgingly let her warn her relatives and allowed them to hide. So she rowed up in a canoe and yelled to warn them of danger, but they refused to go.

Upon returning, Te Ao-Kapurangi again addressed the Ngā Puhi chiefs—even once was

---

* A close runner-up may be Zhuge Liang, who, according to legend, had to defend a town against 150,000 soldiers with just 100. Flinging open the gates and hiding his soldiers, he sat alone on the city walls, strumming a lute. The enemy, convinced this was a trap, retreated. (This is likely apocryphal, but it's a great story.)

unorthodox enough for a woman!—and begged for them to spare her stubborn kinfolk. The war chief, frustrated at her obstinance, put forward a ridiculous condition: he'd let some live, but only those who passed through her legs.*

The Ngā Puhi embarked on their war canoes, circling around the island. For two full days, they menaced the Te Arawa, showing the full extent of their army. On the third day, the war chief's canoe (which also carried our heroine) landed. The war chief stood tall, chanting a war song, his steel helmet† glinting in the sun.

He was immediately shot in the head.

The Te Arawa had only one musket, but they knew how to use it. Sadly, the helmet was well-made, and the war chief was merely knocked over. He'd have a horrible headache for the next three days.

Taking advantage of the confusion, Te Ao-Kapurangi leapt out of the boat and scrambled onto the roof of a nearby building. Straddling the roof post with her legs, she yelled for her people to enter the house. Realizing what she was up to, the Te Arawa, one after another, crammed into the house—through her legs. The Ngā Puhi respected the space as a sanctuary. Some were still killed, but most were saved by packing the house like a clown car.

The next day, they established peace. Although some Ngā Puhi wanted to continue the war, Te Ao-Kapurangi's captor/husband Te Wera made them stop. Calling over Te Ao-Kapurangi's son by her first husband, Te Wera referred to him as "my child"—and in so doing, bonded the Ngā Puhi to peace. Although the Ngā Puhi would continue warring against other Māori for years to come, never again would they fight the Te Arawa.

Little is known of the rest of Te Ao-Kapurangi's life, but her deeds have not been forgotten. Indeed, she gained a sort of immortality in a Māori turn of phrase that lives on to present day: *Ano ko te whare whawhao a Te Ao-kapurangi* ("This house is as crowded as Te Ao-Kapurangi's").

## · ART NOTES AND TRIVIA ·

This is the actual meeting house upon which Te Ao-Kapurangi stood, with each carving replicated as best as possible from photo reference. It's still standing today. It took a very long time to draw.

———

* This was a Māori tradition, symbolizing rebirth.
† A gift from George IV! This dude had been to England!

# Man-deok Kim

## (1739–1812, KOREA)

## *The Mother of Jeju Island*

Man-deok Kim was dealt a rough hand in the karmic lottery. She was born on Jeju Island, a land for banished nobility—basically the Siberia of 18th century Korea. Her father, an exiled noble, married a Jeju native, but when his exile was lifted, he left her, likely without even knowing she was pregnant. Man-deok's father died in a shipwreck some years later, and her mother* died in an epidemic not long after that. This left 11-year-old Man-deok an orphan.

Things got worse before they got better. After living in squalid conditions with a relative, she caught the eye of a noblewoman—who adopted her as a *gisaeng*, an entertainer/concubine/slave of the government. While this afforded her an education and arts training, it also thrust her into the lowest rank in rigidly stratified Korean society and put her every action under a microscope. Being a gisaeng made her a commodity, and one with a short shelf life.

But she did the unthinkable: she regained her status! After learning that her father was a noble, she put her literacy to work and petitioned to be released from servitude, due to her noble birth. Although it took multiple requests, the government eventually relented. She was given the rank of commoner (a step up!), and her name was scrubbed from the official register. She was 22, and she was a free woman.

Which isn't to say she had a ton of great choices immediately available to her. As a former gisaeng, she was still on the fringes of society. Marriage would have been difficult, if not impossible, due to the stigma. Furthermore, women in that era didn't usually have jobs.

However, none of this proved an impediment for Man-deok. She opened a *gaekju*—a type of hotel for merchants—and from there, a burgeoning mercantile empire. Using every contact and skill she learned as a gisaeng, she began trading with the mainland, bringing in clothing, jewelry, and cosmetics—all niceties with which she'd developed some expertise. She sold cheap, and in volume. Not only was she Korea's first female businessperson, she was also, in short order, insanely rich.

She even, apparently, took a lover (whom she may have also employed). Although they

---

* A tangential, super-cool note: Man-deok's mom was a *haenyeo*—a sea-diving hunter local to Jeju. The industry was dominated by women, which led the island to develop a semi-matriarchal structure, since women were the primary breadwinners. Haenyeo were famously independent and headstrong, which is likely where Man-deok got her gumption from.

could not marry, they lived together. In the sources that describe their relationship, some add that the man had two daughters, whom Man-deok fostered after his death.

But as much as the world might have treated her as mere merchandise, she did not treat the world the same way. In 1792, when she was in middle age, a horrific famine struck Jeju. By 1795, it had killed a third of the population. The government tried sending relief, but several of the boats sank in violent storms. To combat this, Man-deok sold most of her belongings and used her private fortune to buy hundreds of sacks of rice, which she freely gave to Jeju residents, saving the lives of thousands.*

When word of her deeds reached the ear of the king, he was so moved that he offered her a boon—material goods, a noble rank, whatever she wanted. Her request was simple: she merely wanted to travel outside of Jeju, to see scenic Mount Geumgang. The king not only granted her wish, but gave her a tour of his palace, a government post, a residence in Seoul, and the official title of *Uinyeo Bansu* ("medicine woman") for having looked after the people of Jeju. She lived the rest of her days peacefully, leaving much of her money to her foster children when she died.

In the years after her death, she's been celebrated across Korean culture. In 1980, an award was introduced in her name; in 2010, she got her own TV show; and in 2016, a memorial hall devoted to her opened on Jeju Island. But perhaps her greatest immortality rests in this Korean proverb: "work like a dog, spend like Man-deok."

## · ART NOTES AND TRIVIA ·

The building in the back is the gaekju inn that Man-deok operated in Geonip-dong. The man in the front is the one with whom she was partnered, and whose children (in the background) she might have helped look after. In the far background, there are rice fields, a callback to her great generosity.

It is hard to see, but she has two pupils in her left eye, a trait to which many records attested.

Lastly, the daughter in pink and white is modeled after Jeanette Wu, a reader whose translation help was essential to covering this story (and many others). Like me, she worried that the glasses would be an anachronism—thankfully, while rare, eyeglasses did exist in Korea at the time.

---

* The exact figures for this are uncertain. She's usually credited with buying 500 sacks of rice, giving away 450, and saving 50 for her relatives, thus saving around 18,000 people. One particularly bitter source claimed she took advantage of men and let her family starve prior to this, but it seems to be alone in this assessment.

# Vera Peters

(1911–1993, CANADA)

## The Mother of the Modern Mastectomy

he room was silent.

It's understandable why. Dr. Vera Peters had just done the impossible. She'd spent 30-plus years poring over the charts of more than 8,000 breast cancer patients. She'd done it by hand, in her home, after putting the kids to bed. She'd proven that the longtime standard for breast cancer treatment was not only brutal, it was unnecessary. She'd just shown her findings to the most prestigious doctors in Canada. And the room fell silent.

Gradually they began to stir. A cough here, a laugh there. Nonsense, they said, and dismissed her.

But Vera Peters would not be so easily dismissed.

She'd been through all this years before, when she'd proved Hodgkin's lymphoma was treatable. Long thought to be incurable, Hodgkin's was, at the time, a virtual death sentence to anyone diagnosed with it. Through years of patiently graphing patient outcomes, Vera had come up with a triage system that would eventually lead to a survival rate of over 80 percent.

But the medical community didn't believe her. When, in 1949, she tried to submit her study to the Canadian Medical Association, it was rejected because there were "too many tables." It took another year to find a journal that would accept it. While physicians would, after about a decade, accept her findings and change their methods, that wasn't the initial reaction. At the time, her peers' response was, as one biographer put it, "go back to Toronto and do your women's work."

It helped that she'd had a wide-ranging view on "women's work." Her father had died when she was young, and she'd grown up on a farm with her mother, aunt, three sisters, and one brother. They all pitched in to make ends meet. By age 11, Vera was milking cows at 4 AM and driving the tractor before school. Her mom and aunt encouraged her to never miss a class—a drive that baffled their rural neighbors. By 16, she'd graduated high school, at which point her family all chipped in for her to go to medical school. By age 23, she was a doctor.

While she was in med school, Vera's mother developed breast cancer. She got the only treatment available at the time: radical mastectomy, a horrifying treatment that removed most of the patient's pectoral muscle. Many patients wouldn't even have a decision in the process. They'd be sedated for a checkup, and when the cancer was found, the doctors would perform the procedure before the patient was conscious again. They would wake up with their bodies mutilated. With Vera's mother, it didn't even provide a cure—when her cancer later recurred, she died while trying an experimental treatment.

The death of her mother—and later, her sister—from breast cancer helped inform Vera's entire professional career. Not only did she specialize in radiation, but she adopted a border-line-heretical patient approach: including them in treatment decisions. Before approaching a patient with a choice, she would collect as much information as possible about their condition, often finding cancerous lymph nodes that others missed. This resulted in her settling on a better treatment for breast cancer: the lumpectomy, where the doctor identifies all cancerous regions, and focuses treatment only there.

In promoting the lumpectomy, she faced the same uphill battle she'd faced a decade earlier, despite her study spanning over 8,000 patients. When Vera gave a speech about it at an American conference in 1968, she was, in her words, "refuted and shunned by most of the outstanding surgeons in the States." Another oncologist around the same time referred to her paper and "was nearly killed for it." The establishment believed they had the last treatment they'd ever need.

As radical as her approach was, she was far from radical in her personal life. Outside of work, she was Mrs. Lobb, loving mother of two, who made sure to eat dinner every night with her husband and two daughters. Having grown up poor, she enjoyed treating herself to nice clothes, and made sure her hair was always well coiffed. She picked berries and enjoyed making jam and pie. Vera mentored many young female doctors, mothering them with the same care she showed her children and patients. She was soft-spoken and hated arguing, which drove her to be that much more careful about her data. She let the work speak for itself.

And eventually, it did. Similar to their reaction to her work with Hodgkin's, after over a decade the rest of the medical community adopted her methods. She was vindicated.

Vera died of lung cancer in 1993, a result of endless nights with a cigarette in one hand and a stack of papers in the other. Shortly before her death, she used her status to release a paper promoting her last revolutionary idea: choice. "I would like a decision made by a discussion among my physician, my surgeon, my radiotherapy consultant, but most particularly myself," she wrote, "because it's my body and I would like to be able to determine my risk if I have radiation, my risks if I have surgical operation, and all the possibilities that might ensue if I live 20 years."

After her death, Vera was lionized by the medical community. She received a smattering of awards, and was posthumously inducted into the Canadian Medical Hall of Fame. And in 2014, Charles Hayter, a playwright/oncologist, commemorated her story in a new play, *Radical*. The entry line ran around the block, and included former cancer patients, a Member of Parliament, scores of physicians, and one very special doctor: Vera's daughter Jenny Ingram, who'd followed in her mother's footsteps.

### · ART NOTES AND TRIVIA ·

Vera is seen here working late at night at her kitchen table, cigarettes and coffee at the ready. Her daughters are coming to peek in on what she's doing, and one is trying to help her out. In the background is a calendar with a diagram of the lymphatic system, and a picture of her mentor, Dr. Gordon Richards.

# Jigonhsaseh

## The Mother of Nations

Nobody could say how long the nations had fought. Mohawk, Onondaga, Oneida, Cayuga, Seneca—they'd warred so long that entire traditions had developed around the conflict. One went like this: the Clan Mothers of any neutral villages had to feed passing war parties, regardless of tribe. In exchange, no harm would come to their village. Kind of a protection racket.

This continued until one day a woman altered the tradition and in so doing helped end the endless war. Her name was Jigonhsaseh.[*] She united the nations and made a constitution so strong that America's Founding Fathers would try to emulate it come 1776.

Jigonhsaseh was a farmer, not a warrior. Originally from a different area, she'd come to convince the people of what is now northern New York State to farm instead of hunting for their food. She settled at the border of several nations, and lived there so long she gained their respect, serving as mediator in intertribal disputes. Thus, when the Great Peacemaker set out on his journey to end the wars, it was only natural that his first stop would be to Jigonhsaseh.

The Great Peacemaker, in most versions of this story, is the main character.[†] Although details of his origins vary wildly from tradition to tradition,[‡] ultimately, he was a man whose experiences had led him to pacifism. Most of his ideas sounded downright Buddhist: confront your pain and fear, and focus on personal growth. "Thinking will replace killing," he envisioned, "and there will be one commonwealth." To help make this a reality, he approached the most politically powerful woman around: Jigonhsaseh.

"Your message is good," she replied. But, she pointed out, it needed to be more concrete. "What form shall this message take when it comes to dwell among people?" That is to say, theory is great, but what's your concrete plan?

We shall make a longhouse, he replied. It will have many hearths, one for each nation,

---

[*] Whose name translates roughly to "New Face of Corn," and indicates a sense of rebirth. Most traditions indicate she was also the reincarnation of Lynx, one of the deities of the Iroquois creation myth.

[†] Most surviving versions of the story are the men's tales. The women had a different tradition, one that European visitors blithely neglected to record and has not survived the years well.

[‡] At birth, his given name was Deganawidah, a name that Iroquois tradition dictates be used only respectfully and only in discussions of this story. Most traditions add that he was the reincarnation of Sapling, one of Lynx's children—thus making him the sort-of child of Jigonhsaseh, weirdly enough.

but ultimately still run under the auspices of a single chief mother: the Mother of Nations, Jigonhsaseh.

Undoubtedly flattered by the proposal, she moved on to negotiate other specifics—including ensuring the place of women under his proposed Great Law. Once that was ensured, she began spreading the Great Peacemaker's message in an ingenious way: she altered the custom regarding housing warriors. Traveling to Clan Mother after Clan Mother, Jigonhsaseh convinced them all to give visiting war parties something extra in addition to the free food: a lecture on pacifism.

While the Peacemaker continued his adventures, including healing a cannibal (Ayonwatha, also known as Hiawatha), she continued the hard work of coalition building. She regularly had to evade cannibals while journeying to council meetings, but her labor eventually brought success. Ultimately, the combined forces of Jigonhsaseh, the Peacemaker, and Ayonwatha brought the five nations together under one banner—except for one holdout, Tadodaho: a mad sorcerer with snakes living in his gnarled hair.

After Ayonwatha and the Peacemaker failed twice to get Tadodaho to join them, Jigonhsaseh had an idea. Under her guidance, the trio gathered supporters from all their nations and approached Tadodaho, silently encircling him to show their strength and unity in the face of his isolation and loneliness. They then began to sing a song of Jigonhsaseh's making:

> My offspring, I come to greet them again;
> The war chiefs, I come to greet them again;
> The body of women, I come to greet them again;
> My grandparents, it was their work;
> My grandparents, do ye continue to listen to them.

This, at last, converted Tadodaho. He agreed to join them, and in return, they offered him chairmanship of their new league. Ayonwatha combed the snakes out from his hair, straightening out his mind in the process. Thus began the long and peaceful reign of the Haudenosaunee (Longhouse) Confederacy.*

Centuries later, Benjamin Franklin and other Founding Fathers of the United States were astonished to find this society that upheld freedom of expression; regarded leaders as servants of the people; forbade unauthorized entry of homes; distributed wealth relatively

---

* Also known as the Iroquois Confederacy. The word "Haudenosaunee" means longhouse, and refers to the building in which they all dwelled. It's also the word that the Iroquois use to refer to themselves.

equitably; and provided political participation by women. "It would be a very strange thing," Franklin wrote, if the Haudenosaunee could achieve this, "and yet a like Union should be impracticable for ten or a dozen English colonies."

After Jigonhsaseh's death, women took her name as a title and continued participating in a similarly revered manner in Haudenosaunee matters. Some were brave—one spent her life fighting to protect the constitutional rights of women. Some were fearsome—one in 1687 led armies to defeat the largest European force ever assembled in North America at that time. Some were despised—one betrayed the position's neutrality by favoring one tribe over another, which led to the abolishment of the position for some time. But they were all the most sacred women to their people, the dealmakers whose word was law. And they all bore the name of one woman whose legacy would not be forgotten.

## · ART NOTES AND TRIVIA ·

Jigonhsaseh's outfit is a mix of Wyandot and Seneca styles, as those were the tribes she was from. The purple-and-white pattern on her belt clasp is the symbol of the Haudenosaunee Confederacy. To her left stands the Great Peacemaker, wearing a *gustoweh* cap with feathers arranged in the Mohawk way. As a nod to his possible Onondaga heritage, he wears a sash with the traditional Onondaga pattern. They are standing underneath a white pine, a symbol of the peace adopted by the Haudenosaunee Confederacy.

In the foreground stands Tadodaho, larger than life and scarred from years of living alone. He is stuck in the darkness, as the arrayed forces invite him into the light with Jigonhsaseh's song. He is wielding an Iroquois war club.

# Rebecca Lukens

(1794–1854, UNITED STATES)

## *The Mom with a Will of Iron*

or Rebecca Lukens, 1825 was a crap year.

In June, her husband suddenly died from fever, joining her father and two of her children, who'd died in the previous year. On his deathbed, her husband made Rebecca promise to continue running the family business, an iron working plant . . . which was heavily in debt and had a massive order to finish. Rebecca's mother, Martha, was so dead set against Rebecca running the plant, she began trying to repossess it.

And Rebecca was pregnant. With her sixth child.

In that situation, what's a woman to do? Well, if you're Rebecca Lukens, you start kicking butt.

Born Rebecca Webb Pennock, the future Mrs. Lukens was from a well-to-do Quaker family in Pennsylvania. She had a pretty sweet childhood: riding horses, getting an education, and even enjoying a fairytale romance. She and her husband fell for each other *hard* (he proposed on the second date—bold move!). Her husband integrated himself into the family quickly, going into business with Rebecca's father. The newlywed couple leased the old Brandywine Iron Works factory from Rebecca's father and began rebuilding it to get in on the manufacturing boom. It was hard work and a lot of it, but they were happy.

Then, in her words, "in summer of 1825, I lost my dear and excellent husband, and I commenced my hard and weary struggle with life."

Challenge number one was keeping the employees. According to family lore, many of the workers were packing their things and ready to leave for good when she ran out the door and called them back, one by one. As Rebecca's granddaughter later put it, Rebecca took some time to brush up on her multiplication tables, and then formally took the reins.[*]

Rebecca not only got the business back on track, she made it boom. Her task was to complete the massive order they'd just undertaken: plates for the *Codorus*, the first iron-hulled ship in the United States. Over the next 22 years, she established Brandyworks iron

---

[*] Neither of these anecdotes are historically confirmed, and are likely a bit of hyperbole, but come on. Just go with it.

as some of the highest quality on the market. When one of their suppliers provided inferior product, she was unafraid to bring them to court. She was not about to let someone walk all over her.

She overcame endless difficulties throughout all this. A financial crisis in 1837 wiped out several iron working plants—but not Rebecca's. Realizing the massive financial instability afoot, she temporarily shut down the plant and put her employees to work upgrading the facilities. When they ran out of work to do, she put them to work on her estate. Not only did her plant survive, she even retained her workers.

But by far her biggest thorn in her side was her mother, Martha. Feeling that a woman running a business was unfeminine, Martha did everything in her power to screw Rebecca over. Martha kept trying to give the plant to Rebecca's brothers—despite Rebecca having rebuilt it herself, and having paid her late father money for the privilege. But due to her father's will being poorly worded and her late husband's will being nonexistent, Rebecca had to fight her mother in court over the deed for 20 years—and when Martha died, Rebecca had to continue fighting her own brothers.

In the end, Rebecca was victorious, but she had to pay for the property two or three times over.

Rebecca's true strength in all of this was realizing she could not go it alone, and reaching out for help. She folded her family life into her professional one—she brought on her brother-in-law to help manage the plant and her daughter to serve as bookkeeper. Additionally, Rebecca relied on the religious community of Quakers for support, and continually referred to the religion's *Rules of Discipline* to conduct business in a moral manner.

After Rebecca spent 22 years hard at work, her health began to decline, and in 1847, she withdrew from running the business. By the end of her life, she'd accumulated over $100,000 in personal property, a far cry from the $15,000 of debt she'd started with. She carefully earmarked much of it for her children—she was intent on not making the same mistakes with her will as had her late father and husband.

After her death, the Brandywine Iron Works was renamed the Lukens Iron Works and later Lukens Steel in her honor. It was a Fortune 500 company for quite some time, and was managed for 125 years by her descendants. In 1994, *Fortune* magazine recognized Rebecca as America's first female industrialist leader, and inducted her into the American National Business Hall of Fame.

Much of the vibrance of Rebecca's story is due to her being able to tell it in her own words. Her diary, found some 150 years after her death, reveals the personal struggles of a woman trying to move on from tragedy. Of the early days after her husband's death, she wrote: "With some fear, but more courage, I began to struggle for a livelihood. I think at this period I must have possessed some energy of character, for now I look back and wonder at my daring. I had such strong, such powerful incentives for exertion that I felt I must succeed."

## · ART NOTES AND TRIVIA ·

This is a decently accurate representation of the Brandywine Iron Works. Thankfully, a depiction of it on a bank note survives to current day, and serves as excellent reference. The furnace embers are a bit of artistic license. Of course the iron workers would not want embers floating around a wooden building, but they added a bit of wonder to the composition.

# Bella Abzug

(1920–1998, UNITED STATES)

## The Mom Who Went to Washington

She wasn't motherly enough, the other moms said. Their protest was about to go in front of the cameras, and she wasn't good PR. "She doesn't have that innocent image of just being an angry and concerned mother of children." She was too bossy, too aggressive, too much.

It's easy to see why they felt that way. Bella Abzug (née Savitsky) was a loudmouthed wrecking ball of a human being, with a voice that, in the words of Norman Mailer, "could boil the fat off a taxicab driver's neck." He didn't like her. Lots of people didn't.

But it didn't matter. Put a wall in front of Bella Abzug and she'd tear it down. She was too "unladylike"? Well, then, she'd change your mind on what a "lady" was—and everyone else's too, while she was at it. As Geraldine Ferraro* put it, "she didn't knock lightly on the door. She didn't even push it open or batter it down. She took it off the hinges forever! So that those of us who came after could walk through."

And good God, the doors she took down. In six short years in US Congress, she pushed through an unbelievable amount of civil rights legislation, most of which the country is still debating, decades later: she ensured equal rights for women in education, made banks treat women fairly, instituted comprehensive privacy protections, mandated government disclosure of information, introduced bills for child care and LGBT rights, and got within inches of amending the Constitution itself to enshrine equality for women.† All while trying to stop the war in Vietnam, calling for Nixon's impeachment, and mothering two girls. She kept busy.

The point is—and there's a reason this entry comes early on in this book—almost everyone gets uncomfortable when women behave outside the norm. It'll happen to you too, as you read on (just wait till you get to the chapter on **Ranavalona I**)! But here's the deal: Bella, and others like her, was *necessary*. The world needed the work Bella would do, and Bella could not have done it if she was not a hemorrhoid-level pain in the ass.

---

\* The first woman to run on a major party presidential ticket in the United States; she was the Democrat's candidate for vice president in the 1984 elections.

† The pieces of legislation mentioned here were, respectively, Title IX, the Equal Credit Opportunity Act, the Privacy Act, the Freedom of Information Act, the Child Care Act, the Equality Act of 1974, and the Equal Rights Amendment (ERA). The ERA was narrowly defeated, but in the wake of the 2017 Women's March, has regained momentum, and may pass within the next couple years.

Bella started her tuchus-paining early, in her orthodox Jewish community. Already frustrated that the women had to sit in a separate section in synagogue, she grew only more so after her father died. Jewish tradition dictates that children should do daily prayers of mourning at the synagogue for a year after their parents' death, but her strict synagogue didn't allow women to do so. She ignored this prohibition and did so anyway.

As she grew up, she kept finding bigger and bigger authority figures to antagonize. In law school, she argued with her teachers (it's little wonder she'd become a professional arguer), showing many of them what to expect from this upcoming wave of female lawyers.* She also got so into activism that proto-McCarthyist New York legislators began investigating her. By the time she graduated from Columbia, her phone was already being tapped.

Now working at a law firm, she commenced fighting anyone who showed her a hint of disrespect. She butted heads with union leaders she was representing, who referred to her as a "secretary" and demanded to see their actual lawyer. She refused to blindly respect firm partners unless they respected her first. She didn't last long in that world before she went into business for herself.

The case that brought her notoriety was that of Willie McGee, a black man from Mississippi accused of raping a white woman. The charge was bogus: it was a consensual affair, and she had turned on him as an "out" for cheating on her husband. These sorts of cases were depressingly common, and played into all kinds of racist fears about out-of-control black men. Willie faced the death penalty. Nobody would take up his case. Nobody but Bella.†

The work was grueling. As the case stretched on in appeals, it became a cause célèbre: everyone from **Josephine Baker** to William Faulkner to Albert Einstein tried intervening. Unfortunately, this did little to lessen public vitriol for Willie, and for Bella. A local newspaper wrote that "they should burn Willie McGee's white woman lawyer along with him in the electric chair."

In the end, they lost the case. Come 1951, McGee was executed. Bella miscarried from the stress. She'd been eight months pregnant when she went to Mississippi in 1950. It was her third miscarriage.

To get her through, she relied heavily on the man who was her foundation: Martin Abzug, her husband. The two had met in college and married shortly thereafter. They were utterly devoted to each other, and eventually had two daughters, Liz and Eve. Martin supported Bella in every way he knew how—an activist friend described it so: "Martin

---

* This was during World War II, when women were entering the workforce in record numbers, due to the number of men off at war.

† She managed to draft two local lawyers to help, one of whom she described as a perpetually drunken war vet.

cleaned! Martin got the girls' first brassieres. Martin did everything! Martin was the guy who danced with all the frizzy wives of all the crappy Congress people. That was a *love affair. A love affair.*"

His help was necessary: Bella was often working and not at home. After the McGee case, she turned to helping those Joe McCarthy was targeting with his famous communist inquisitions. She often worked until three in the morning. Most of Liz and Eve's day-to-day care fell to Martin and the Abzugs' housekeeper, Alice Williams. Bella would make time for all their important events, like recitals and graduations, and she enjoyed teaching her daughters Joan Baez, Bob Dylan, and labor union songs. But she was also as hard on them as she was on everyone else around her, and screaming matches, especially in her daughters' teenage years, weren't uncommon.

As the McCarthy era ended, Bella began seeing the limits of the legal system. Realizing the thing to do was shape the laws instead of merely argue them, she set her sights on the biggest authority figures around. She decided to run for Congress.

It was a tough race. Her enemies spread rumors about her being antisemitic for advocating for a diplomatic approach to help Israel instead of a military one.[*] When a protestor began yelling about it at a rally, she, in characteristic Bella fashion, told an assistant, "Hit that bastard in the mouth for me, I can't do it where people see me." In the end, she won over the Jewish vote by spreading an image of herself as "a Jewish mother with her gefilte fish recipe."

She won the election, and then immediately was faced with having to run again—the electoral maps had been redrawn, and she'd have to run against a representative whose district was merged into hers. She got beaten in the follow-up election, only for her opponent to die of cancer almost immediately thereafter. She then had to run against her opponent's widow—who publicly blamed Bella for causing his death by having run against him at all.

Finally, she won, and in 1970 Shirley Chisholm[†] swore her in as a new Democrat in the House of Representatives. Her first day in office, she introduced a bill to end the Vietnam War.

Bella's race for Congress was just a preview of what she'd go through on the job. Remember that big list of accomplishments, the one at the beginning of this chapter? Understand that every single one of those was an ungodly, knock-down, drag-out fight, not unlike the McGee case or her run for office. Her staffers described working for her as getting five years of experience in a single calendar year. There's a reason one Republican referred to her as "the only man in the House."

---

[*] A staunch Zionist in her youth, Bella came to realize the horrors that had been perpetuated on the Palestinians. She supported Palestinian rights well before that was even close to being acceptable in Jewish circles.

[†] Two years later Chisholm would become the first black woman to run for president. She was a longtime ally of Bella's and an all-around rad woman.

It was that sort of respect that gave her political power. Her ideological opponents may not have liked her, but they respected her. She was willing to take an extreme position to let others look moderate. She traded votes on smaller bills to pass larger ones. She was pragmatic. She quickly mastered obscure congressional rules and got an ungodly amount of work done.

But six years in, she made a fatal mistake. She decided to run for Senate, a seat which would give her even more influence in politics. She lost by a single percentage point—devastating those who'd wanted her to stay in her safe House seat and accrue seniority in the House, becoming a lifelong influence in American politics.

After that, her political enemies worked hard to keep her from ever having influence again. In 1977, she chaired the first National Women's Conference—a huge, diverse event where over 20,000 women from all across the country and a wide range of backgrounds came together to create proposals for the president to enact into law.

It was sabotaged from the get-go. The state delegations were packed with organized opposition: one was almost entirely Ku Klux Klan members. Another brought in busloads of Mormon women and one man, who instructed them how to vote. Saboteurs would get in line to vote just to make the line longer, then leave and get back in line when they got near the front. People jammed the elevators so delegates couldn't even get to the voting area. This was largely the doing of Phyllis Schlafly and the never-to-be-sufficiently-damned antifeminist movement.

Bella managed to mitigate the chaos and rally everyone around a strong proposal—but it was for naught. Once she presented it to President Jimmy Carter, he let it sit. When members of her committee criticized him for the delay, he publicly fired Bella. Most of the rest of the advisory committee quit in protest, and the entire effort was sunk.

Bella proceeded to lose every race she entered for the rest of her life: for mayor of New York City (she was the first woman to ever run), and twice more for the House. The final blow came in 1986, when she was running for the House, a race her husband Martin didn't want her to enter. A day before the primaries, he had a heart attack and died.

Bella went to pieces. She stayed with his body for hours, unresponsive to anyone, just berating herself in a low wail. Martin had been her anchor. Her fire would never burn as brightly without him. After she lost the race, she moved in with her daughters, and lived a quieter life.

Although she was never as active again, she hardly remained idle. She worked with international organizations to help women. Much of the influence and processes that nongovernmental organizations (NGOs) have today is thanks to her.

By 1992, her health had started to fail. She was diagnosed with breast cancer and had a double mastectomy. A day after giving a 45-minute speech in front of the UN, she was hospitalized, and died shortly thereafter.

The eulogies came in from all over. Figures from United Nations Secretary-General Kofi Annan to Hillary Clinton mourned her loss. Each of them had Bella stories—of times she'd fought, of turns of phrase, of times she'd made them laugh. One of the best came from her ex-staffer Judy Berek. She talked of a campaign event she and Bella had attended, shortly after Judy had gotten divorced. Everyone was asking about Judy's husband, and it was driving her into a deep depression. Bella realized this and stood by her the whole night, deflecting any mentions of her marriage.

"The entire evening standing there with her arm around me like a human flyswatter," Judy recalled. "It could've been the worst night of my life. And she had work to do at that party; she didn't need to be standing there with one person, but it was the point at which I knew that deep down inside she was a mother."

## · ART NOTES AND TRIVIA ·

Bella is seen here working the phones late at night—as she was known to do, calling her colleagues at all hours—while Martin massages her shoulders. Atop her desk is a packed Rolodex (we used to store people's contact info in them!), a mug with her actual senatorial campaign imagery on it, and her oft-used bullhorn.

In the background are a number of magazine covers that she graced, as well as actual political signs she used or was affiliated with. Above the door is a whip, given to her by House Majority Leader Tip O'Neill when she was appointed deputy whip. Additionally, there are her two daughters and a rack full of hats (she was never seen without one).

# Amanirenas

(C. 60 BCE–C. 10 BCE, SUDAN [KINGDOM OF KUSH])

## The Mother Who Invaded Rome

**T**his is the story of why Rome never ventured south of Egypt. It is also the story of one of history's most famous decapitated heads.

The head in question belonged to the Roman Emperor Augustus, or rather, a statue of him. Augustus had recently defeated Marc Antony and Cleopatra VII (aka *that* Cleopatra) and annexed Egypt. The underlings he installed, with his apparent approval—although it's a little tricky to tell how much he knew, more on that in a bit—began to push farther south, taking Ethiopia and setting their sights on the kingdom of Kush.*

Kush, located in what today is Sudan, does not get nearly enough play in the history books. While initially dismissed by historians as mere Egypt-imitating fans located to the south, the reality is that Kush was more of a rival. Kush was a thriving competitor that at one point actually *conquered Egypt*.† They had their own distinct culture (with pointier pyramids—take that, Giza), they worked their own metal, they repelled a ton of outside invasions, and had an army of archers so renowned that Egypt referred to Kush as the Land of the Bow.

And come 27 BCE, Kush was being led by a fearsome one-eyed queen (*kandake*‡) named Amanirenas.

Convinced that Rome was about to attack, Kush made the first move. Amanirenas's husband died in an early battle, and she and her son continued the fight. They captured two major Roman cities, took captives, and expanded Kush's borders. And in a final sign of disrespect, they defaced Augustus's many statues of himself (seriously, the things were everywhere).

This did not amuse Augustus. He struck back hard: he recaptured his cities, invaded Kush, and burned the Kushite capital of Napata to the ground. He sold thousands of Kushites into slavery (which was only fair, as they'd done the same with their Roman captives). In the

---

* No, the name is unrelated, stoners. Stop giggling.

† The 25th Dynasty, also known as the Nubian Dynasty, around 700 BCE. Lasted for about 45 years, which ain't bad! Yep, undeniably black pharaohs! Deal with it, racists!

‡ This title is the apparent origin of the name Candace, and is often spelled that way. You may have stumbled across the tale of Candace of Meroe (a Kushite city), whom Alexander the Great purportedly met, or Candace, Queen of the Ethiopians, who made a cameo appearance in the Christian Bible—both Kushite leaders.

end, as the Roman soldiers marched back north, they seemed to have delivered a debilitating defeat.* They had not.

Amanirenas counterattacked quickly and repeatedly, likely using some terrifying war tactics. One carving depicts a later kandake with two swords, feeding captives to a pet lion. Other accounts describe kandakes using war elephants on their foes. It's safe to say she made an impression.

Before long, the war ended, with the two nations agreed to a permanent peace. Kush had proved too difficult for Rome to continue fighting—the climate was taxing on Roman soldiers, the Kushites would not stay down, and the far-flung geography taxed Roman supply lines. In the end, Rome didn't even make Kush pay tribute, and they never ventured south of Egypt again.

The politics behind this is somewhat murky. It is this author's speculation that the whole thing may have even been a bit of a misunderstanding. Strabo described the Kushites suing for peace, citing grievances with previous Roman administrators, ones who'd been demoted for waging expansionist campaigns without Augustus's knowledge. The Kushites displayed surprisingly little awareness of Rome, and were unaware of its size, its leader's name, and where to find him. All this indicates (to this author, at least) that the overreaching administrator, Cornelius Gallus, was provoking Kush in ways that didn't make it into the histories, and that when Kush started fighting, it was against him—they didn't really know who they were fighting. Egypt had swapped hands a lot in the years leading up to the war, so confusion is understandable.

We don't know Kush's take on the war. Kush died out around 400 years after these events, leaving ruins that were largely unstudied until the 1900s. To this day, nobody has been able to translate their hieroglyphs, and so we don't have any words directly from Kushite mouths. But we do have a hint as to how they viewed the conflict.

The hint came to us in 1913, on an archaeological dig that unearthed a Kushite temple. With the Roman-Kushite war not terribly well-known at that point, it proved quite shocking to the assembled archaeologists to find the head of a Roman statue, hundreds of miles from Roman borders. It proved to be the best-preserved Augustus head to survive. It is one of the great treasures of the British Museum.

They found it resting by a mural of a Kushite ruler—positioned under the ruler's foot.

---

\* The Roman historian Strabo—who was a personal friend of Augustus—describes the sack of Napata with the Kushites flailing about ineffectively, due to poor leadership. This would almost certainly have been under Amanirenas' son, Akinidad, as Amanirenas was elsewhere. However, given the eventual peace terms, this author views the finer details of Strabo's "Kushites are bad at everything" account with mild suspicion.

## · ART NOTES AND TRIVIA ·

Amanirenas's outfit is a stripped-down version of the one portrayed in the above carving (of Kandake Amanitore, who reigned about a hundred years after Amanirenas). In reality, it's more likely she would have worn something like a leopard pelt. She's standing on the head found in the Kushite temple. In the background, Roman captives are being led to a Kushite pyramid, under the watchful eye of soldiers, elephants, and a lion.

# Madam C. J. Walker (Sarah Breedlove)

### (1867–1919, UNITED STATES)

## The Mother Who Made Her Own Fortune

he did it for her daughter.

No child of Sarah Breedlove's was going to suffer like she had. Her daughter would not work cleaning clothes. Her daughter would not spend her days breathing in chemicals. Her daughter would not wake up one day to find her hair falling out. It didn't matter that Sarah was orphaned, that she was widowed, that she was poor and without prospects. She was going to send her daughter to school. Lelia was going to have a good life, everything else be damned.

That need to provide for her daughter was powerful—so powerful that it would change Sarah's life until nothing old remained, not even her name: Sarah would remake herself as Madam C. J. Walker, the wealthiest black woman in America.

This was an astonishing transformation, especially given her origins. Like so many children of ex-slaves, Sarah didn't exactly start life with a ton of options. Orphan by age 7, laundress by age 10, wife by age 14, mother by age 18, widow by age 22: most of her early life was just her making the best choice available. She didn't have an education, she didn't have money, she often didn't even have a safe place to sleep. After her parents died, she moved in with her sister, who was married to an abusive man. Sarah married early, in large part just to escape her brother-in-law. When Sarah's husband died,[*] she moved to St. Louis to be closer to her brothers. It was the best option available.

Things turned around in St. Louis. The biggest change to provide stability was her new membership in the African Methodist Episcopal (AME) Church. This provided almost everything she needed: community, adult education classes, and most importantly, day care. Over the next 15 years, the church would help see her through rough waters: a turbulent second marriage to a cheating alcoholic; the deaths of her three brothers; constant deterioration

---

[*] Nobody is sure how Moses McWilliams died. Three separate accounts indicate he was lynched, but they were published after her death—Sarah herself never mentioned it in any interviews. Biographer A'Lelia Bundles, who wrote the book on Madam C. J. Walker, finds the prospect dubious.

of her neighborhood. With the help of the church, she kept her head high and even sent her daughter, Lelia, to boarding school.

But the church's second-biggest impact was to introduce Sarah to self-made women. In particular, she met—and began working for—a hair-care magnate named Annie Turnbo. Hair care in the 1800s was far more than frivolous beauty products: it was often the difference between having hair or not. Due to bad nutrition, chemical exposure, and poor hygiene (most people didn't even have running water yet), dandruff, lice, psoriasis, and outright losing your hair were commonplace occurrences. Most "medicines" just made the problem worse, by treating the scalp with harsh chemicals. Turnbo's was one of the first wave of modern shampoos.

Having a good job and healthy hair changed Sarah's life. Poor hair had always been one of the instant tells that Sarah was lower-class. Suddenly, that was gone, and everyone treated her differently. As she traveled from place to place, selling Turnbo's products, she saw repeatedly how improved appearance turned people's lives around. For the first time in her life, she felt she had options. She could go her own way. And that was just what she was going to do.

Within a year, Sarah started making moves. She moved to Denver and began developing her own hair-care formula.* She married a fast-talking raconteur named C. J. Walker, and started her own business. She bad-mouthed Turnbo's product while promoting her own (she had chutzpah). By the end of 1907, she headed back to the South to sell her goods to its black clientele. She sold her products under her new name: Madam C. J. Walker.

Her first year, she made $3,600. It was likely more than she'd made in her entire life to that point.

She was just getting started. Using the AME Church to make contacts across the South, she traveled from town to town and state to state, bringing on customers (and employees) by the truckload. Soon Walker had more work than she could handle, so she brought in Lelia to handle accounts, and began grooming her to lead. Her company was growing so fast she had to change headquarters twice within three years.

It wasn't all sunshine, though. Furious at Walker's betrayal, Turnbo fought her expansion tooth and nail, in court and out. Lelia married, only for her husband to leave shortly thereafter. Walker experienced similar heartbreak: after years of her husband C. J. shirking responsibility and spending her money, she found out he was cheating on her. As legend has it, Walker went to his hotel with a revolver, ready to end his life, but froze in the hallway. Realizing all she had to lose, she left, and divorced him soon thereafter.

---

* In the grand tradition of showmen throughout history, she said the formula came to her in a dream. This claim is questionable at best.

This left just Walker and Lelia, mother and daughter, together against the world. But it wasn't just the two of them for long: feeling the need for a family heir, Lelia adopted a daughter, Fairy Mae. She was bright. She was curious. She had great hair. Before long, the face (and long braids) of 13-year-old Mae were part of their business's newspaper ads.

Now exceedingly wealthy, Walker turned her attention to activism. Initially this too was a business interest: she wanted to network through established organizations, like she had through church circles. She came after Booker T. Washington *hard*, insisting to join his National Negro Business League (NNBL). He rebuffed her, feeling that beauty products were frivolous, and didn't fit with the image he wanted to project.

She wasn't about to take no for an answer. First she showed up to his house unannounced, which somehow failed to win him over. Next she appeared, without prior notice, at the NNBL annual meeting. She arrived in a chauffeured Model T (although she usually drove herself), and joined the group for several days, hoping to win a chance to speak.

On the last day, after Washington had highlighted virtually every other black entrepreneur there, Walker called him out. From the audience, she stood up and shouted: "Surely you are not going to shut the door in my face!" From there, she gave an impassioned speech, telling her story, proclaiming her pride in rising up from poverty, and declaring that she wanted to use her privilege to help others. She capped it off by announcing her plan to fund the creation of another Tuskegee Institute: this one in Africa.[*]

She stole the show.

It wasn't a lie. Sarah remembered vividly how much her life had changed, just by having a good job. She wanted to give the same opportunity to everyone. Initially she'd done this just by employing people, but she soon expanded into outright philanthropy. Beyond bankrolling organizations like the NAACP, she encouraged her army of sales agents to likewise become agents of social change. Improving the lot of African Americans became part of her company's mission.

Which isn't to say she was purely selfless—far from it. She and Lelia spent lavishly, flaunting fine clothes and new automobiles. Walker bought a massive New York mansion, which was soon dubbed Villa Lewaro, after the first letters from each part of Lelia's full name (**Le**lia **Wa**lker **Ro**binson). Naming it after Lelia was appropriate, for she had drifted away from the business, becoming an arts patron and socialite.

This drift caused no shortage of mother-daughter conflict. It was frankly unavoidable: the two were stubborn, hot-blooded, and independent. One secretary described their relationship as "fire and ice," alternately fighting bitterly and making up with lavish gifts and affectionate declarations. They'd both been abandoned by people they'd loved, and had a need to control

---

[*] This appeal to Africanism became a growing theme in Walker's work. She'd amend the story of her "formula dream" to include a bit about the ingredients needing to come from Africa.

the world around them. The one person they couldn't control was each other, and it drove them nuts.

After World War I, Walker threw her weight behind an unsuccessful movement that deserves its own "what if?" alt-history TV drama. With the German Empire collapsed, there was a question of what to do with its African colonies. Walker, and many others, advocated for a "supernational" coalition of educated black people from around the world to govern and develop Germany's former colonies. It never happened, but seriously, put down this book for a second and imagine what the world would be like if it had.

It should come as little surprise that, due to her involvement with this campaign, Walker was spied upon, denied a passport, and labeled as seditious. This was the same era, after all, that was tossing **Marie Equi** and **Mother Jones** in jail.

The African mission was to be one of her last major campaigns. Her health had been declining for some time because of her nonstop work, and she fell ill. Sensing the end was at hand, Walker altered her will to give much of her wealth to charity. Some of her last recorded words were "I want to live to help my race."

Walker died at 61 years old. Newspapers celebrated her as America's first female self-made millionaire, but she was only worth around $600,000 at the time (which is worth many millions of dollars in today's money, so hey, let's just let her have the title).

Unfortunately, her company did not thrive after her death. Devastated by the loss of her mother and uninterested in running the business, Lelia left matters to the trusted company lawyer, and went to find herself. Renaming herself A'Lelia, she had a turbulent life. She married and got divorced again; she became one of the central figures of the Harlem Renaissance; she made an intellectual salon that went under within a year. The Great Depression sent company revenues into a tailspin, and A'Lelia died not long thereafter.

Mae went on to run the company through some of its roughest times, and was succeeded by her daughter, A'Lelia Mae Perry Bundles. She in turn gave birth to A'Lelia Bundles, who in 2001 honored her great-grandmother by producing the most thorough biography ever written on Madam C. J. Walker. In 2017, the biography was optioned to be turned into a TV series, with Octavia Spencer playing the titular role.

## · ART NOTES AND TRIVIA ·

Walker is pictured here driving her Model T about town, as she was known to do. In the back seat are Lelia and Mae—Lelia is, of course, doing Mae's hair. Walker herself is handing a copy of her ad to a woman out of frame, as she was always trying to recruit young women and encourage them to pull themselves up by their bootstraps. Walker is wearing a badge from the national convention of sales agents for her company, identifying her as the CEO. In the background is the Philadelphia Union Baptist Church, site of her first company convention.

While both Lelia and Walker are flashy, Lelia stands out a bit more visually, while Walker dominates the frame. They are dressed in complementary colors, but still clash somewhat: Walker is more muted, while Lelia is vibrant and saturated.

## Straightening Hair

During the 1970s, when the movement for black people to rejoice in the natural state of their hair was in full swing, the story of Madam C. J. Walker fell out of favor. Many associated her with skin bleaches and hair-straightening products—there was a persistent rumor she invented the "hot comb" straightener. However, it was all a myth. The hot comb was created in France around the 1870s, and while Walker provided some straightener products, she only presented them as an option and didn't advocate for their persistent use. In a sharp retort to a newspaper article where Walker had been called the "dekink queen," she said, "I deplore such an impression because I have always held myself out as a hair culturist. I *grow* hair."

# Masako Hōjō

(1157–1225, JAPAN)

## *The Mom Who Became Shogun*

**P**op quiz—you find your significant other has, during their "hunting trips," been cheating on you with another woman. Do you: a) Leave them quietly? b) Toss them to the curb? c) Try to work it out? d) Hire an army to reduce the other woman's house to a pile of smoking rubble?

If you answered *d*, you have something in common with Masako Hōjō, unofficial seventh shogun of Japan.

This was to be expected from her torrid relationship with her husband, Yoritomo. Both Masako and he had acted like hormone-addled teenagers from the get-go. For her part, she left her fiancée on the eve of their wedding night to be with Yoritomo, pissing off half of Japan in the process. As for Yoritomo, the man had a rightly earned reputation as the bad boy of the Heian era. His father had led a failed uprising against the government, and despite living in exile, Yoritomo was all but shouting from the rooftops that he intended to do so too.

Surprisingly, he actually did, and he did so well. Over the first several years of the marriage, Yoritomo crushed western Japan and became the fourth shogun in history. Simultaneously, though, he continued his horndog antics: while Masako was pregnant, he started cheating on her with several women, including one Lady Kame. It is at this point that Masako (with the aid of her family) got a small army to flatten Lady Kame's house. Lady Kame survived, somehow.

It should be noted: this was not that uncommon! Old wives would get revenge on mistresses so often in olden Japan that there's even a word for it: *uwanari-uchi* (literally "strike of the after-wife," which sounds like the world's most acrimonious ninja move). Traditionally, the wife's family would be the one handing over a dowry in the marriage, so they had a lot riding on it. It was entirely sensible for families to band together in deterring husbands from straying, and thus them from losing power. So while, yes, it was an jerkwad move, it was also called playing the game. And Masako Hōjō played to win.

And this was hardly the last time Masako openly defied her husband (you know, the most powerful man in Japan). When Yoritomo impregnated another lover, Masako ordered the woman dismissed and then run out of town. Later, Yoritomo started crushing on a court dancer named Shizuka Gozen, who didn't want anything to do with him—and let it be known by publicly insulting him in poem form. This delighted Masako, and she took Shizuka under her wing, even trying to help her get out of town.

Some years after that, Yoritomo died in fairly klutzy fashion, by being thrown from a horse. This resulted in such a loss of face that rumors immediately started springing up that he'd actually been assassinated, or that a jealous Masako had somehow detached her spirit from her body and haunted him to death. That particular rumor got popular 500 years after his death, which shows just how long-lived Masako's reputation was. The truth of the matter is that she probably loved him (possibly overly) intensely to the end of her days, but that doesn't make for as good a story.

Immediately after Yoritomo's untimely demise, Masako became a Buddhist nun, but she kept getting pulled back into politics. Her son Yoriie assumed power and started being a total turdbiscuit, killing people he didn't like, seizing property, and playing sports (which, to read the accounts, was apparently a more grievous offense than the first two). When he made plans to murder a governor named Morinaga, Masako left her temple, stood in front of Morinaga's house, assumed her best "come at me, bro" stance, and said, "If you're gonna kill him, you gotta go through me first."

The straw that broke the camel's back was when a bunch of dudes tried to kill both Masako and Yoriie. Seeing how utterly incompetent her son was at dispatching these weak-tea assassins, she stepped in to show him how it's done. She took control of the shogunate, obliterated the assailants, and made her son give up the claim to the throne. From there on, she ruled pretty much directly—despite the fact that she was, on paper, just a common nun.

Masako was a very successful leader. With the aid of her brother, she immediately quashed other claimants to the throne. When her brother died, she wiped out his remaining family as well (to be fair, they were kind of jerks). She established the Hōjō dynasty, which survived for 100 years, an enormous length of time for the era. The Hōjōs only went down after a decade of simultaneous assaults from other samurai families, when an invasion fleet sailed in from Korea and the friggin' Mongol Horde landed in Japan simultanously.

We'll wrap up with an anecdote from late in Masako's life: at one point, she was given an enormously high-profile award, made even more impressive by her being only the second layperson to ever get it. When the emperor of the time set up an imperial audience to give it to her, she didn't even show up. Instead, she remarked that an old country nun had no use for such things, turned to go home, and presumably dropped the mic in the process.

## · ART NOTES AND TRIVIA ·

The image here is a bit of a mishmash of her life as opposed to any specific moment. She's dressed in nun robes, even though the destruction of Lady Kame's house (depicted in the background) took place well before she ever became a nun. You may note that Lady Kame (in purple) has blackened teeth and weird eyebrows. This was actually the practice at the time—fashionable Japanese women would blacken their teeth in a practice called *ohaguro*, and totally eliminate (and then paint on) their eyebrows in a practice called *hikimayu*. The scene takes place at sunrise, since Japan is the land of the rising sun (literally, the Japanese word for their nation means "root of the sun"). And yes, that's Mount Fuji in the background. The siege weapon being used by the excitable soldiers is a little-used mega-crossbow called an *oyumi*, which was sometimes used to sling rocks. Nobody is 100 percent sure what they looked like. Japan never used catapults much, and didn't start until a century or two after this. Mostly they used fire.

# Freydís Eiríksdóttir

## The Mother Who Fought While Pregnant

he trip to Vinland was not going as expected.

Leif Eiriksson and his band of Norsemen had come to the shores of Vinland, as they called North America (present-day Canada, to be precise), in the late 900s, and had made an uneasy truce with the local Native Americans (whom they called *skrælingjar*). Unfortunately, that peace had fallen apart,[*] and a large war party had the Vikings on the run. But one of them wasn't about to turn tail. Striding toward the red-painted native warriors, Leif's extremely pregnant sister, Freydís, insulted the courage of her fellow Icelanders and proclaimed, "Let me but have a weapon, I think I could fight better than any of you."

The weapon only came to her after she was totally surrounded by skrælingjar, with nary a live ally in sight. Grabbing a sword off a dead clansman, she bared her chest at her enemies, beating her breasts with the flat of her sword and screaming bloody murder.

The skrælingjar, realizing that their foes had left but a single person to fight all of them—and that this person was a pregnant alien striking herself with a foreign weapon and shrieking indecipherable obscenities at them—decided they weren't about to stick around and figure out *why* any of this was happening. They wisely ran for the hills.

And that would basically be the beginning, middle, and end of Freydís Eiríksdóttir's story. Except historians wanted to hold her up as an example. So things get messy.

The story you just read comes to us courtesy of the *Eirik the Red's Saga*, and it's one of only two sources on Freydís's life. The other source, the *Greenlanders' Saga*, tells a *totally* different story. While it ostensibly covers many of the same events as the *Eirik the Red's Saga*, the *Greenlanders' Saga* paints Freydís as a conniving, nasty lady who married for money and only went on the Vinland trip for yet more money.

In the *Greenlanders'* version, she convinces two brothers to help lead a private expedition to Vinland with her, but she double-crosses them. Lying that the brothers had offended her honor, she orders her husband to avenge her, and threatens to leave him if he doesn't. Her husband dutifully murders the brothers and the brothers' men, and Freydís finishes the job

---

[*] Which was not a terrible move on the part of the Native Americans; historically speaking, there are few benefits to having Vikings as neighbors.

by using an axe to kill all the women in the brothers' party. From there, Freydís takes the brothers' boat, divvies up their wealth, swears everyone in her party to secrecy, and returns to the main Viking expedition.

It does not stay a secret for long, though. Her brother (and expedition leader) Leif senses something amiss and tortures a confession out of some of her men. Once the truth is revealed, Leif does not punish her—she's his sister!—but the moralizing narrator of the *Greenlanders' Saga* notes that "after that, no one thought anything but ill of [Freydís]."

So . . . that's just a *smidge* different than the previous version. How to reconcile?

Well, historians have done some digging into the stories, and they've found some telling information to help flesh things out. The basic consensus is that the *Greenlanders' Saga* was, in some part, Christian propaganda. It refers to Freydís as a heathen who'd refused to conform to Christianity, holding her up as an example of a "bad woman" who wouldn't obey the rules, a Norse parallel to the biblical **Jezebel**. Which helps explain some of the details that don't make sense. Like, why would she ever think mere gifts could keep 35-plus people quiet? Why would Leif need to torture people to get information, when he could have just ordered them to tell him? It has the hallmarks of cultural revisionism about it, meant to steer people toward a new way of thinking.

Strangely enough, the *Eirik the Red's Saga*, although conclusively proven to be a Norse revision of the *Greenlanders' Saga*, seems to be a bit more objective, according to historians. *Eirik the Red's Saga* was a conscious rewriting of the Vinland expedition events, using the *Greenlanders' Saga* as well as other texts, many of which are now lost to history. While the exact details of Freydís's story are hard to prove—they distantly echo other shield-maiden stories— they were put in there as a conscious effort on the part of Norse historians. Almost as if to provide a counterexample, saying "look how awesome Norsewomen are!"

## · ART NOTES AND TRIVIA ·

It's a bit difficult to tell which tribe the Vikings actually met when they confronted the skrælingjar. Freydís's confused foes, standing around in befuddlement, are modeled off the Beothuk, a tribe that lived in the area in the 19th century and was known to have red-painted faces and mohawks.

In the background sits a Viking ship and the longhouse where they might have lived (Freydís's sword is pointing to it). This image is based off a modern-day re-creation of the longhouse.

# Ilona Zrínyi

(1643–1703, HUNGARY/CROATIA)

## The Mom Who Held a Castle

You know what's surprisingly common? Women defending castles by themselves. History's chock-full of them. **"Black" Agnes Dunbar** of Scotland,* Mary Bankes of England, Christina of Saxony, Fannu of Marrakech, Maud de St. Valéry, Nicholaa de la Haye—all of them put in strong showings. But one of the greatest of this admittedly obscure category of heroism is undoubtedly Ilona Zrínyi, who held a castle for three lonesome, siege-filled years.

Ilona was part of the last generation of one of Croatia's† most famous families. It's hard to understate this family's importance: the names Kennedy, Khan, and Medici come to mind by way of comparison. At 23, Ilona made a fateful marriage to the hunky rebel of Hungarian politics: Ferenc Rákóczi I. He threw his life into freeing Hungary from its foreign oppressors, the Hapsburgs (cue *booo* sounds), and so did she.

While her first husband was defeated (and died shortly thereafter), she continued her crusade for independence by marrying the newest bad boy on the block: Imre Thököly (clearly she had a type). Despite the age difference—she was 39 and he 25—she fell madly in love and followed him into almost every skirmish against their foreign oppressors.

Unfortunately, Thököly was less than successful. He began to lose almost every battle, despite Zrínyi's presence (she left the kids with the nanny). With this unfortunate track record, Thököly's Ottoman allies began to blame him for their losses, and wonder if he had enough skin in the game. They requested a token of loyalty—his stepson Ferenc, Zrínyi's son from her first marriage. But she would not let her own son be torn from her, and refused outright. Family came first.

This proved an unfortunate choice for Thököly. Reading this refusal as treason, his Ottoman "partners" imprisoned him for some time, and his loyal troops sought to free him—by joining the Hapsburgs, the guys they'd been fighting all this time. By the time Thököly was finally released, the Ottomans had captured virtually every one of the castles he'd defended. All of them, that is, save Palanok Castle, where his wife lived.

---

\* Whose remarkably funny story is recounted at www.rejectedprincesses.com.

† At the time, Croatia and Hungary were essentially one nation, ruled by the Austrian Hapsburgs. It's a bit of a conundrum as to which country's name to use throughout this entry—Ilona was Croatian but her husbands were Hungarian, and they all fought for the same cause, to free themselves from Hapsburg rule.

Zrínyi held the castle for three years.

This was no mean feat. Using the Military Field Guide of her famous uncle Miklos Zrínyi, she pushed her 4,000 troops to their utmost, repelling every Hapsburg assault. At one point, Palanok Castle was bombarded for seven weeks straight. In response, she flew red flags of defiance, and burned down all nearby villages that could have supplied the enemy troops. She even managed regular correspondence with her husband via secret couriers.

Part of Zrínyi's correspondence was with the enemy. She wrote to the Hapsburg's General Caprara, saying "If you try to harm us, I will resist . . . although I am only a weak woman, neither the loss of neighboring fortresses nor the terror of siege could force me to forget my obligations toward my children." When Caprara ignored her and began shelling the castle, she became an icon for her resistance. Before long, she was the talk of Europe, with Louis XIV of France extolling her virtues and Poland's King Sobieski calling her "the greatest woman in Europe."

But in January 1688, after three years, Zrínyi had to give up. Her traitorous chancellor had deliberately wasted their supplies to the point where resistance was no longer feasible. She went to Vienna to surrender in person, on the twelfth birthday of her son, Ferenc. One day later, she was separated from her children. Realizing her son was out of her reach, she entered a convent so she could stay with her daughter, Julianna. She remained there for another three years. She would never see her son again.

Zrínyi lived the rest of her life in relative quiet. After a short-lived counteroffensive against the Hapsburgs on the part of her husband, she reunited with him. He'd aged considerably, having suffered serious injuries during his campaigns. Whereas previously she'd needed him, suddenly he was the one to need her. Overcome by their enemies, they went into exile in Constantinople, where they lived until their deaths.

Shortly before Zrínyi died in 1703, she heard word of her son, Ferenc: he was following in her footsteps, fighting his country's oppressors. Like his mother, father, and stepfather, he was ultimately doomed to failure, but he—as well as all of the rest of his family, his mother chief among them—would be recognized as heroes centuries later by a finally freed Croatia.

## · ART NOTES AND TRIVIA ·

Zrínyi is seen here at the ramparts of Palanok Castle with her son, Ferenc. His hand is on the military guide of Zrínyi's uncle. Behind Zrínyi is her daughter, Julianna, who was also there for the siege. In the background, beyond the surrounding castle wall and forest, is the enemy's camp and the burned-down remains of the villages that once surrounded the area.

# Mother Lü

## (1ST CENTURY, CHINA)

## The Mother Who Overthrew the Xin Dynasty

he middle-aged woman known as Mother Lü wasn't exactly the ideal candidate to overthrow the government, but when a local magistrate messed with her son, she did exactly that.

The Lü family was a wealthy, peaceful bunch, well-integrated into their rural province. Mother Lü's son, Yu, was a town clerk in the town of Haiqu. However, all that changed in the year 14. With the government recently usurped by the unpopular Wang Mang,* government officials began instituting stricter policies. And when Yu committed a minor offense, the local magistrate reacted by having him executed.

This was a mistake.

Mother Lü quietly swore to get revenge, but outwardly only showed the face of a bereaved mother. She began investing her resources into small acts of charity: She used the rice from her family fields to make wine, which she'd let young men take on credit. She'd buy up clothes, and if she came across a young man in need, she'd clothe him and give him money.

After several years of this, she'd spent her family's fortunes. The legions of young men she'd helped came to her with offers of help, to which she responded with the story of her slain son. "All I desire," the unassuming old woman told them, "is my vengeance, if only you would take pity and help me!"

It is at this point that the little old lady revealed that she'd spent her remaining money on buying a massive stockpile of weaponry.

The young men, suitably wowed, began gathering backup: hundreds and hundreds of men. Then, following Mother Lü's lead, they went into a neighboring region and began recruiting fugitives (and, for a brief spell, became pirates). Once her forces numbered in the thousands, sweetly Mother Lü appointed herself General Lü and laid siege to Haiqu.

She conquered without pity. The clerks and the magistrate all begged for mercy, and were told, "my son made one small mistake, one that did not deserve death. Yet he was killed by the magistrate. The punishment for murder is death, what good is your plea for clemency?"

---

\* Wang Mang was a government official who'd usurped the throne and instituted some deeply unpopular measures, the most well-known of which was the abolition of private ownership of land. As with so many other rulers throughout history, he tried to do too much, too fast, was too set in his ways, and all too soon his (well-intentioned) efforts failed.

Mother Lü beheaded the magistrate and laid his head as an offering at her son's grave. Then, her honor satisfied, she went back home, her troops in tow.

She died of an illness in 18 CE, and her troops soon joined other rebels, known as the Red Eyebrows, in overthrowing Wang Mang and ending the short-lived Xin dynasty. She went down in history as China's first female rebellion leader. The moral of the story? Do not mess with a mother's family.

## · ART NOTES AND TRIVIA ·

The composition here presents the unassuming mother as sweet and hunched over, lit by heavenly rays. This stands in stark contrast to the carnage around her. In the foreground, a magistrate is made to kneel before Mother Lü. The clothing and armor is patterned off that of 1st-century Chinese dolls.

# Sor Juana Inés de la Cruz

### (1651–1695, MEXICO)

## The Mother of Mexican Literature

I t was unlikely that Juana Ramirez would make the history books. An illegitimate child born into poverty in 17th-century Mexico, her prospects were dim. And yet, through force of will and fierceness of wit, this precocious young woman rose to become one of the greatest heroes of Mexican history: Sor Juana Inés de la Cruz, known as the Tenth Muse and the Phoenix of Mexico.

From early on, Juana wanted one thing above all others: knowledge. She begged her mother to dress her in men's clothes and send her to university. As early as age three, she would sneak into her sister's lessons and hide in her grandfather's study to read his books.

Juana taught herself, and she was a harsh teacher. If she wasn't learning fast enough, reasoning that her head should not be "adorned with hair and naked of learning," she would cut off her own hair. It's a testament to her learning prowess that her hair soon grew long. She taught herself math, mythology, history, philosophy, the sciences, and above all, the art of writing—all subjects usually closed to girls.

By her teens, word had spread about Juana's brilliance, but some doubted her abilities. The viceroy of New Spain (as Mexico was known at the time) decided to put her to the test:* he gathered 40 of Mexico's brightest minds and had them quiz her, to determine if she was a charlatan. She blew them away. "In the manner that a royal galleon might fend off the attacks of a few canoes," the viceroy said, did Juana acquit herself against the crowd's inquisition.

From there, Juana became a lady-in-waiting for the vicereine, Leonor Carreto, a feat almost unheard of for illegitimate children. While she and Carreto became very close—some historians suggest that the two had a lesbian affair†—the court of New Spain proved a poor home. Although she was respected and supported, she was surrounded by gossip and intrigue.

After it became clear that Juana could not stand the court, she was faced with a tough

---

\* Poet Octavio Paz, who wrote extensively of Sor Juana, finds it unlikely that this scenario actually occurred, or that it did as described—he notes that it veers very close to the account of Christ before the learned sages at the temple. Juana's first biographer, who knew her in life, described the event with some detail, and even quoted the viceroy himself, but it is entirely probable this was hyperbole.

† While totally possible, it's tough to say whether this happened or not. The two definitely wrote flowery, affectionate letters to each other, but that was also the style of the time. Given that it's nigh-impossible to prove one way or another, that this author is in no way an authority on the matter, and that Juana's primary focus was scholarship, this book is also going to focus on that.

MATURITY 2

DOWN WITH IMPERIALIST WAR

choice. Mexican society at that point virtually required women to be married, as they had little way of supporting themselves. Juana had received a steady stream of marriage proposals, but she had less than no interest in marriage: exposure to the philandering men of the court and to her sisters' unfaithful husbands had turned her off to the idea entirely.

So she did the unthinkable: she became a nun,* Sor ("Sister") Juana.

Sor Juana quickly found that the convent was not the quiet haven she'd imagined—the nuns were just as gossipy as the courtiers—but she adjusted and began to blossom. She established herself as a renowned poet with many wealthy patrons, the viceroy and vicereine chief among them. Her work grew internationally famous, and she spent her earnings amassing a huge personal library.†

In private, Sor Juana pushed her writing further and further. In her greatest work, *First Dream,* she wrote of her soul's journey, once freed of her sleeping body. She imagined it rising above the world, taking in all of creation. But at the pinnacle of her soul's journey, some inherent flaw in her being proved unable to take it all in, and she fell.

It was to prove a prophetic dream.

At age 39, at the height of her career, Sor Juana wrote a critique of another priest's sermon. It was a mild political attack, with the aim of keeping a misogynistic priest from silencing her.‡ She was confident it would blow over, but she was wrong. From all throughout the church, priests replied with outrage, questioning how a woman could dare to critique a priest. Her allies, one by one, chastised and abandoned her.§

Sor Juana responded with an unimaginable act of defiance. Penning a defense of women that was centuries ahead of its time, she left no bridge unburned. Defending women's intellectual prowess, she then went on the attack: "Had Aristotle cooked, he would have written

---

* She initially joined a very harsh order, the Carmelites, but found them too restrictive and left after a couple months. Afterward, she joined the Hieronymites, with whom she was to stay the rest of her life.

† Estimates peg her library at between 1,500 and 4,000 books, a truly astonishing number for the age. Moreover, her work was internationally acclaimed on the order of only a handful of other, male writers. She accrued a fairly substantial amount of wealth and property while in the convent.

‡ The details of the political intrigue are long and boring. There was a political struggle going on between two priests—Manuel Fernandez de Santa Cruz and Francisco de Aguiar y Seijas. Sor Juana was allied with Fernandez, who basically contracted her to critique a 40-year-old sermon. The sermon was by one of Aguiar's allies, and so a critique on it would be an attack on Aguiar. Juana's reasoning for doing this was seemingly fear that the misogynistic Aguiar would doom her career if he rose to power. He hated women to a disturbing degree—thanked God he was nearsighted so he didn't have to see them, refused to be in the same room as them, and really didn't like Sor Juana's work.

§ Part of the reason Aguiar won this power struggle was that a famine struck the town and he positioned himself to help the townfolk faster than anyone else—and so nobody could talk against him, and everyone turned their back on Sor Juana. Otherwise, with various well-positioned benefactors behind her, Sor Juana would likely have weathered the storm.

a great deal more." Although it was not published until after her death, it was to be her blaze of glory.

The priests put her under the microscope. Rooting through every word she'd ever written, they decried her for being too secular. Her choices dwindled down to one: renounce her works and cease writing.

Signed in blood, the signature on her confession was some of the last words she ever wrote. She signed it: Juana Inés de La Cruz, the worst of all.

After that, traces of her prove hard to find. Silenced by the church, ████████ ████████████████████████████████████ sold all her books for a pittance ████████████████████████████ ████████████████████ ████████████████████████████ a plague hit Mexico, █████████ ████████████████████████████████████████████████ contracted the plague while taking care of fellow nuns █████████ ████████████████████████████████████ died in 1695. █████████████████████████████████ ███████████████████████████████████████████ the vicereine saved some of her writing, ████████████████████████████████████ ████████████████████████ the Mexican Revolution, Sor Juana's writings were found ████████████████████████████ scattered her remaining works ████ ████████████████████████████████████████ ████████████████████████████████████ ████████████████████████████████████ ████████████████████████████████ she was studied in higher academia, but she remained largely unknown to most. ████████████████

*renounce
these works
as heresy.*

*— Juana Ines
— La Cruz
the worst of all*

▮▮▮▮▮▮ Octavio Paz's study on her, *The Traps of Faith* ▮▮▮▮ ▮▮▮▮▮▮, more of her work was found in antique booksto▮▮ ▮▮▮▮▮▮ ▮▮▮▮▮▮ gradually gave life again to her voice.

The resurgent interest in her led to ▮▮▮▮▮▮▮▮▮▮▮ appearing on the 200-pesos bill and a 1,000-pesos coin. ▮▮▮▮▮ statue was established at the convent where she ▮▮▮▮▮▮▮ story was told in a 1990 movie and a 2016 miniseries on Netflix. Thus, centuries after her death, did the Phoenix of Mexico rise again.

## · ART NOTES AND TRIVIA ·

This is an illustration of Sor Juana's poem, *First Dream*, where she envisioned herself floating above the earth. She is being buoyed upward by wings made from her writing—literally. The actual Spanish used in her poem is written throughout her "wings." The wings are a series of looping curls, similar to the cursive writing she used in her own work. Subtly laid into the background are shadowy purple claws reaching out to pull her back down to earth.

Midway through this entry, the text is blacked out, and we get only bits and pieces of her story, mimicking the story of Juana herself. Written in the margin is "I renounce these works as heresy. Juana Inés de la Cruz, the worst of all." The redacted text details her death by plague while helping her fellow nuns; how the vicereine saved her works, only for them to be scattered during the Mexican Revolution; how interest in Juana flourished due to the intercession of figures like Octavio Paz; and how the Phoenix of Mexico has risen again to public consciousness.

# Sojourner Truth

### (1797–1883, UNITED STATES)

## *The Mother Who Sued to Save Her Kids*

It was an unusual sight for 1800s America: a black woman towering above a white man, arguing him into submission. Uncommon as it was, this exact scene would play out many times in public across the country, always with the same woman. Reporters would gleefully recount her quips with a tone usually reserved for circus sideshows, but she would not be sidelined. She'd already had the grit to endure a lifetime of slavery, and the wits to legally win her son's freedom. She'd use both traits to bend the press to her own ends: she'd make a name for herself.

The name she chose was Sojourner Truth.

She was born into slavery in 1800s New York as Isabella Baumfree,* although she went by Belle. She was one of the last of the dozen or so children born to her parents. Nearly all the others were sold to other slaveowners. Belle herself was separated from her parents at age 11 and shunted from slaveowner to slaveowner, in a variety of horrific living situations: sleeping on planks in an unventilated cellar with 12 others, being beaten into unconsciousness for not knowing English,† and forced to marry someone she'd just met.‡ By age 19, she'd had five kids.

Belle knew that, come July 1827, under New York State law, she would be freed—but the new law would not free her children. Nevertheless, it gave her something to aim for, and she worked hard, with the eventual goal of living under one roof with all her kids. But she lost heart after her slaveowner reneged on his promise to free her a year early. Unable to take any more, she escaped, carrying her infant daughter. She found refuge with a nearby Quaker couple (Quakers were staunchly antislavery), who negotiated to buy the

---

* Also spelled "Bomefree." People were pretty loose with spelling back in those days.

† The Hardenberghs, whom she'd grown up with, had engaged a cruel, cynical, and sadly commonplace tactic: they spoke only in Low Dutch around the house, and never taught Belle's family English. This so destroyed her parents' prospects that when they were told they were freed, they couldn't make a living, and had to stay working for the Hardenberghs. Belle would learn English under another slaveowner, but her parents were not so lucky. After her mother died, her invalid father, unable to provide for himself, ended up starving to death, forgotten and alone in a basement.

‡ This, despite the fact that she'd met and fallen for a neighboring enslaved man named Robert. Robert's slaveowner, having other ideas on whom he should marry, beat him mercilessly when he snuck out to see Belle. In the end, she married a man named Tom.

services of Belle and her daughter, and house the two of them until the emancipation went into effect.

However, once freed, Belle found that her only son, Peter, had been sold, and was en route to Alabama. When she confronted her old slaveowners, the wife mocked her: "Why, haven't you as many of 'em left as you can see to take care of?" Belle replied, "I'll have my child again"—and, to the astonishment of everyone, she did.

With the assistance of local Quakers, she filed a legal complaint, on the grounds that New York State law prohibited out-of-state slave sales. It wasn't a smooth process. After the defendant dodged a court summons and put up some delaying tactics, Belle managed to employ a lawyer and get a trial. But to her shock, when Peter appeared, he proclaimed that Belle was not his mother, saying "I don't want to leave my master. He's so good to me."

Thankfully, this did not fool the judge. Glimpsing numerous scars on the six-year-old, and realizing his obvious terror regarding the slaveowner, the judge determined his testimony had been coached. He awarded custody to Belle. She became one of the first black women to ever win against a white man in American courts.

Unfortunately, the episode left Peter with severe emotional scars. Even after being re-united with his mother, he began to steal and run with the wrong crowd. Sensing a lack of opportunities for her son in upstate New York, Belle left her youngest daughter with her other daughters—most full-grown by now—and moved with Peter to New York City.

New York City was overwhelming. It took some time for Belle to find her feet, and when she did, it was in religion. She found community in the AME Church, and even reunited with two of her long-lost siblings. When she asked after her sister Nancy, who'd been sent away before her young eyes, she was told that Nancy had died a short time ago. It was then that Belle realized she'd actually prayed with Nancy shortly before her death, even held her hands—but didn't recognize her. "What is this slavery," she cried, "that it can do such dreadful things?"

In addition to the AME Church, she was briefly involved in a cult. She never grew comfortable there, and left within a year. However, after she left, one of the cult leaders was murdered, and the ensuing drama pulled her back in. A novel came out that was clearly about the cult, and blamed a "black witch" for the murder—clearly Belle. She was being savaged in the press for the high crime of being in the wrong place at the wrong time. Belle, however, brought the authors to court for defamation of character, and won. Because she was awesome.

Peter's situation only got worse. Only 11 years old, the boy Belle fought so hard to save was getting into fights and stealing from employers. Belle would continuously bail him out, but eventually he pushed his luck too hard and got arrested. She resorted to tough love. She refused to post bail, and then got him placed on a naval vessel, hoping that the experience would straighten him out. He sailed away in 1839. He wrote several letters to her, but seemingly never got any of hers. When his ship came back, he was not aboard—to this day, his fate remains unknown.

After Peter's disappearance, Belle was adrift. She was 46, and her daughters were adults now. She prayed for guidance, and felt a message to go east. She followed suit, wandering in search of a purpose. Reborn as an itinerant wanderer, she took a name to match: Sojourner Truth.

Soon in her wanderings, she found her calling in public speaking. Stumbling upon an outdoor religious meeting where anyone could approach the stage and speak, she began to preach against slavery. Illiterate and largely uneducated, she used the details of her life and her loud voice to drive home her argument. The audience was wowed. Even when she was interrupted by stick-wielding ruffians and momentarily cowed, she remembered what she'd been through, and stood her ground. She ordered them to leave, and they did.

Sojourner Truth would never stand down again.

Word of her prowess spread, and she was soon integrated into the abolitionist and suffrage movements. She befriended movement leaders, like orator Frederick Douglass and *Uncle Tom's Cabin* author Harriet Beecher Stowe, and got the confidence to publish an autobiography, dictated to her friend Olive Gilbert—*The Narrative of Sojourner Truth: A Northern Slave*. Now in her fifties and a published author, Sojourner hit the speaker circuit.

Often the only black woman at various conferences, Sojourner was both sharp and blunt in her comments. Appalled by chatter over dresses and wedding rings at a suffrage convention, she remarked, "If women want any rights more than they've got, why don't they just take them and not be talking about it." When a man called her a fool, she replied by asking who he was. "I am the only son of my mother," he replied—to which she said, "I am glad there are no more!"

Her most-lauded speech came in response to a misogynist argument at one of these conferences. A common argument to keep down both women and black people was that the Bible stated they were inherently inferior. Sojourner replied, "He says women need to be helped in the carriages and lifted over ditches and to have the best everywhere. Nobody ever helps me in the carriages, over my bottles, or gets me any best places. And *ain't I a woman*?"

Baring her arms, she exclaimed, "Look at me! I have ploughed. And I have planted. And I have gathered into barns. And no man could head me. And ain't I a woman? I have borne thirteen children* and seen them sold into slavery, and when I cried out in a mother's grief, none heard me but Jesus. And ain't I a woman?"

She brought the house down.

She continued giving speeches and going on book tours for years. The press breathlessly covered her, harping on her height and appearance. She used it to her advantage, bolstering her book sales and drawing bigger crowds. Even though she ostensibly retired to Michigan with much of her family in 1857, she stayed involved. Realizing that nationwide emancipation was coming (she had her grandson Sammy read the news to her), she went back on tour to help make the case for abolition.

The tour didn't go smoothly, but she was undeterred. With tensions high and civil war imminent, Sojourner, now a senior citizen, faced threats almost everywhere she went. One group threatened to burn down the meeting hall where she was to speak—to which she replied, "I'll speak on the ashes." Another group insisted she was, in fact, a man disguised as a woman, and demanded she disrobe to prove herself. She began to do so, and they were silenced.

When the Civil War broke out, Sojourner volunteered herself as best she could. Although she wished she could fight alongside her grandson—"I'd be on hand as the **Joan of Arc**"—she put herself to work helping the newly freed southerners who'd relocated to Washington, DC. Besides helping with sanitation and nursing, she used her legal prowess to advise women who'd had their children stolen about how to get them back.

Indeed, she never lost sight of her legal standing. Refused seating on a streetcar,† she sued the conductor, and won—in the 1860s!

In her twilight years, she took on one last crusade. Realizing that many freed slaves had no prospects, she pushed for the government to award them property out west, as had been done with so many homesteaders. She was ultimately unsuccessful, when the senator backing the effort died,‡ but the government would eventually come around on this (see the entry on **Marie Equi**).

Sojourner died not long after. She'd lived a long, full life, in an age where one could

---

* This would seem to describe her mom's life, not hers—Sojourner had only five kids—but just let it slide.

† For a period after the Emancipation Proclamation, there were no Jim Crow laws enforcing segregation, and so people like Sojourner Truth attempted to force the desegregation issue through acts like this. She also tried voting, almost 50 years before women got the vote.

‡ Okay, sidebar: This guy was Charles Sumner, a staunch antislavery politician who was the unfortunate subject of one of the most messed-up parts of US history. While Sumner was writing at his desk, a South Carolina representative, Preston Brooks, beat him unconscious with his cane—on the floor of the Senate! Other senators tried interceding, but another South Carolina representative, Laurence Krett, took out a pistol and told them to back off. Sumner was an invalid for three years. Brooks, meanwhile, had hundreds of new canes mailed to him. Seriously, this was 1856—not *that* long ago.

scarcely be expected to live beyond 40. In the years since her passing, she has been celebrated in a huge variety of settings—everything from postage stamps to a Mars rover. The name remembered is not that given to an enslaved child without agency or recourse. It is the name of a free woman. It is the name of a woman who beat the system, who said what she liked, who used the law for justice. It is the name she chose: Sojourner Truth.

## · ART NOTES AND TRIVIA ·

Sojourner is seen here in court, fighting for custody of her son. She stands taller in the frame than anyone else, a visual indication of how she rose above her foes. Her hand on the Bible indicates her deep religious ties, while the weathered nature of her hands, which she often pointed out in her speeches, shows the difficulties she's been through. A shaft of light streams in from the heavens, as if to bless Sojourner's efforts.

# Naziq al-Abid

## (1898–1959, SYRIA)

## *The Mother of Syrian Independence*

aziq al-Abid had one of the best resumes ever: she spoke five languages, started the Syrian Red Crescent (and half a dozen other organizations), became the first female general in Syrian history, and possibly held the world record for greatest number of times sent into exile.

The first thing to know about Naziq is that she was fair-minded. The second is how much it got her in trouble. Exhibit A: She's a young student in Mosul. She sees the Turkish teachers discriminate against Arab students (she was Kurdish, so she didn't get treated the same). Her response? Organizing a mass protest to get the teachers fired. This resulted in her getting kicked out—of the school, of Mosul, of the entire country—and sent back to Damascus.

For those counting, that's exile number one.

Having now been kicked out of one country for agitation, she decided to try for a second by starting a women's rights club (the first in Syria) as soon as she got back. The club advocated for the right to vote . . . as well as Syrian independence from the Ottoman Empire. Cue the unamused powers-that-be kicking her (and her family) out of Syria. That's two.

Well, the Ottoman Empire fell and she headed back to a Syria with a lot of questions on its mind. Newly free after 400 years of being others' subjects, Syrians wondered what issues to tackle first. Naziq, now 16, had an answer: give women the right to vote. Now. Right now. Did you hear me? Now.

Again, an unpopular opinion. How unpopular? Let's let Ahmad Qudmani, a high-ranking government official from the time, answer: "God created her with half a mind, how can we give her the right of political decision-making?"

Yeah . . . At least he didn't pelt her with rocks (others did).

Nevertheless, she continued her crusade, giving speeches and eventually meeting the US ambassador (without a veil!) to pressure the United States for help. The ambassador, from his description, had a total crush on her. Soon suffrage got put to debate—had it passed, Syria might have given women the vote before the United States. Unfortunately, it didn't, due to France destroying the government.

The French, somewhat incensed at the idea of Syrians governing themselves, decided they owned the place. The Syrian king, realizing that his country was all of four months old and had no real army, surrendered to avoid mass bloodshed. His minister of defense, however, was all, "I ain't going out like that!" Independent of the king, he scraped together some decrepit weaponry and volunteers for a suicide mission, with the idea to go out with middle fingers blazing. France had 9,000 well-armed troops. Syria had 1,500 untrained conscripts. One of them was a woman: Naziq.

The image of her in military attire, sans veil, rifle slung over her shoulder, was in every newspaper. The articles called her "The Sword of Damascus" and "The Syrian Joan of Arc." The reaction, in her words: "Some were very critical, accusing me of blasphemy, but most people supported me. I was off to battle, not to a cabaret!"

The resistance predictably fell to the French (by some accounts, Naziq, as a medic, was the only survivor) and you can guess what happened next: exile number three.

Two years later she was back, on the condition she give up politics. Technically, she did. Instead, she enabled others to do her kind of work. She opened her women's rights organization (Noor al-Fayyha, or Light of Damascus), co-administered a school for orphans, and started the Red Crescent (Syria's version of the Red Cross). At some point, she pissed off yet another politician and was exiled to Jordan (that's four).

She came back to Syria again, this time spending her time smuggling food and munitions to anti-French rebels, and caring for the wounded. During this time, she also founded yet another women's society, because presumably the life of an outlaw was not actually keeping her busy enough. Eventually the French had enough, issued an arrest warrant, and she fled to Lebanon (that's five—okay, technically she was fleeing arrest, but it counts).

It's in Lebanon that she met her future husband. She didn't marry him until she was in her forties, though, as she was too busy getting things done.

By the time she died, she was back home, Syria was a free nation, women were joining the workforce, going out in public alone, and unveiling with abandon. A decade later, women began being elected to parliament. Regardless of what came later for Syria, for a period it made great strides toward equality, due in no small part to Naziq al-Abid: a woman born into every conceivable luxury who traded it all to fight injustice.

## · ART NOTES AND TRIVIA ·

Naziq is seen here ripping off a veil, since going veil-less was a big part of her life. Not that there's anything wrong with choosing to wear a veil; Naziq just didn't have that choice, and wanted it badly. She didn't actually carry a flag through the streets, but since she kept getting compared to **Joan of Arc** (who's always depicted carrying a flag), it seemed like appropriate symbolism. There is one white journalist in the crowd, to represent that someone there managed to popularize the term "Joan of Arc of the Arabs" to the Western world. That's the actual flag for the short-lived Arab Kingdom of Syria. There's a ton of light streaming in as a reference to her Light of Damascus organization.

# Zelia Nuttall

## (1857–1933, MEXICO)

*The Mother of Mexican Archaeology*

MATURITY 2

elia Nuttall did not suffer fools.

One of the first—and most important—Mexican archaeologists, Zelia was a mama bear to what mattered to her: her protégés, her work, and especially her daughter (whom she raised alone). Most of the time, she was nurturing and kind, a welcoming host and well-regarded socialite. But cross her, and hoo boy, the claws would come out.

From the start, Zelia* wasn't interested in a conventional life. While the other girls were engrossed in fairy tales, eight-year-old Zelia was head down in her copy of *Antiquities of Mexico*, realizing what she wanted to be when she grew up. She married and had a kid early on, but four years into the marriage, decided to go it alone.† She got a divorce, sole custody, and her freedom—under her maiden name.

From there, her career took off. Her first archaeological dig resulted in a published paper, which led to a special assistant position at Harvard University that she kept for 47 years. She discovered the most complete set of pre-Conquest Mexican writings that still exist, uncovered lost manuscripts from Sir Francis Drake, presented at the World's Fair—she did it all.

Moreover, she paid it forward. Early on, she partnered with philanthropist Phoebe Hearst (mother to William Randolph), and set about educating local peoples to preserve their own heritage. One of her indigenous proteges, Manuel Gamio, would go on to become Mexico's most famous archaeologist—after Zelia fought tooth and nail to secure his education.

None of this was easy. Besides the omnipresent sexism, Zelia also had to fight the status quo of archaeology, which was replete with sleazy treasure hunters. It's here that she had the incident that really cemented her reputation.

The dustup revolved around the Isla de Sacrificios, a tiny (haunted!) island that, Zelia discovered, housed the ruins of a site for human sacrifice. Once Zelia set up shop there to

---

* Properly Zelia Maria Magdalena Nuttall.

† From the sound of it, her husband may have been one of the fools she did not suffer. Although there aren't a ton of details available on him, he did apparently spend no small amount of money buying a crystal skull—yes, like the ones in the crappiest Indiana Jones movie—from a shady French antiques dealer. Zelia was a woman of science. It's not a leap to assume she did not exactly approve of this move.

DOWN WITH IMPERIALIST WAR

excavate it, the Mexican government immediately presented her with three setbacks: they slashed her funding; they limited the area in which she could work; and, because she was a woman, they gave her a supervisor. This was Salvador Batres, son of her archenemy, Leopoldo Batres.

Zelia haaaaaaated them. The Batreses, besides being corrupt jackholes who'd sell off priceless treasures to even bigger jackholes, were staggeringly incompetent. Upon starting work at the National Museum of Anthropology in Mexico, Salvador completely reorganized their classification system, turning a decent setup into a nigh-unusable one. Similarly, upon starting work at the Isla de Sacrificios, he destroyed an ancient fresco in the process of unearthing it. But the thing to top it all off: they sent out a press release claiming to have discovered the ruins themselves.

Zelia was not amused.

In short order, a couple things happened. She resigned in disgust from her post at the National Museum. She got the *Mexican Herald* newspaper to run a correction. And, most importantly, she wrote a 42-page article in a major academic journal that burned her enemies to the ground.

The article laid out the backstory on finding the site, talked about Zelia's methodology, and, midway through, took an aside to eviscerate Salvador and Leopoldo for their incompetence. Soon thereafter, the Mexican government followed through on Zelia's suggestion to hire "competent and honorable engineers and architects," and got rid of the Batreses.

She lived out the rest of her life as a nurturing host and advocate. She threw a lot of weight into trying to revive native traditions of solar worship, and wanted to see annual festivals celebrated in schools. She also grew to be quite the botanist—collecting seeds from ancient Mexican plants and growing them; cultivating medicinal herbs; re-creating foods from olden times. But more than anything, she was known for her gracious hosting, whereupon one finds an anecdote that perfectly sums her up.

At one point, two young men came to visit Zelia. As she descended a staircase to greet them, her dress snagged on something and came right off. Without missing a beat, she walked up to them, shook their hands, and continued with the pleasantries—as her maid frantically grabbed the dress and ran off.

## · ART NOTES AND TRIVIA ·

The location here is the Casa Alvarado, where she lived most of her life. She's tending a garden both as a reference to her interest in botany, but also to how she nurtured the field of archaeology, her daughter, and her protégés.

You can see in the flower bed by Zelia some bits of pottery scattered about. That's historically accurate—she found a ton of Aztec pottery fragments in her own garden, and did an excavation on them. It was actually the first-ever academic study of Aztec pottery, and it happened in her house.

The maid in the background is, of course, running off with the snagged dress.

The book Zelia holds is based on a copy of *Antiquities of Mexico*. Her baby daughter is reading it, just like Zelia herself did early on.

Her necklace has an Aztec swastika on it. This is a callback to her research into the worldwide symbolism of swastikas, which she linked to astrology. For a journey into the bizarre, check online for conspiracy theories about her.

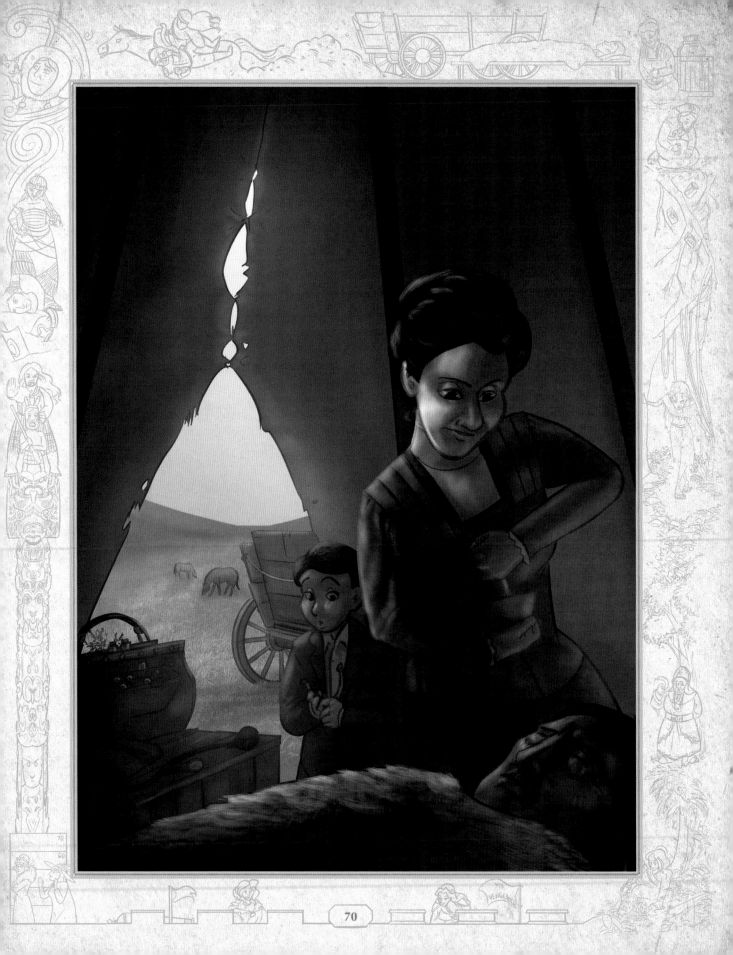

# Susan La Flesche Picotte

### (1865–1915, OMAHA NATION/UNITED STATES)

## The Mom Who Built a Hospital

usan grew up surrounded by sickness. It had been a way of life with the Omaha for generations, ever since the whites came. The Omaha would get tuberculosis or influenza, and they'd have to wait for the whites to show up and help, since the Omaha needed permission to leave their lands.

As a child, Susan once sat at the bedside of a sick old Omaha woman, caring for her as a messenger went to the white agency doctor. Four times the messenger went, and each time the doctor said he'd be there soon. But he never showed up. Susan could do nothing but watch through the night as the old woman slowly died in agony. Years later, she'd recall the doctor's attitude: "It was only an Indian, and it [did] not matter."

That was the moment she vowed to do something none of her people, male or female, had ever done before: she would become a medical doctor.

It wasn't *that* surprising: she was already a conscious blend of Western and Native heritage. The daughter of two half-white, half-Native parents, she was raised with both Omaha traditions and a Christian education. She spoke Omaha, but her father, a tribal chief, never gave her a Native name, or let her get a "mark of honor" tattoo. He wanted all his children to assimilate. Unlike most Omaha, he'd been to the cities of the whites: he knew the Omaha were vastly outnumbered, that the future of the whites was coming, that the Omaha needed to adapt or die.

It would require a lot of sacrifice. The assumption at the time was that by becoming a professional, women would be giving up any chance to have a family—quite literally. A Harvard Medical School professor wrote in 1873 that women who studied too hard would become infertile. Women had to choose to educate or menstruate, because their "system never does two things well at the same time." His book on this went through *seventeen printings*. It was accepted as fact.

Susan was undeterred.

Through some family connections,[*] Susan managed to get into Hampton Institute,[†]

---

[*] Her oldest sister, Susette (aka Bright Eyes), was a famous Native rights activist. Through her, Susan met well-connected ethnographer Alice Fletcher, who'd become one of her greatest supporters. Naturally, they met while Fletcher was sick. Susan nursed her back to health.

[†] This college had predominantly black and Native American students, and was the alma mater of Booker T. Washington.

where she proved an incredibly dedicated student. She got up at 5:15 every morning, sewed and sold clothes to help pay her tuition, and threw herself into her studies. Even when she fell in love with a classmate, a sickly Sioux boy named Thomas Ikinicapi, she pushed thoughts of romance aside and kept to her books. Although she did tutor and take care of him (it was kind of her thing). She graduated second in her class, salutatorian. But she wasn't done with her education yet.

Medical school proved to be harder. The first challenge was paying for it. She didn't get a scholarship, as women going into medicine weren't highly regarded (one yahoo claimed working women would tear America apart by becoming "incompetent mothers and inferior wives"). Determined to not only prove that wrong, but also provide a hero for the so-called vanishing race of Native Americans, her connections organized a huge number of women from across the United States to pool together funds and pay for her education.

The second challenge was the cultural stigma. Susan went to the only medical college in the world to accept women,[*] which was small enough that it had to pair with other schools at instructional surgeries. For weeks leading up to the first surgery, the boys belittled Susan's class mercilessly, saying that female constitutions couldn't handle the sight of blood.[†] True enough, just before the first surgery began, one of the students did faint: the boy who'd been taunting the loudest.

The first two challenges surmounted, the third one began: the workload. The amount of memorization and study was intense, but the girls found support in one another. They shared their notes and studied as a group, helping everyone forward in solidarity.

Susan struggled to keep her focus. She was intensely homesick, and moreover, lonely. Even as her sisters were settling down and having kids (and she was providing pregnancy advice in her daily letters), her love life was nonexistent. She and Thomas, despite mutual attraction, had effectively broken up due to communication skills so poor they'd make Jane Austen roll her eyes.[‡] Susan had promised all the women who'd paid for her college that she wouldn't get married and disappear as soon as she graduated. She was already a role model for everyone back home. She had a lot on her shoulders.

Then her father died. It was sudden and unexpected, just weeks into her final semester. He was the pillar of the community, the man holding everything together.

---

[*] The Woman's Medical College of Pennsylvania, which drew a staggeringly international crowd. Her classmates included some of the first female doctors from Japan, Syria, and India—the last of whom, Anandibai Joshi, was possibly the first native-born Indian woman to set foot on American soil.

[†] They evidently had not yet done the lesson on menstruation.

[‡] They'd spent Christmas together at various social gatherings, side by side for hours on end, and barely talked. Just reading about it will make you want to reach through time and shake them.

Susan didn't attend his funeral. Instead, she finished her studies, as he would have wanted. She gave him the best posthumous gift she could have: graduating as valedictorian. She had become the first Western-educated Native American medical doctor in history. And she was going to hold the community together in her father's stead.

Susan's workload only increased when she moved back home. Starting at 7 AM and ending past 10 PM, she rode on horseback to treat patients spread out over 1,350 square miles. She earned the trust of her people so fast that the one white doctor left within a year, because she'd taken all his patients. She had to buy an entire team of horses and a buggy just to reach some people without breaking her medical equipment along the way. But she would never turn someone down, never let someone die because she didn't feel like leaving the house.

However, her job rapidly grew well beyond medicine. In no time, Susan was providing advice on business matters, legal questions, financial actions, marital problems, religious concerns, and much more. She started a small library. She helped run community events for the local church. She led health awareness campaigns, educating the Omaha about the dangers of alcohol and urging them to put up screens to keep flies out—all while keeping exhaustive records on each of the 100 to 130 patients she treated a month.

And Susan was deliriously happy. She was making a difference. It's what she'd always wanted.

Not that it wasn't hard. The winters were brutal, forcing her to make house calls to families too sick to make the trek to her. She had limited funds, poor customers, and dwindling supplies, so she often had to resort to herbal remedies. And alcohol was a growing problem: whenever the Omaha voted on local prohibition ordinances, white whiskey peddlers would trick the illiterate Omaha about what their votes meant, and sabotage the bills.

After several years of this, Susan began slowing down. She'd had a number of personal difficulties. At the beginning of 1892, her sister's husband, Charles Picotte, died of tuberculosis. He was followed soon thereafter by Thomas, the only man Susan had ever loved. Topping it off, following the death of Susan's father, her mother's health had started failing. And so had Susan's: she had begun experiencing bouts of debilitating pain, symptoms of a chronic ailment that she couldn't diagnose.

But more than anything, she was *lonely*. All her life she'd devoted herself to others. She'd been an icon, but she'd never been a person. She was 29 and unmarried, an extreme rarity for the era. She wanted something for herself.

And so, to the massive shock (and disappointment) of almost everyone, Susan quit her job. She retired as a physician and went to look after her mother. And within a year, she married.

Her husband was Henry Picotte, a Sioux tribe member and brother of her sister's late husband. They were an odd couple: she was one of the most educated women in the world, and he was an ex–circus showman. While she'd worked for a decade elevating the status of her people, he'd been playing a racist half-man, half-beast caricature for money. Nobody really liked him.

But the marriage got her out of her slump. Within a year and a half of the wedding, shortly after giving birth to their son Caryl, she began practicing medicine again. She'd get up at daybreak, work all day long, come back for supper, and then set out again. She initially brought Caryl with her on the long buggy rides, but after one particularly harrowing journey, she left him at home. Henry became a stay-at-home dad, looking after Caryl and, soon, Caryl's young brother Pierre.

For a decade, Susan was a tireless advocate for the Omaha. She did it all: practiced medicine, fought whiskey peddlers, spread hygiene awareness, protested unfair land treaties, lobbied the government for funds. It wasn't easy: her health would fail periodically and she had bouts of depression, where she'd feel that nobody recognized her endless struggle. During one of these bouts, word got out about her depression, and she was awash in thankful visitors who showered her in gifts. She resolved to remember that feeling whenever melancholy struck again.

In 1905, her husband died. Like so many others with little to do, few career prospects, and nowhere to go, he'd taken to alcohol. It had aggravated his tuberculosis and taken his life. He'd known better. Susan, 40 years old, in failing health, and deaf in one ear, was now the single mother of two young boys, ages nine and seven.

Miraculously, from there, things got better. For one thing, the Omahas' public health finally started to improve: a prohibition law went into effect, and the government began encouraging the Omaha to cultivate crops. Susan built a dream house across the street from her sister Marguerite's home, and they shared the responsibilities of raising each others' kids. Susan saved up enough money to send both her sons to boarding school. She managed to slow the spread of tuberculosis by banning the practice of communal cups and installing drinking fountains. She even successfully got the government to grant full land ownership to the Omaha.*

But she had one last project. Ever since her husband's death, she had dreamed of having a modern hospital, one with decent supplies, where her husband, or any of the numerous

---

* The government had granted 160 acres to each household 25 years earlier, but held it in trust, feeling that the Omaha didn't understand property law well enough to not get swindled. Susan went back and forth on whether this was patronizing or a good idea. In the end, the government granted full ownership to those they felt showed legal competence. Unfortunately, they did not test this very hard: the vast majority to receive full ownership rights were illiterate or barely understood American law. Within two years, 90 percent had sold their land rights. They didn't have much else in the way of wealth, and few ways of making more.

orphaned children she treated, could have received ongoing treatment. She pulled in every connection she'd ever made as a public figure, contacted every woman who'd ever pushed her to go to med school, practically everyone she'd ever met. She called and wrote for days and weeks and months.

And on January 8, 1913, her hospital opened. It was a tiny affair: 39 beds, two general wards, and a surgery room, named after her father. It was funded entirely from private donations. In an interview with the local paper, Susan said, "My greatest dream in having the hospital built was to save the little children."

Soon thereafter, she fell sick, and her chronic ailment was at last identified: bone cancer. She went through two surgeries. She spent her recovery time with her two boys. Pierre had just graduated high school as salutatorian, and Caryl had started med school. But her health continued to decline, and despite the intervention of Marie Curie herself,* she died.

Susan was eulogized by the entire community as one of the greatest Omaha people ever. The next edition of the local paper added an extra page just to fit in all the condolences. She would not have accepted it, as indicated by some of her dying words: "I cannot see how any credit is due me. I am only thankful that I have been called and permitted to serve. I feel blessed for that privilege beyond measure."

## · ART NOTES AND TRIVIA ·

Susan is portrayed here as the mix of cultures she was: She bears modern medical equipment in a briefcase, but she is mixing herbs in a bowl. She is missing several vials in her briefcase, a nod to how she was perpetually underfunded. She's clearly made a house call to a remote Omaha man, as seen by the wide open space outside. Her son Caryl is playing with her stethoscope, although that is a bit of artistic license: in reality, Susan stopped bringing Caryl on house calls while he was still an infant.

---

* Made aware of Susan's condition, Curie sent a radium pellet in a lead-lined box from France, to help treat Susan. Unfortunately, the doctor accidentally lost it in Susan's ear and had to spend several painful hours digging it out.

# Molly Craig

### (C. 1917–2004, AUSTRALIA)

## The Mother Who Walked Across Australia—Twice

*(Aboriginal and Torres Strait Islander people should be aware that this chapter
contains images and names of people who have passed away.\*)*

In the 1930s, Australia had some really crazy ideas about Aboriginal people.
One of the most dangerous of these sanity-bereft "ideas" was to kidnap
all mixed-race Aboriginal children and raise them in concentration camps.
The "logic" was: because Aboriginal tribes would give these kids a hard time
for their skin color,† and because Aboriginal tribes were undoubtedly going
to die out, it was only moral to forcibly wrench children from their mothers' arms, reeducate
them in youth prison camps, and train them as domestic servants, in a twisted update to
slavery. This plan actually went into effect.

Fourteen-year-old Molly Craig was one of those kidnapped—except she *escaped*. Using
wit, cunning, and traditional hunting expertise, she led her two sisters‡ on an almost 1,000-
mile walk back home across the Australian outback, while evading the police. And when
they caught her and her children years later, Molly did the same trip again, this time while
carrying a toddler.

Molly was part of the Mardu people, who'd traditionally lived in the western deserts of
Australia. Starting in 1907, many of them had come to live in the area near Jigalong, which
the Australian government had spent significant effort making livable. There they'd created a
maintenance depot for their massive rabbit-proof fence: a continent-spanning attempt to keep
the foreign-introduced pests from spreading west. Molly's father, a white man, was one of the
fence's inspectors.

In 1931, under government edict, Molly and her sisters Daisy and Gracie were taken
from their families. As they watched their relatives wail, bash themselves with rocks, and

---

\* As you'll see in this entry, feeling extreme grief at the loss of a loved one is a cultural reaction for these popula-
tions. Offering warnings against the exposure to mentions of those lost is a tradition and courtesy.

† Admittedly, Molly and her sisters did have a hard time due to their skin color. Their grandfather would rub
charcoal on them to try and darken their skin, and other kids would tease them in their youth. But in time, the
Jigalong community grew used to them and the harassment largely subsided.

‡ They were actually first cousins, but in Aboriginal tradition, they thought of each other as being closer to
sisters.

cut themselves—traditional Aboriginal forms of expressing sorrow—the girls were spirited hundreds of miles away to Moore River Native Settlement, their reeducation camp. There they were forced to speak only English, eat horrible food, and use a bucket as a toilet. Those who disobeyed were often beaten and put in solitary confinement.

It didn't take long for Molly to plan an escape.

Nobody had ever escaped successfully, although not for lack of trying. Not only was the area's environment utterly unfamiliar to most, the government employed an Aboriginal tracker to hunt down any fleeing children. The tracker had been as successful as he was cruel, and there was no shortage of stories about girls returned with whip marks all over their bodies. Molly was undeterred.

One day, during the rainy season, she grabbed Daisy and Gracie and forced them to make a run for it. She quickly proved her skill as a hunter. Sussing out the cardinal directions despite the cloudy weather, she guided them up a river to disguise their tracks. Back when they'd been abducted, she'd paid close attention to the sun, and memorized which direction they'd been taken. She aimed to get to the rabbit-proof fence about which her father had taught her so much. If she found that, she knew, she could follow it back home.

They walked about 15 to 20 miles a day, living off the land in areas teeming with some of the world's most infamously dangerous wildlife. They crawled around dueling kangaroos. They slept in dug-out rabbit warrens. They caught and killed game.

Most of all, they avoided capture. Walking under trees to avoid being spotted by planes and marching during rain to cover their tracks, they frustrated their pursuers. When they encountered farms, they would beg for food and clothes, which the farmers would usually give them. But the girls would always approach and leave the farm from and to the opposite direction of which they were really headed. They consistently gave false plans to anyone who asked, often saying they were planning to hitch a ride on a train. When they left, their hosts would then almost inevitably call the government, and inadvertently lead their pursuers astray.

It's worth mentioning at this point that Molly was only 14. Gracie was 12 or 13, and Daisy was only 9.

The trip was incredibly difficult on them. The acacia branches scratched up their legs terribly, and eventually their wounds got infected. Gracie and Daisy were so debilitated by this that Molly carried them. When Molly grew too tired, they would take turns carrying each other. After almost two months, when they were getting close, Gracie, exhausted, irritable, and in pain, left her sisters and headed to a nearby train station. She made it to a nearby Aboriginal colony where she heard her mother had moved, but was eventually caught by the authorities.

The search for the missing girls became a nationwide sensation. While A. O. Neville,

Chief Protector of Aborigines,* had kept the story out of the news for some time out of fear of embarrassing his department, the girls had been gone so long that he had no choice but to ask the public for leads. Many wrote in with sightings of the girls, leading Neville to deploy constables and hire trackers. None of them ever caught Molly or Daisy.

After nearly nine weeks, Molly and Daisy reunited with their families at Jigalong. The day after their tearful reunion, the families left Jigalong and moved into the desert, to prevent the government from taking their children again. Neville's department determined, at last, that they would be too difficult to recapture. "I am afraid," one employee said, "you will never get them now as by this time they will be back in their own country and well and truly camouflaged." And so Neville let Molly, "a very costly woman to the Department," to her own devices.†

Unfortunately, it was not to last. Molly settled down and married a stockhand named Toby Kelly and had two children, Anna and Doris. However, in 1940, after going to a hospital for appendicitis surgery, Molly and her children were apprehended and again taken to Moore River. Her family was apopleptic: her niece literally died of self-sustained injuries from her grieving. But Molly was not one to give up. Within a month and a half, she'd left with 18-month-old Anna in tow, and walked the same route back to her home, along the rabbit-proof fence. She'd had to leave Doris behind.

Her victory was again short-lived. Within three years, the authorities came back and took Anna from her. They let Molly stay.

Doris would not see her mother again until 21 years later. It took her many years to shake off the indoctrination of her government-sponsored upbringing and accept her heritage. She initially accused her mother of abandoning her, not realizing the government had snatched her away, or that her mother had twice run away from the reservation. In 1996, Doris published *Follow the Rabbit-Proof Fence*, a telling of her mother's story, which was adapted into a film in 2002. Molly died two years later—only a couple months from finally being reunited with her lost child Anna, who'd been told all along that she was an orphan.

Aboriginal children continued to be stolen from their families until 1970, in what is known as the Stolen Generation. Starting in 1998, Australians have taken to commemorating this mistreatment with National Sorry Day, as the government steadfastly refused to apologize until 2008.‡

---

* Yes, revolting as it is, that was his official title. This was a guy who asked, after doing the job for 23 out of 25 years, "Are we going to have a population of 1 million blacks in the Commonwealth or are we going to merge them into our white community and eventually forget that there ever were any Aborigines in Australia?"

† When officials caught Gracie, they exchanged no shortage of letters regarding remuneration and how to imprison her most cheaply. Her health and well-being were not discussed in these letters whatsoever.

‡ For reasons that will increasingly infuriate you the more you look into them, this continues to be an ongoing debate, as some pigheaded jackholes argue that Australian colonization was largely well-intentioned and beneficial. One of the most infamous turdblossoms of this "movement" has gone so far as to claim Molly Craig/Kelly's story was inaccurate and negatively misrepresented the treatment of children at Moore River.

# Sister Rosetta Tharpe

## (1915–1973, UNITED STATES)

## *The Mother of Rock 'n' Roll*

er music shaped Elvis Presley, Johnny Cash, Chuck Berry, and many others. Her career paved the way for everyone from Aretha Franklin to Whitney Houston to Beyoncé. She was a bisexual black woman who toured across the Jim Crow–era South, playing sold-out show after sold-out show. Yet almost nobody remembers Rosetta Tharpe.

Let's change that, shall we?

Tharpe[*] was born in rural Arkansas, where she was put on a fast track from a young age. Recognizing her daughter's musical talent, her mother[†] put her onto the gospel church circuit as a solo act by the time she was six. It was the sort of childhood you'd associate with Mozart or Michael Jackson—starting out, she was so small she could barely hold a guitar, but that didn't stop her from being incredible at playing it. She learned to improvise, sing over crowds, and entertain so well that even orthodox Jews would visit out-of-town churches just to hear her.

Although she tried living her life in line with the gospel music she sang, she was soon lured away by secular interests. She was married to a preacher by age 19, but he was abusive and un-faithful—leading her to divorce him and keep only his surname, Tharpe. Simultaneous to step-ping away from her marriage, she began to depart the core gospel circuit for the more secular one of New York. One can see traces of her ambivalence about this in the stage name she hit the scene with: Rosetta "Vashti" Tharpe, after the biblical queen who disobeyed her husband.

But once she set foot in New York, her career took off fast. Within two months of mov-ing to town, she was singing at the famous Cotton Club and playing Carnegie Hall. She befriended luminaries like Duke Ellington, Cab Calloway, and Dizzy Gillespie, and began playing music alongside each of them. She was a star.

But in her fame, Tharpe found herself walking a tightrope: she had to not be too religious for the secular New York clubs, and not too inauthentic for the church audiences down south.

---

[*] Her surname at birth was likely Atkins, or perhaps Nubin. She went by a number of different names in her youth, including Rosa, Rosie, Rosether, and Rosietta. Makes it a bit hard to pin down!

[†] Her mother, Katie Bell Nubin, left her husband and took Rosetta to Chicago when Rosetta was six. The reason why is murky—speculations have included a bad marriage, Rosetta being born out of wedlock (and the social scrutiny that came with that), and Nubin wanting to make money off Rosetta's talent. Nubin, quite a singer herself, would perform on the same ticket as Rosetta regularly for the rest of her life.

Instead of bending to one or the other, she pushed ahead with her own unique blend of the two. She refused to be pigeonholed as a novelty for New Yorkers, and she refused to stick to the calcified history of gospel tradition. She instead kept pushing her blend of gospel and dance music further and further.

And thus was born what we know as rock 'n' roll.

Now, there's certainly no shortage of influences on rock 'n' roll, and there's no end to the men that could claim to be the fathers of the genre—but it's hard to argue that anyone before Tharpe was its mother. The combination of her knockout voice and virtuoso guitar work led endless musicians to idolize and imitate her work. This book alone cannot possibly communicate this properly—please, go look up video of Tharpe's "Didn't It Rain," "Strange Things Happening Every Day," and/or "Up Above My Head." When you do, you'll likely realize, as this author did, how shockingly rare it is to witness such an accomplished black female guitarist. It's an experience you owe yourself.

This move into a new genre marked the end of her prolonged adolescence. She dumped her old producer, her old husband, and her old name: she was now Sister Rosetta Tharpe.

She began touring with a number of partner acts. The first, and most important, was a younger woman named Marie Knight, with whom, according to many, she had a romantic relationship.[*] Others included an all-girl band that she dubbed the Rosettes,[†] after herself. In dealing with partner acts, she developed a keen sense for business, promotion, and self-preservation that would serve her well—especially as she toured the hostile southern states of the Jim Crow era.

Heading down south was downright dangerous for black women in that era, but Tharpe persevered and even thrived. Knowing she wouldn't be able to book a hotel or even eat or shop in many places due to racist Jim Crow laws, she brought along a tour bus that had all the necessary accommodations, including a place to change and sleep. For extra security, she made sure to hire a white driver, who could enter areas she herself couldn't.

The climax of this era of her career was undoubtedly her wedding concert. Sensing her star beginning to fall, she agreed to a scheme concocted by two rakish producers: a combina-

---

[*] Upfront, it is important to note that both Knight and Tharpe denied the relationship during their lives. However, a ton of people have come forward in the years since to paint a different picture, including one man who claimed to have seen the two of them and another woman together in bed—shortly after Tharpe's third wedding, no less! They would certainly not have been the only instances of black LGBT singers from the era: Little Richard was gay, "Ma" Rainey was lesbian or bisexual, and Clara Ward had several sexual relations with women.

[†] They were initially called the Twilights, but she first renamed them the Angelic Queens Choir. This was a cutthroat business move on her part—there was another act gaining popularity at the time called the Angelic Gospel Singers, and the similarity in names was meant to confuse audiences into coming to see her act instead of theirs. Once she got called out on it, she redubbed them the Rosettes.

tion concert/wedding. The only problem was that she didn't have anyone to marry. Undeterred by this small detail, she signed on, with seven months to find a husband. Yes, it sounds like a rom-com setup, but it happened! She found herself a groom (her third*) and the concert was a massive success.

Unfortunately, the success was not long-lasting, and she fell on a hard period of failed reinventions. While other acts like Elvis Presley and Mahalia Jackson were on the rise, Tharpe's style of pop gospel began to seem old-fashioned. She tried partnering with some country musicians, then eschewed pop and returned whole-heartedly to gospel, but neither worked well. By 1957, she'd lost her house, in part due to her falling fortunes, and in part due to her spendthrift manager/husband.

She reestablished her footing while touring Europe, which had recently been hit by a craze for gospel music. By the time she returned, the American gospel scene had edged more to accept her blend of pop and gospel, and welcomed her back. Even though she was well into her forties, she hit the ground running, recording album after album, playing high-profile gigs, and humiliating all challengers in onstage guitar duels. For a full decade, despite her friends begging her to slow down, Tharpe played as hard as she ever had.

But nobody can go on forever. In 1968, her health got the better of her. Struck by a numbness in her arms, she was rushed to the hospital, to find she had undiagnosed diabetes—and that the doctors would have to amputate one of her legs. Determined not to let it get the best of her, she soon returned to the stage, literally hopping about on one foot as she played, working just as hard as before. But her health continued to decline, and she died a few years later, one day after she was supposed to record a new album.

Sister Rosetta Tharpe's name vanished into the footnotes of history surprisingly fast thereafter. This was partly due to an estate mismanaged by her manager/husband, Russell, who didn't even have the finances put forward to buy her a gravestone—to this day, Tharpe rests in an unmarked grave.

But perhaps the larger issue with her legacy was the difficulty in summarizing her. She was a study in contradictions: a gospel singer with a secular bent; a conservative persona who'd swear like a sailor; a sweet and sincere soul who manufactured her own wedding for publicity; a boisterous, flawed, magnificently human soul.

---

* Her first husband, Thomas J. Tharpe, she had left in 1938. Her second husband, unmentioned until now, was a man named Foch Pershing Allen. She married him around the time she began going by "Sister" Rosetta Tharpe, in 1944. This marriage lasted only two or three years. Her third and final husband, Russell Morrison, she married in 1951.

# Sutematsu Ōyama

### (1860–1919, JAPAN/UNITED STATES)

## The Godmother of Japanese Girls' Education

he first Japanese girl to go to college didn't have a choice.

Her name was Sakiko Yamakawa.

She was only eight years old when troops came for her town. As samurai of Japan's Aizu clan, her family were on the losing end of a civil war that would end the age of the sword. Their last stand came when enemy forces closed in on Aizu castle. Behind those walls, Sakiko did a woman's duty: she ran ammunition to the gunners and empty shells to the storehouse. And when artillery fire landed nearby, she smothered the shells with wet quilts to prevent explosions.

Which is how her sister-in-law Tose died. She was running to a shell when it burst. Most of the shrapnel hit her in the chest, with an errant piece slicing Sakiko in the neck.

But this did not kill Tose immediately.

As she laid there bleeding, Tose begged for Sakiko's mother to give her an honorable death—but the mother could not bear to do it. Sakiko watched as her sister-in-law died slowly out in the open. Sakiko's neck would bear a shrapnel scar until the end of her days.

After the war, the Japanese government ended its centuries of isolation. Humbled by foreigners who'd forced their ports open at gunpoint, the government viewed learning from these "barbarians" as a matter of survival. To that end, they offered a kingly sum for volunteers willing to go abroad for 10 years. But despite mass poverty and starvation, there were almost no applicants.

That is, until Sakiko's brother signed her up to go to America.

He didn't ask her, he didn't ask their mother—he just did it. For him, it solved two problems: it increased the family profile, and it gave him one less mouth to feed. Sakiko didn't know any English. She'd never left Japan. Almost nobody ever had.* And so, at age 11,

---

\* Her brother Hiroshi, who'd made this decision, was not only now caretaker of the Yamakawa clan after the wartime death of his father, but also tasked with looking after many of the surviving Aizu rebels. He did not have altogether that many options. In the end, at least two others of Sakiko's family would go abroad, although their level of consent is unknown—her brother Kenjiro was already taking classes at Yale before Sutematsu got to the United States, and her other sister, Misao, would end up going to St. Petersburg and studying French. For many years, Sakiko and Misao would have no common language.

Sakiko joined a group of four other girls, ages 6 to 14, as the first women to go to the West. None of them had been asked.

The last time Sakiko saw her mother, she was given a new name: Sutematsu. It was an odd, sorrowful name, combining the symbol for "discard," the name of the defeated lord of Aizu, and the Japanese word "to wait."* Her old life was over.

Her name was Sutematsu.

She arrived in the United States six years after the American Civil War. As she and the four other girls made their way from west to east across the country, they were bewildered time and time again. In San Francisco, they witnessed blackface for the first time. In Utah they saw their first snowball fights. In Illinois they visited the smoldering aftermath of the Great Chicago Fire. In Washington, DC, they went to dinner with some young notables. When Sutematsu asked one if he spoke Japanese, he replied with an invented string of foreign-sounding gibberish, and then burst into laughter.

Terrified, she and the other girls kept to themselves, even as the press hounded them, trying to get a glimpse of the exotic "princesses." (They weren't princesses, not that anyone would listen.)

But gradually, they were separated. First to go were the two eldest, for whom the stress was too much: they returned to Japan. The remaining three—Sutematsu, Shige, and Ume— clung together so tightly that even after several months in the United States, none had learned any English. To fix this, they were separated and sent to different foster homes.

Her name was Stemats.

Everyone in her new family kept tripping up over how to pronounce her name, so they simplified it. She was warmly welcomed and soon sent off to a public school. Despite a bumpy start—in which she was required to rank the civilization levels of the United States and Japan on a scale from "savage" to "enlightened"—she excelled. Not only did Stemats get top grades in high school, she was the only girl in her class to go to college. She went to Vassar College, which had only been open for a little over a decade, and graduated near the top of her class, giving a speech at graduation. She was the most educated Japanese woman alive.

After over a decade away from her native land, she headed back, to live with a family with whom she could barely speak a common language. She had changed so much after spending her formative years in another country. When asked how she felt to return, she replied, "I cannot tell you how I feel, but I should like to give one good scream."

---

* The first character, "sute" (捨), is the base of the verb "suteru," to discard. The second character, "matsu" (松), means "pine tree," and was the first character of the family name of the defeated lord of Aizu—Katamori Matsudaira. "Matsu," besides being the first part of the Matsudaira's name, is a homophone for the verb "to wait" (待つ). Her mother was telling her she was waiting for her to return.

Japan welcomed her back courteously, but the political winds had shifted. Where once had existed a fervor to modernize, instead was growing a conservative backlash. Tradition, not change, was on the rise. Japan had little use for Stemats. She was an alien in her own country. So she set out to change her country.

She and the other two girls sent abroad—Shige and Ume*—began spending more time together. They began pursuing a common goal: opening a school for girls. But they needed funding, and social standing. It came from the place Stemats least expected.

His name was Iwao Ōyama.

He was high up in the Japanese army, where he'd served for many years. He'd been at the battle of Aizu. He'd been on the opposing side. He bore scars from bullets fired from Aizu—bullets that may have been carried by Stemats. He had fired shells in return—shells that may have killed Stemats's sister.

He was asking for Stemats's hand in marriage.†

Her family said no immediately. But she thought through it. She'd been back for years, and isolation had worn her down. She wanted to do more. Iwao afforded her that. She did not love him, but what was her life, save a series of sacrifices for her country? In the end, she said yes.

Her name was Sutematsu Ōyama.

Her new surname was appropriate for one who had—for the first time willingly—given her life to Japan. It translated to "great mountain." And fittingly, in the shadow of Mount Fuji, she got to work.

With the empress's patronage, Sutematsu started the Peeresses' School, which taught noblewomen. She brought on Ume as one of the teachers, and her foster sister from America as another.

But as her profile grew, she became a target for gossip. She was not Japanese enough. She was too close to the empress. When her stepdaughter died of illness, a "fiction" novel blamed a proxy Sutematsu for it, painting her as a cruel, power-hungry villain. It became a bestseller.

Her successes came with a trade-off of more isolation. The higher she rose, the more she was obliged to do official functions, and the less she could directly work on teaching, or see

---

* Shige had gone to Vassar too, but did not get a bachelor's degree, just a certificate in music. After, she married a Japanese naval officer who'd also been sent abroad, and settled down to have a pretty normal life. Ume, the youngest of the group and the most isolated by far, didn't speak any Japanese at all when she came back. She was treated as an exotic invalid who couldn't do anything properly, and it really upset her. She'd eventually go back and get a full degree at Bryn Mawr College—she had been so young that she had only graduated high school by the time she returned to Japan.

† Iwao is an interesting character. He'd also spent time abroad—in France—and was recently widowed. He wanted a wife who would be a good companion for him on the international stage, and Sutematsu was the most eligible woman in Japan. He was by all accounts a good man who'd become Minister of War and lead forces in the Russo-Japanese War.

her friends Ume and Shige. She was eventually even given the title "princess," after years of being called one. In one letter to her foster sister, she wrote: "My husband grows fatter every year, and I thinner."

But her sacrifices paid off. In 1899, the government mandated each prefecture create at least one girls' school. The next year, Ume left the Peeresses' School to start a women's college open to all women, not just nobles. Sutematsu helped fund it.

In 1919, the Spanish Flu ravaged Tokyo—the same illness that had claimed Sutematsu's stepdaughter several years earlier. Ume, her health already declining, had recently resigned from running the school. Sutematsu faced a choice: flee the plague, or look after the school. Sutematsu stayed behind. She had to make sure the school continued.

The day after she found a replacement, Sutematsu awoke with a sore throat. She died two weeks later.

Today, Japanese students often learn about Ume Tsuda, the public face of girl's education. But they rarely learn the name of the woman who fought for her, who journeyed alongside her, who gave all.

Her name was Ōyama.

Her name was Stemats.

Her name was Sakiko.

Her name is remembered.

## · ART NOTES AND TRIVIA ·

Sutematsu is seen here looking at herself in the three major eras of her life: as the young Sakiko, as college graduate Stemats, and as married woman Ōyama. In each, she is caressing the scar on her neck, remembering from whence she came. The design of her clothing slowly covers up the pinks of her childhood with muted grays. Pink and gray were also the school colors for Vassar at the time, although they were later changed when Vassar began accepting men in the 1970s. Rumor has it the change was due to male athletes complaining about feeling effeminate in pink, although the Dean of Studies from the time denies it.

The flags behind her are those of Aizu (left), the centennial US flag of 1876 (center), and the Japanese flag (right). The jewelry box is a lacquered Japanese box with a design on the inside lid, typical of the times. The portrait on the right is that of her brother Hiroshi.

# Ada Blackjack

## (1898–1983, SIBERIA/ALASKA/UNITED STATES)

## The Mother Who Survived the Arctic

MATURITY 3
CHILD LOSS C
ABUSE A
SELF-HARM H

It was a dumb, dumb plan.

The idea, if you can call it that, was to claim Wrangel Island, a desolate wasteland located 200 miles northeast of Siberia, for the British Empire. The theory went that after the expedition to claim it spent a year there, the grateful British would shower these four young men (and their savvy backer) with praise for gifting the queen with such a strategically valuable plot of land, from which they could keep tabs on Russia. Never mind that the UK didn't want the land; or that several of the men had nearly died there years before; or that they only brought six months of supplies for a one-year stay; or that even though their entire plan hinged on them hiring several dozen Inuit helpers, they'd only been able to employ one ill-reputed Inuit woman. They were bold, confident white men, and they could do anything.

In the end, everyone died. Everyone, that is, except their Inuit helper, Ada Blackjack—and the expedition cat, Vic.

Wrangel Island would prove as alien an environment for Ada as for anyone else on that trip. Born Ada Deletuk, she'd grown up in towns instead of igloos, towns devastated by the Spanish Flu, towns where she'd had a hard life. At 16, she married a hunter who went by the name of Jack Blackjack (no, really; if there's another name for this guy, it's lost to history). In a stunning betrayal of the good name Blackjack, he turned out to be abusive, alcoholic, and unfaithful. The couple had three kids, two of whom died in childhood, before Jack deserted her.

By age 24, Ada was so destitute that she had to give up her five-year-old son, Bennett, to an orphanage. The orphanage was in Nome, Alaska, and she was so poor that she couldn't afford transportation there, so she walked the entire forty miles to Nome with Bennett in tow. He had contracted tuberculosis, and she didn't have the money to see to his treatment, or even feed him properly. She vowed to make enough money to be reunited with him one day, and to get him the medicine he so badly needed.

Which is how she met the Wrangel Island expedition. The trip was arranged by Vilhjalmur Stefansson, a famous Canadian-born explorer who'd already been to Wrangel Island. In 1913, he'd led a voyage that destroyed the ship *Karluk* and killed nearly half its crew, stranding many of them on Wrangel Island before they were rescued. Undeterred by this harrowing brush with death, Stefansson set about arranging a 1921 return trip, engaging two of his previous employees and two college students as crew.* He led them to believe that he had funding, government backing, and that many others were vying for positions on the trip. All of which were lies.†

Ada desperately needed money for her son, and so approached the sailors. She'd been working as hired help for several years, but hadn't been very successful. She was terrified at the prospect of the voyage, but her friends vouched that the crew was moral, if unskilled.

The sailors were in a similarly dire spot: nobody was interested in joining, and their "plan" factored in Inuit assistance heavily. They only had six months of supplies, and planned to hunt for the rest, for which they needed hunters. Ada didn't fit the bill whatsoever: she'd lived in cities and missions all her life, and barely knew how to sew, forget hunting. Moreover, she had a reputation as a prostitute and a drunk.‡ Nevertheless, when everyone else dropped out, she was their only option. They brought her on board.

On September 21, 1921, they landed on Wrangel Island. They'd had to trick their boat captain into taking them there—since they were on a secret mission, they refused to tell him where they were even going until they got there. When they disembarked, they refused to tell him why they were there. But as the captain left, he grabbed his binoculars and saw them plant a British flag on the island. He determined to alert the authorities.

The first months on the island were rough. They were so far north that the winter brought 61 consecutive days without sunlight. Ada quickly succumbed to a condition known as Arctic Hysteria, where the victim vacillates wildly between severe depression and manic episodes, characterized by hypersexuality. Ada, severely homesick and crippled by her fear of the omnipresent polar bears,§ would regularly wander from camp, and at one point even tried killing herself by drinking a bottle of liniment.

Making matters worse, the four men she was with had never heard of such a condition. None had any medical training (or, for that matter, knew how to shoot a gun—they literally

---

* The experienced sailors were Lorne Knight (age 28) and Fred Maurer (28), both alums of Stefansson-led adventures—Maurer had been on the *Karluk* expedition, and had signed up for the return trip to confront the trauma he'd experienced on the first one. Allan Crawford (20) and Milton Galle (19) rounded out the crew.

† Stefansson had even reached out to the Canadian government (through which he could contact Britain) to see if the Crown would be interested in Wrangel Island, and was told no. He proceeded anyway, sure that they'd change their minds within a year's time. He was convinced it would make a strategic air base. His goal was to angle a lease on the island, so he could raise reindeer. No, seriously. That was his endgame. Reindeer tycoon.

‡ It's very difficult to determine how true this was. As you'll see, she had mental health issues and some substance abuse ones, but she was also repeatedly the subject of outrageous rumors spread by crappy dudes.

§ The fear of polar bears was a cultural thing. Although Ada had become a fervent Christian in her childhood at an Alaskan mission, her Inuit background stayed with her, giving her a petrifying fear of the polar bear god Nanook. In particular, she feared being eaten and left forever inside his stomach.

couldn't hit a sleeping walrus). While their initial reaction was to coddle Ada, they eventually decided that she was harming their chances for survival, and they took a harsher stance. They denied her food, they made her sleep outside, and they strapped her to flag posts and sleds until she started working. When she developed a crush on Crawford (due in part to Arctic Hysteria), they mocked her, and began to drift from calling her The Native or The Woman to calling her Oofty or The Nymph.

But come mid-December, she had adjusted, the condition subsided, and life settled into a regular routine. Throughout the winter, the men would trap and shoot—usually without much success, leading Knight to muse that their names should be "hard luck" or "incompetent." They'd compose poetry, read books, and make bets on information they'd look up once they got back home (ah, the days before Wikipedia). Come warmer weather, hunting improved, and they lived in relative comfort. Sure, one had a mouth ulcer, another a busted hand, and Knight himself developed trouble walking, but the year was nearly up. The supply ship was set to arrive any day.

Except it wasn't. Their trip, since reported by the captain who'd dropped them off, had caused a minor international incident: Americans thought Wrangel Island was part of Alaska, Russia thought it was part of Russia, and the British Empire wanted nothing to do with any of it. Accordingly, Stefansson, completely broke, had trouble raising funds. When he finally did, the relief ship set off too late—the route there was only navigable a couple weeks a year—and was unable to get to the island. Stefansson cavalierly shrugged this off in the press, saying that the Arctic was perfectly hospitable and that they'd be fine living there another year.

Meanwhile, in temperatures dipping to 45 degrees below zero, the group began making contingency plans. With winter coming, their hunting prospects had again dwindled, and their supplies were running low. Realizing no relief boat was on its way, they came up with a plan B that was somehow worse than their plan A: sled across the frozen waters to Siberia. Plan C, if that didn't work? Sled to Alaska. Making the plan even less palatable was the fact that Knight, one of the most experienced on the trip, had grown extremely irritable and less mobile, symptoms of his slowly developing scurvy (the second bout he'd had with it!) that he stubbornly refused to tell anyone about.

Come January, the three men in decent condition set out for Siberia on a dog-pulled sled.* Knight, by this point extremely sick, stayed with Ada.

Knight terrified Ada. He had been inhospitable to her even when he was well, but now that he was bedridden, he became outright despotic. As she cooked, hunted, and cared for

---

* Knight and Crawford had made an abortive attempt in early January, only for them to come back a little bit later with blackened faces and frostbite.

him, he called her lazy and stupid in between throwing books at her. Privately, the sore-covered invalid, smelling of vomit, wrote he was sure she was in love with him (she wasn't), and that there's "no chance as far as I'm concerned" (there wasn't). At one point, in what is a strong contender for the title of "most hurtful thing any human being has ever said," he informed Ada that her two young children had probably died due to her incompetence at caring for others.

However, Ada wasn't about to die on that island. She began to teach herself to shoot (the noise terrified her) and trap. She had some success with both, but when she began to improvise, she blossomed: she jury-rigged a shooting rest to reduce gun kickback; she made new traps out of oil cans; and she constructed a platform on top of their ramshackle house, from which she could watch for bears. She built her own stove, bed, and gun rack. She even managed to make a functional Inuit skin boat, despite never having seen one built or even ridden in one before.

All the while, she continued to feed and care for Knight, changing his bedpan and keeping a fire going continuously. She combatted loneliness by reading the Bible and keeping a journal, despite her low level of literacy. In the journal, she documented her attempts at hunting and trapping, and the lessons she learned. She regularly dreamed of her son Bennett.

On June 22, 1923, Knight died. Ada had kept him alive for six months through sheer force of will.* Ada was alone.

After that, Ada moved into a neighboring tent, as she could not bear to bury or even move Knight. She spent her days teaching herself photography by taking pictures of birds. She looked after the voyage's inquisitive cat, Vic, whom the men had nicknamed Snoops. Occasionally she would sit with Knight's decaying body because she was so lonely.

On August 20, 1923, a rescue boat came to Wrangel Island. It had shown up late in the season for several reasons: pissed-off Alaskans refused to sell Stefansson's men supplies, Stefansson took forever in wiring money, and Russia threatened to shoot any relief vessel. Nevertheless, it arrived, headed up by Stefansson's colleague, Harold Noice.

"I want to go back to my mother," Ada said upon meeting him. "Will you take me back to Nome?" She then collapsed.

Upon making it back to Alaska, the expedition was barraged by reporters, surrounding Ada everywhere she want. She avoided the spotlight, and wanted nothing more than to put the whole matter behind her and return to her anonymous life. Not interested in haggling or profiting unduly from her struggles, she signed over her story rights and handed over the men's effects—including Knight's journal—to Noice. She collected her salary, sold her furs, and moved to Seattle with Bennett to seek treatment for his tuberculosis.

---

* Knight had insisted on having his food overcooked, which killed the nutrients his body so needed. If you have one takeaway from this book, let it be that if you're dying of scurvy, don't overcook your food.

Unfortunately, her rescuer, Noice, proved unworthy of his surname, and turned out to be just as much a greedy conman as Stefansson. Realizing he had a potential gold mine on his hands, Noice refused to hand over Knight's journal to Stefansson or Knight's family, and drummed up a scandal to increase the journal's worth. He strategically erased and ripped out parts of the journal to cast doubt on Ada's role in the journey, and her character.

The story he concocted to legitimate the erasures netted him a firey place in hell. He told the press that he'd censored the journal to protect the men's legacies. These portions, he claimed, said that the Ada had been a prostitute and that the men of the expedition had brought her along for that purpose. Moreover, he continued, she'd been fat and well-fed when he'd rescued her (she wasn't), and that if she hadn't eaten his rations, Knight might have survived.*

After this story hit the papers, Ada traveled south to give an interview. In it, she cleared the air, revealing much of what Noice had studiously kept out of the press. "I don't think I could have pulled through if it hadn't been for thoughts of my little boy at home," she told the *Los Angeles Times*. "I had to live for him." The press turned on Noice, and his career was ruined. Ada then traveled back to Alaska and disappeared from public life.

It is difficult to reconstruct the remainder of her life. She kept loosely in touch with the men's families, and visited them a handful of times. She moved regularly, working odd jobs and plunging again into poverty in the wake of the Great Depression. She married three more times (none lasted long—she had poor taste in men), and had one more child, Billy. Some claimed she spent a lot on alcohol, which is possible—although the lion's share almost certainly went to Bennett's treatment. Her constant care worked: despite also contracting meningitis and becoming deaf and blind in one eye, Bennett lived to 58 years old.

Her youngest son, Billy, grew up largely unaware of his mother's past. A disaffected youth who resented his impoverished childhood and maintained few ties to his Inuit heritage, he spoke of being irritated by a traditional song his mother would regularly sing to him. When he asked, later in life, what it meant, she replied that it simply meant "I love you."

She died in an Alaskan nursing home in 1983. Billy, having late learned of his mother's struggles as a young woman, campaigned for years to make sure she wasn't forgotten.† "She

---

* Noice was unrepentant human garbage, it's true—he even cheated Ada out of money when he bought her furs—but part of the blame for this goes, weirdly enough, with his wife. After Noice concocted a tamer version of the story, merely insinuating that Ada had slept with the men on Wrangel Island, his paranoid wife became convinced that Ada had slept with Noice too, on the ride back to Alaska. She became so determined to destroy Ada's reputation that she threatened to join with Stefansson and ruin Noice's career unless he came out with even wilder accusations against her. In the end, Noice's wife left him for lying about Ada in the first place.

† It is worth noting that as of this writing, one of the main results to surface when searching her name is an "Ada Blackjack" clothing brand. This was started by a Dutch woman who seemingly has no connection whatsoever

survived against all odds," he wrote. "It's a wonderful story that should not be lost of . . . a mother fighting to survive to live so she could carry on with her son." A little over two weeks after her death, Alaska recognized Ada as a hero. Stefansson and Noice carry no such legacy.

Ada Blackjack is buried in an unmarked grave, that she may at last return to the anonymity she'd craved.

## • ART NOTES AND TRIVIA •

Ada wrote that she often looked up at the sky and thought of her son Bennett, and so she is portrayed here doing just that, with the ship's cat, Vic, in her lap. Below, her camp is being inspected by a polar bear, while a rescue ship approaches with the breaking of the morning light. Knight's grave can be seen just below the camp.

Her outfit, the cat's stripe patterns, and even the layout of the camp are accurate. Moreover, Ada did actually witness the northern lights regularly while on Wrangel Island.

to Inuit culture. In 2008, she decided to use Ada's name to sell expensive handcrafted goods out of her Barcelona home.

# The Mirabal Sisters

(1924/27/35–1960, DOMINICAN REPUBLIC)

## The Mothers Who Toppled a Dictatorship

The Dominican Republic of the 1950s was a totalitarian nightmare. Obsessively controlled by cruel dictator Rafael Trujillo—a man for whom no slight was too small, no grudge too big—the nation's citizens quickly grew fearful of expressing any dissent. It was not until a group of sisters slapped Trujillo in the face (both literally and figuratively) that the nation finally found the courage to follow their example and oust the despot.

These women were the Mirabal sisters. And they willingly gave their lives to end Trujillo's.

The Mirabals were from a relatively well-to-do provincial family. The sisters—Minerva, Patria, Maria Teresa, and Dedé—all went to Catholic boarding school, married good men, had children, went to church . . . in short, not obvious candidates for revolutionaries.

But Trujillo was a true monster. He used his secret police and extensive spy network to keep the nation's eyes open and mouths shut. He owned or directly controlled much of the country's most vital utilities—the radio, the mail, the press, the airlines, and the passport office. Those who spoke out against him often died in unexplained, brutal circumstances.*

However, it was Trujillo's vicious lust that pit him directly against the Mirabals. Throughout his reign, Trujillo employed scores of "beauty scouts" to scour the countryside for young girls—often *very* young—for him to romance, kidnap, and/or rape. One such mission resulted in him forcing the Mirabals to come to one of his parties. Minerva soon realized that she was his target, and politely turned down his entreaties. When he forced the issue, she slapped him in the face, gathered her family, and got the heck out of Dodge.

Thereafter, Minerva struggled as Trujillo personally toyed with her life. Despite being a brilliant student, upon starting her second year at law school, Minerva found she was barred from classes until she gave a public speech extolling Trujillo's virtues. When she graduated years later—summa cum laude no less—the government denied her a license to practice law.

Minerva's parents were not spared either. Shortly after Minerva first refused Trujillo's

---

* Including people from other countries. Notably, he once unsuccessfully tried to kill Venezuelan president Rómulo Betancourt with a car bomb. When that plot was revealed, many of his international allies, including the United States, turned on him.

advances, her father was imprisoned. After a period of brutal treatment, he was released, only to die shortly thereafter. Some time later, Minerva and her mother, on a visit to the capital of Santo Domingo, were kept as virtual prisoners in their hotel. Minerva learned that if she slept with Trujillo, they would be released. She refused. Eventually she and her mother escaped.

Gradually, Trujillo's wrath also turned Patria, Maria Teresa, and their husbands into activists. With the Mirabal family finances ruined by Trujillo's meddling, and the family's every word monitored,[*] the entire Mirabal clan were primed for transformation. The final push into all-out rebellion came after a failed attempt by exiled Dominicans to oust Trujillo. The Mirabals decided to continue the work.[†] They distributed pamphlets, gathered materials for weapons, and even made makeshift bombs out of firecrackers around Minerva's kitchen table. Collectively the three activist sisters became known by the code name Las Mariposas (the butterflies).

When their attempt to assassinate Trujillo at a 1960 cattle fair was exposed, the entire group was thrown in jail. Due to international pressure stemming from some of Trujillo's dumber moves,[‡] the women were quickly released. When Trujillo's political fortunes continued to worsen—despite all the male conspirators being imprisoned—he began to blame the Mirabal sisters for his every problem. So he ordered them killed.

The assassination of the Mirabals was a clumsy, brutal affair. First, Trujillo transferred their imprisoned husbands to a remote jail that required travel across a mountain range. The three activist sisters knew this was a trap—their friends begged them not to visit their husbands—but they did so anyway. True enough, when they did, secret police ambushed their jeep in the mountain pass. Knowing their ends were at hand, Patria ran to a nearby truck, told the driver who they were and that they were about to get killed, and to spread the word. The truck sped off.

The three activist Mirabal sisters were killed shortly thereafter. The secret police strangled and beat them, then put them back into the jeep and threw it over a cliff, to make it look

---

[*] Once, a traveling car salesman tried pitching Minerva a car by saying that Trujillo himself owned one. She replied "all the more reason not to own one"—and was reported. At a later dinner, she declined to toast Trujillo's health, and was again reported. Trujillo had created an atmosphere of betrayal and suspicion that pervaded the entire country.

[†] This attempt, the Luperón invasion, was made by the Dominican Liberation Movement on June 14, 1959. Trujillo's troops slaughtered the expat-led troops. Following that, Minerva's husband, Manolo Taváres, helped organize the 14th of June Movement, of which he served as president, to further these goals. This was also the jumping-on point for Patria. Maria Teresa joined earlier, due to her extreme fondness for Minerva and attendant hatred of Trujillo.

[‡] The aforementioned attempted assassination of the Venezuelan president.

like an accident—despite clear fingerprints all over the vehicle, and the obvious trauma on the Mirabals' bodies.

The Mirabals' deaths served as a catalyst for overthrowing Trujillo—six months later, military leaders assassinated him. Although many factors were at play in Trujillo's downfall, in the words of one historian, "the cowardly killing of three beautiful women in such a manner had greater effect on Dominicans than most of Trujillo's other crimes. . . . It did something to their machismo. They could never forgive Trujillo this crime."

In the years following, the Mirabal sisters became hallowed icons for the Dominican Republic. Dedé, the sister who didn't participate as actively, and survived Trujillo's reign, raised her late sisters' children, many of whom entered the government.* Virtually all Dominican towns today bear some commemorative marker, school, or street bearing the names of the Mirabal sisters. Their home province was even renamed Hermanas Mirabal—an ironic inversion of Trujillo's renaming the capitol city Ciudad Trujillo (a name that did not stick).

Gradually, their fame spread internationally. In 1994, novelist Julia Alvarez commemorated their story with her historical fiction novel *In the Time of the Butterflies*, which imagined much of the smaller details of their story that were lost to time. In 2001, the book was adapted into a movie of the same name starring Salma Hayek. And on every November 25th—the date of their assassination—the world celebrates the UN-designated International Day for the Elimination of Violence Against Women, in their honor.

## · ART NOTES AND TRIVIA ·

The scene here is of the sisters around the kitchen table, working out their plot to assassinate Trujillo. The scene is based on model 1950s homes, to evoke the sense that these were normal (if well-to-do) women, provoked into something extraordinary.

Minerva is overseeing the work, while Maria Teresa pours out the gunpowder from fireworks to make bombs and Patria cuts up paper to use as fliers.

Dedé is in the upper left, cleaning up after the three, and worrying about their fates. In the upper right, their children are sneaking out from bedtime to witness their mothers' plotting. At the bottom, their husbands are taking apart and cleaning weaponry.

The fireworks have symbols of butterflies on them as a reference to their code name.

In the background are some toy cars. Two black VW bugs—a favorite of Trujillo's police—overlook a fallen jeep, in reference to the Mirabals' assassination. In the corner, driving off toward the kids, is a beaten-up old truck.

---

* Minerva's daughter became the Under Secretary of Foreign Relations, and Dedé's son, the Vice President.

# Angela Jiménez

(1896–1982, MEXICO/UNITED STATES)

## The Mom Who Lived a Dozen Lives

trap in, because you are about to go on a *ride*—for the story of Angela Jiménez is more like a dozen biographies: the tomboy who swears revenge; the daughter who joins her father's army in disguise; the spy who escapes by hanging onto a rail car; the widow who adopts over a dozen children; the innkeeper who finds fortune in gold mining; the nurse who fights for special needs children; the native trying to keep her language from dying; the veteran who finds love in her twilight years.

Angela Jimenez doesn't need a movie so much as a mini-series.

Even the story of how her parents met is interesting! Her father was a well-to-do Spaniard who was running things in the southern Mexican town of Tehuantepec. Her mother was quite different: a Zapoteca native orphaned in her youth and raised by her aunt. Angela's father, being quite the lothario, slept with Angela's mother (as he did with many women), and she got pregnant. At a town gathering some time later, he saw men whispering cruel things about the poor pregnant woman. He did the stand-up thing (literally) by bolting to his feet, declaring to all that the child was his, and that he intended to marry the woman. They did, and the child—who would otherwise not have been accepted, and been doomed to menial labor as an illegitimate child—was put on a different path. That baby was Angela.

She had a short, but happy, childhood. While she was often in conflict with her strict father (he wanted her to study; she wanted to climb trees), they had a good relationship. From her mother, she learned to give to the needy, an act which simultaneously exasperated and delighted her father.

Angela's childhood came crashing to a halt at age 15. The Mexican Revolution had erupted, and president Porfirio Díaz sent a platoon to stamp out any potential rebels in Tehuantepec. Although her father hadn't publicly taken sides, he'd heard rumors of Díaz's cruelty. To be safe, he ordered Angela to hide in the basement with her mother and sisters. His fears were well-founded: when Díaz's captain found them anyway, the captain ordered everyone to leave—save Angela's sister Blanca, whose waist he began to suggestively caress.

Blanca's response was immediate. She grabbed the captain's gun, shot him three times in the heart, and yelled that she would "rather die than become a bone that goes from mouth to mouth of Porfirist pigs." She then shot herself.

While everyone was frozen in shock, Angela and her father escaped. Her father committed fully to the revolution and began to organize local natives against the government. Angela tried to join, but he convinced her to return home. She did so, but it was empty: the others had been taken away. Try as she might, Angela couldn't sleep. Visions of Blanca kept coming to her head. "Right there in the house of living horrors," she later said, "I swore that I would be a soldier, not a woman soldier, but a man who would fight with every bone of courage in my body against the government of Díaz."

She put on men's clothes and began going by the name Angel. She walked eight days on foot through the Sierras just to learn her father's location—and then rode by horseback the rest of the way. He was enraged to see her, but gradually settled down and began to teach her the arts of war: how to aim, how to shoot, how to make grenades[*] and how to throw them. You know, father-daughter stuff.

Her father couldn't bear to put Angela in harm's way for long, though, and ordered her home once more. Again, she refused—instead, she joined with another revolutionary group. She kept her male disguise up well, to the point where she had to spurn the affections of a young woman (who grew rather foul-mouthed upon learning her secret). Some soldiers knew she was a woman, but they posed no problem: "It was made clear and simple that if I was approached in any abusive way I would in no way hesitate in blowing out their brains."[†]

She would switch back to a feminine guise if it suited her, as it often did when it helped her to spy. She'd sometimes visit nearby towns in a dress, gossip with the locals, and return with information on enemy positions. Once, when her comrades were ambushed and taken prisoner, she escaped by donning a dress and pretending she was merely a camp follower. She then offered to take care of the new prisoners, secretly smuggling out their weapons in laundry bags, hiding them nearby, and planning their jailbreak.

She did this again in 1916, in an incident that would mark the end of her time in the war. She'd reunited with her father—even busted him out of jail once—but she, her father, and many others had been captured and were facing imminent execution. She bribed a woman named Maria to smuggle her out in women's clothing. Reluctantly, she agreed, and Angela escaped.

The guards soon realized she was gone and arranged a search party. Angela hid at the bottom of a well for three days and nights for the pursuit to die down. Eventually the guards gave up, but not before destroying everything in Maria's house in their hunt. Angela took a fake identity and worked as a shopkeep for a time, using her pay to reimburse Maria. She

---

[*] Out of gunpowder, sulfur, and black beans. I'm not sure how it works either.

[†] This sentiment was not unique: many female soldiers (*soldaderas*) did this, often also disguising themselves in male garb. One of the most well-known was **Petra "Pedro" Herrera**, covered in Volume One—she and Angela knew each other!

spent her free time plotting to save her father, but she could not figure out how to do so by herself. In her work, she attracted the affections of a young man—she was apparently irresistible to both men and women!—who worked on a railroad. This gave her something to work with. She began to form a plan.

She promised to marry the young man[*] on one condition: if he could also get Maria and her two sons (whom she'd promised to look after) to Ciudad Juárez. He agreed, and helped her to a passenger compartment on board the train where he worked. However, Angela had no intention of marrying him. As soon as he was out of sight, she swung underneath the train car, where she rearranged a bunch of hanging wires into a sling, and *rode hanging under the train in a makeshift hammock*. Once they got to Juarez, he looked for her in the passenger compartment, but she was nowhere to be found.

Let's repeat that: Angela Jiménez rode 230 miles. Hanging onto a speeding train. From underneath. To avoid getting married.

If you have a new hero now, you're not alone.

In Juárez, Angela learned her father had been executed. In a daze, she headed to El Paso, Texas, and there, the reality of her life slowly set in. She was in exile: she'd been unable to save her father, she was cut off from her mother and sisters, and she couldn't return. She was alone in a country where she didn't speak the language. As she contemplated this, staring for hours into space, she was approached by a pharmacist who asked if she was okay—and then offered her work.

So she landed on her feet. She began doing odd jobs, learning English, and before long, she'd relocated her family (and Maria's family) to El Paso. Life went on. She began leading a more conventional life, making friends and going out dancing.[†] "My lack of English was never an obstacle in finding jobs," she later said, "much less boyfriends. After some romantic mishaps, she settled down with her first husband, Felix Romero.[‡]

Around this time, Angela received news that she would not let change her life: she couldn't bear children. As a soldier, she'd downed hideous quantities of a traditional Mexican Revolution cocktail (gunpowder and tequila), and it had rendered her infertile. But she soon took to being mother to Felix's young daughter. Then she adopted three children. Then she adopted three more.

---

[*] "He proposed to me without knowing anything about me, which was probably better."

[†] A funny anecdote: Early on, she was out dancing and accidentally stepped on her dance partner's foot. Still learning English, she said "squeeze me" instead of "excuse me"—which her partner did. She repeated her utterance, and he squeezed tighter, much to her dismay. While the mistake was eventually explained, the damage had been done: "I didn't care, I never wanted to dance again with handsome blonde boys."

[‡] She'd gotten engaged to Felix, but when World War I broke out, she called him a coward for not enlisting. He did so to prove himself to her, and while deployed, went missing in action, presumed dead. She was despondent, but eventually moved on, getting engaged to another man—only for Felix to return alive! (*dramatic violin sting!*) In the end, she went with Felix.

"I had a difficult time turning away children," she later said, in what you will soon realize is the understatement of a lifetime.

After some minor adventures in El Paso and a brief trip back to Mexico* they moved to Jackson City, California, a mining town. She ran a boarding house, while her husband worked in the mines. During this, Angela befriended an old prospector, and took care of him when he got sick. When he died, she found out that he had left her the deed to a gold mine in his will—and quite a profitable one.

(Yes, this reads like she was pulling out random Monopoly Chance Cards, but it really happened! Angela Jiménez was a real-life Forrest Gump.)

Angela and Felix brought in another couple to help finance the dig, and things went bad. Unable to directly communicate with them (her English was still quite poor) and feeling something was off, Angela looked at their accounting books. She realized she had been allotted no shares in the mine, even though she had invested as much money as they had. Her husband was unwilling to confront them, and she grew more frustrated as they showed her escalating levels of disrespect.

When, one day, Angela arrived at the mine cabin to find the couple's mangy dog eating from Angela's plate, she snapped. Grabbing the wife of the couple, Angela hurled her out to the patio, intending to hit her—only, Angela threw her too hard, and the wife went hurtling over a cliff. Mortified at the sounds of the woman's moans at the bottom of the cliff, Angela fled. She stayed in the wilderness for some time, and eventually made her way back home. Felix joined her several days later, with news that the woman was hospitalized. The other couple successfully sued for full ownership of the mine, and received profits from it for at least twenty years.

"I found the Mexicans in this country own nothing of value," Angela would later grumble, laying out a valid critique while passing over the part where she borderline murdered someone. "For one reason or another the 'Americans' know how to gain control and possess what they want."

She returned to running the boarding house, and Felix returned to mining—which, due to his poor health, soon resulted in his death. Angela was heartbroken—"Felix had become such an integral part of my life that losing him was like killing part of me"—but she refused to lose herself to depression. Instead, she threw herself into taking care of her expanding brood (now at *eighteen children*), and running the boarding house, where she looked after seventy-five others.

After several years of this work, she caught the eye of a local named Ramon Vasquez,

---

* At one point, she and Felix went after a secret cache of Pancho Villa's gold buried in the desert, which she knew about from her time in the revolution. Unfortunately, just before digging it up, they were discovered by unfriendly soldiers, who threatened to shoot them on sight. She got them out of it by pretending to be a raving lunatic who'd made the entire thing up. Yes, she had her own Indiana Jones treasure-hunting episode. Seriously, Angela needs a miniseries.

who asked for her hand in marriage. Eyeing him skeptically, she replied that she would accept, but she had some preconditions: "I would marry him if he accepted me as his equal and not as his weak wife who he could boss around. My children needed warmth and affection and if he was to accept me he must also accept all of my children."

He did, and the massive flock moved to San Jose, California.

There life grew quieter and time passed quickly. Angela began working in a hospital, a job she would keep for some time. Her children grew up and moved out. Eventually she found herself without any children to care for*—and remedied the situation immediately by getting a license to look after developmentally disabled people. She began working in the foster system, where she found such horrible conditions that she adopted five *more* children. She sheltered them, taught them to speak, and nurtured them until they could enter state-run institutions.

She also opened three small restaurants throughout this time, which would *seem* like a big deal, but she literally only once ever made a brief mention of it, and then never brought it up again.

In 1960, she went back to Mexico to find out if any of her family had survived the revolution. She paid for radio ads and through them tracked down her sister Rosa, now a single mother of two. Angela later insisted on paying for the children's education, essentially adopting them from afar.

In her twilight years, she continued reconnecting with her past and her roots. She became involved in veterans organizations and in teaching her culture to the young—particularly her Zapoteca way of speaking, which was rife with profanity. Constantly marching in parades and doing outreach, she never slowed down. Even when she had a stroke, she insisted that she had "no time to pamper a heart attack," and went on her way.

In part, this showed her distrust of the American medical system. Her husband Ramon died from, as Angela described it, medical malpractice. Given three pills to take and no Spanish language instructions, he fatally overdosed. This drove Angela into a rage: "Why is it that doctors who are serving Mexicans or Latinos don't seem to know enough to put the instructions for medicine in Spanish? . . . Our people have contributed to the progress of this country and in return physicians should deal with us in our own language instead of killing us off one by one."

She spent her twilight years in the company of her fellow Mexican Revolution veterans, and after some time, even fell back in love. On Christmas Day 1974, in front of their friends and family, Lieutenant Nicolas Duran proposed to her. It was a bit of a May-December relationship—he was 87, she 77. She said yes.

"We are fighting our battle for a longer life for each other," she said, "and if I am allowed to see the blooming of springtime flowers then Duran and I will marry in the Spring of this year."

---

* Except for a brief stint in the 1940s, when two of her sons died, leaving behind children whom Angela, you guessed it, immediately adopted.

# Marie Equi

## (1872–1952, UNITED STATES)

## *The Mom Who Broke Every Taboo She Could*

nce upon a time, there was a lesbian Wild West abortion doctor. She was jailed in San Quentin prison for radicalism. She was dubbed "Queen of the Bolsheviks" by Margaret Sanger. She was in the *New York Times* for horse-whipping a jerk in the face.

To the surprise of no one, she lived in Portland.

Marie Equi was a study in contradictions from day one. Described by her teachers as both a "very earnest scholar" and "exceptionally unruly," she grew up in Massachusetts as the American-born child of poor immigrants. Although she didn't love school, she was set on going—a goal made impossible by her family's poverty. After a year of high school, she had to drop out to help provide for them. She seemed destined to work 14-hour days in the textile mills, agitating her childhood tuberculosis.

Her salvation came from an expected source of funding: her girlfriend, Bessie Holcomb. Well, they might not have been going out at the time—but that certainly wasn't the case for long. By 1892, once Marie had spent more time in school, they moved to Oregon together and built a house. Homesteading like this was a good option for some minority Americans:* for no money, you could legally claim a plot of land,† provided you cultivated it. Not only did this cater extensively to the black population (which created tons of largely forgotten rural settlements), but to women as well: upward of 15 percent of the settlers were women.

A year into their stay in Oregon, Marie made a name for herself. Bessie, who'd taken work as a school teacher, hadn't gotten paid in months. When they confronted the superintendent—widely viewed as a con man and fraudster—he refused to pay and kicked the two of them out. This did not sit well with the hotheaded Marie. She got a rawhide whip and began pacing outside his office, threatening loudly to whip him if he didn't pay

---

\* Not only was Marie homosexual, but she was also half Italian—a population despised as an "inferior" race at the time. Funny how the concept of "white" shifts over time, isn't it!

† "Legally," as in according to US law—the Native Americans already living there weren't exactly advised. This resulted in decades of wars and atrocities that generally get swept aside in history books as "resettlement" or "displacement." The majority of the conflicts had ended by the time Marie was a teen, mostly because virtually all the Native Americans had been forced onto reservations at gunpoint.

up. She continued to do this for a full hour, wearing a skirt in oppressive July heat, gradually drawing a crowd.

After an hour, the superintendent tried escaping, only for her to whip him across the face. But it didn't stop there: the crowd grabbed him and held him down while she punched him. The crowd then took turns punching him, let him up, and let Marie punch him again. For this, Marie was jailed with a $250 fine, which was quickly paid by a town druggist. Locals sent her flowers and held a raffle to buy the whip. The story made its way into newspapers (under the headline "Flogged by a Woman") across the country, including the *New York Times*.

She was a hero, but not to everyone. Unsurprisingly, some decried her with the age-old insult "unladylike," but a larger problem was on the horizon. A "scurrilous report," which the press quickly put down, spread that Marie and Bessie were lesbians. This was a problem because there were not, to put it mildly, good depictions of lesbians in those days. The previous summer, the press breathlessly covered a domestic violence case between two women. After a summer of public conjecture on lesbianism as a form of mental illness (telltale warning signs: being a tomboy, liking sports, and seeking a job), the courts concluded that the defendant was insane and committed her to an asylum. Marie and Bessie preferred to avoid being a sequel to that case.

The next year, amid an economic downturn and rising social tensions, the two moved to gay-friendly San Francisco, then referred to as "Sodom by the Sea" (a nickname that is absolutely ripe for a comeback). There, after ten years together, the two began to drift apart, entering new relationships. Marie, becoming close friends with Mary Parker, a female doctor, entered medical school.* Bessie began dating her new boss—a man—and within three years had settled down and started having kids. Marie switched schools after two years and moved back to Portland.

Med school was rough. The only woman in a class of five, Marie was the subject of endless harassment. She didn't suffer it gladly. On one occasion, when she objected to a proposed student fee to fund campus football (which was only open to men), a male student called her a fool. She rebutted his argument by slapping him in the face. This again made the papers.

After graduation, Mary and Marie headed as far away from big cities as they could, to the frontier of eastern Oregon. There Marie regularly traveled long distances on horseback to provide care for cowboys and Native Americans. Her practice thrived, but the more proper Mary had trouble making ends meet. After several years, they ended up back in Portland.

---

* Despite having never actually graduated high school. She just had to pass a written exam. Med school was a lot different, way back in the day.

It was here that Marie met the great love of her life: Harriet Speckart.* Heiress to a rich family, Harriet, at 22 years old, was 11 years younger than Marie. They fell for each other hard, which disturbed Harriet's mother so much she moved the entire family to San Diego. But Marie was not to be deterred. When the Great San Francisco Earthquake hit, Marie went down to California to help.† Afterward, since she just *happened* to be nearby, she visited Harriet in San Diego.

The two quickly devised a plot to be together, whether Harriet's family liked it or not. As it turned out, the family decidedly did not, and got into a massive fight with Marie shortly after she arrived. But the groundwork had been laid: Marie "diagnosed" Harriet with tuberculosis and dropsy, necessitating a return to Portland for treatment. The family grudgingly agreed, but their simmering hatred soon erupted into all-out war in the newspapers. The Speckarts accused Marie of being a gold digger, and hired an investigator to dig up dirt on her. When he found nothing, the affair died down somewhat, but the two women now had the dubious distinction of being one of the first publicized lesbian couples in the Pacific Northwest.

Emboldened by her vindicated social status, Marie grew more brash. Due to her visibility, she became the focal point of a growing LGBT movement (many of whom, weirdly enough, were seemingly named either Mary or Marie). In 1906, she and Harriet entered the Rose Carnival together, winning second place. Shortly after, the two moved in together. And because being the talk of the town and the linchpin of an underground lesbian society wasn't enough to keep her occupied, Marie also began providing abortions.

Abortions were illegal and poorly understood at the time. While idiots would regularly make claims that abortion doctors incinerated babies, the truth was that the procedure was safe, private, and all around better for the patient than the nondoctor alternatives. Without experienced doctors performing the operation, the poorest women turned to back room operators, attempted to do it themselves, or committed suicide. Marie quickly grew a reputation as the best abortion doctor in Portland—a woman who treated her patients with discretion, dignity, and grace.

This work also began getting her into activism. She once attempted to help a destitute 18-year-old unmarried woman give up her newborn child for adoption, only for the orphanage to demand the mother's identity. Marie wouldn't let this stand. She brought this up to the Medical Club of Portland and the local newspaper, and made the orphanage back down. In another incident, she visited a trans man named Harry Allen, who'd been arrested for "white

---

* It's worth pointing out that it's unclear how involved Marie and Mary were—it was likely more on the platonic side. This sort of "Boston Marriage" wasn't an uncommon arrangement at the time.

† Here she became a local hero again. The earthquake was the greatest disaster in living memory, flattening the city. She was the only woman on the Oregon relief mission. She delivered numerous babies and received a medal for her efforts. She was only the second woman ever detailed for service at a US general hospital.

slavery"—that is to say, transporting his wife across state lines for "immoral purposes" (living together). Marie interceded on his behalf and he was freed.

And that still wasn't enough for Marie! From there, Marie joined the labor movement, which was shutting down large parts of the United States (ref. **Mother Jones**). Seeing several women striking at a cannery, she joined them. As a well-known upper-class citizen, Marie became the public face of the strike. Marie being Marie, it wasn't long before this escalated into her getting into fights with cops. Once, when arrested, she stabbed a police officer with her hatpin,* claiming it was dipped in a virus that would cause a "slow, lingering death." It wasn't, but the story certainly added to her reputation.

Her troubles with the law put a strain on her relationship with Harriet, who was no radical. The two began seeing other people—Marie, a woman named Elizabeth Gardiner,† and Harriet, a man named James Morgan, whom she would marry for a period of eleven days. Soon after the ill-fated marriage, Harriet reconciled with Marie. The couple, likely spurred on by Harriet's desire for a more conventional life, adopted a baby girl two weeks later.‡ Their daughter was, of course, named Mary.

Thus did Mary Equi, alias Mary Junior, join the family.

With her commitment to Harriet renewed—Marie even turned down an ultimatum from Gardiner to leave Harriet—Marie again ramped up her activism. This time, she became involved with the women's suffrage and birth control movements, providing a medical viewpoint to many of their publications. She and Margaret Sanger were lovers for a brief spell, and wrote tender letters to each other to the end of the lives. "She was like a crushed falcon," Sanger wrote, "which had braved the storms and winds of terror and needed tenderness and love."

It's important to note that despite these kind descriptions, others said Marie was outright abusive, and there's evidence to support that. One woman tried to prevent her graduating med school with stories of how she'd been violent to her first girlfriend, Bessie. When she was fighting with Harriet's family in San Diego, she shoved Harriet's mother and choked her brother. She was always on the razor's edge of taking it too far, and the outbreak of World War I sent her spiraling out of control.

---

* This was not uncommon. In the early 1900s, women regularly carried massive hatpins that were essentially foot-long blades. Chicago actually banned pins longer than nine inches.

† The timelines for most of these relationships are hard to establish, as is the level of monogamy practiced and expected. This author's supposition, reading up on her relationships, was that Marie likely both practiced some variety of nonmonogamy and broke whatever rules she and her partner had established by cheating.

‡ In those days, adoptions were handled mostly by doctors, with final sign-off by a judge, so Marie sped up matters.

Always staunchly antiwar,* Marie grew frustrated that World War I led some activists to drop out of the peace movement, if not outright support American imperialism. This was somewhat understandable: the Sedition Act, in a massive legislative overreach, allowed the government to imprison dissenters. Mostly this was used to shut up anyone the government didn't like. But Marie was never one to shut up. She decried the war in the strongest terms possible, climbing telephone poles and unfurling pacifist banners. She even brought Mary Junior to rallies (she carried Marie's valise) and gave inflammatory speeches. Eventually, Marie was ratted out by a secret informant and put on a watchlist. This led to the feds indicting Marie and putting her on trial.

Her time in court was a sham. All 12 jurors were men, nine of whom hailed from small towns that reviled women like Marie. The trial centered on her patriotism: if, in the eyes of these random men, she lived up to their idea of the country, she would go free. Shocking nobody, this aging lesbian doctor did not fit the standards of rural America. After some attempts to escape (she tried faking the Spanish Flu), she was sentenced to three years in San Quentin prison, one of the harshest institutions in the United States.

The stay was difficult on her. She wrote to the outside world constantly—and it often wrote back. No correspondent was more prolific than Harriet, who wrote almost daily about Mary Junior's goings-on. Marie sent back fairy-tale allegories of her experiences, describing prison as a "Palace of Sadness," with an enchanted princess imprisoned by an Old Ogre. Margaret Sanger sent notes to cheer Marie up, describing Marie as "Queen of the Bolsheviks." She wrote, "It is such a milestone to meet a real woman and you are a dozen of them packed into one."

She was released in less than a year, but by then, her world had changed. She didn't realize it immediately: her first impulse was to start advocating for prison reform. But this didn't go anywhere. By this point, she was pushing 50 and had been in prison for some time. She didn't have the resources to support herself, much less launch an offensive on the government. The war and the Sedition Act had gutted activist circles. Many had dropped out or committed suicide. To punctuate the end of an era, Harriet had a hemorrhage in 1927 and died. Marie was now a single parent to a 12-year-old girl.

With her health starting to fail, Marie began spending more time looking after her daughter, Mary Junior. However, Mary Junior, who absolutely took after Marie, did not take well to this supervision, or anyone else's. She took up flying, becoming a solo pilot despite social stigma against it. She rebelled against Marie's wishes, and eloped with a male classmate. Just like the parent she always called "da," she lived her own life. Although they didn't see eye to eye for some time, Marie and Mary Junior reconciled later in life, after Mary Junior had children.

---

* She'd been against it from the days of the Philippine-American War, covered in the entry on **Trinidad Tecson**.

The final years of Marie's life saw her attempting to cement her legacy. She kept up her letter writing to her comrades from the movement, even as they grew old and died. As she slowly lost mobility, she grew chattier, regaling anyone who'd listen with stories of her youthful indiscretions. For this, she demanded some respect. When a conservative group began circulating a list of dangerous radicals that did not include her, she threatened to sue until she was included, as "Queen of the Bolsheviks."

She died at 80 years old, a venerable age for anyone who'd gone through so much. She was interred next to Harriet, likely due to Mary Junior interceding. Although she'd outlived most of her contemporaries, Marie was eulogized by a great many activists—perhaps the best summary came from Oregon labor activist Julia Ruuttila, who said simply: "I think she's the most interesting woman that ever lived in this state, certainly the most fascinating, colorful, and flamboyant."

## · ART NOTES AND TRIVIA ·

Here Marie is seen climbing a phone pole to unfurl her antiwar banner, while Harriet (carrying Mary Junior) and a policeman follow her. Below, a crowd of labor activists and suffragists crowd the streets. The entire scene is tinted yellow and purple—the colors of the suffrage movement. At her hip is the whip she used to attack the corrupt superintendent. This is an actual Portland square from the era, and all of the banners are slogans from the time.

# Funmilayo Ransome-Kuti

## (1900–1978, NIGERIA)

### The Mom Who Deposed a King

Somewhere, in a parallel dimension where teaching history isn't an afterthought, there is a woman whose name comes in the same breath of Western teachers as that of Gandhi, Mandela, and Martin Luther King, Jr. Her name is Frances Abigail Olufunmilayo Thomas Anikulapo Ransome-Kuti, or Funmilayo Ransome-Kuti for short.

(Okay, it might take more than one breath.)

She was an activist whose tenacity won women the right to vote, a teacher whose lessons taught a generation of Nigerians how to fight, a mother whose words felled a king.

Said king, Alake Ademola II, did not go down easily. When the British started meddling with Nigeria, he'd been the big winner: all traditional leadership roles besides his had been absorbed or eliminated, including the few offices that gave women a political voice. He was the sole authority figure. For a long time, this didn't cause a huge stir: Ademola was popular and life was fairly peaceful. He was even friends with Funmilayo and her husband, two of the most well-regarded teachers in the country.

But as World War II broke out, Ademola let the British walk all over Nigeria, which put him in Funmilayo's crosshairs. The British committed a series of outrages. First, they confiscated food and forced all imports to be bundled: for example, anyone who wanted to buy sugar would pay more, but also get a bundle of cutlasses.* But by far the most outrageous act was the (re-)implementation of direct taxation. This was hugely stupid on their part—not only did it effectively double taxes on women, but it had already sparked a women-led conflict in Nigeria not 15 years earlier.†

They'd lost that conflict, and history was about to repeat itself.

Funmilayo *tried* to work within the system. She and her political groups were careful not to simply complain; for every demand they made, they backed it up with specific alternatives. They would hire accountants to look at government expenditures and submit detailed budget

---

* Truly, one of history's strangest Cracker Jack prizes.

† Nigeria already had a method of taxing women, in the form of marketplace sales taxes. This new taxation allowed tax collectors to enter a woman's house, which resulted in several assaults. This exact provocation was the cause of the 1929 conflict—for more info on that, this author humbly recommends the entry on **Nwanyeruwa** in Volume One.

counterproposals. They provided long lists detailing the government's abuses of power and instances of corruption. The government response? Tear gas.

By 1947, Funmilayo had run out of patience. She publicly refused to pay her taxes, and led 10,000-woman marches in protest. When they were denied protest permits, she proclaimed their demonstrations to be "picnics." When the police fired tear gas canisters, she would throw them back at them. When her colleagues were arrested, her organization would pay for lawyers. When one woman's husband refused to allow her to join, she and her colleagues grabbed the man and rolled him in the dust. "Now," Funmilayo announced, "we have no more opposition from men."

Most shocking to Nigerian society, she snatched "*Oro.*" Both object and ritual, *Oro* is part of the behind-the-scenes power of Nigerian society, a symbol of a secret society of kingmakers—think skull and dagger. During *Oro,* women are compelled to stay inside as men march around, swinging an ornamental stick above their head (also called *Oro*) in a supernatural rite that compels others to obey. Funmilayo not only didn't stay indoors, but she walked right up, took the *Oro,* and hung it up in her home. This is like snatching the Pope's hat and putting it on your coat rack. That is the sort of woman Funmilayo was.

Not all men stood against her—her greatest supporter was her devoted husband, Reverend Israel Olodotun (Dotun) Ransome-Kuti. They'd met in childhood, and endured 13 years of celibate courtship to finish their schooling before getting married. They had four children[*] and worked hand in hand as teachers in the city of Abeokuta. Throughout their lives, he had her back. Late in life she made this recollection:

> He hated women being exploited. Many times he was sent for and told, "Come and see what your wife is doing, O!" He merely smiled and told them to leave me alone as I had my own mind. He never went against anything I did.

Funmilayo didn't make much of a distinction between time at home, time at school, or time in activism. In all arenas, she and her husband were strict, always looking to set an example. Their children grew up feeling distant from their mother, but also awash in her values. Each was a stubborn workaholic who went to college and became a leader in their field. Each internalized the importance of looking after others, and continued Funmilayo's work in their own ways (more on that in a bit).

As her protests continued from one year to the next, tensions intensified. While her colleagues loved her—they made a song calling her a king and a goddess—the newspapers decried her as a "dictatrix" and Ademola compared her followers to "vipers that could not be

---

[*] They had three sons—Olikoye (Koye), Olufela (Fela), and Bekolari (Beko)—and one daughter, Dolupo (Dolu). In addition, they had a child who died in infancy, and one who died from a miscarriage.

tamed." Rumors of assassination attempts swirled. At one point, a British official yelled at Funmilayo to "Shut up your women!" She replied, "You may have been born but you were not bred! Would you speak to your mother like that?" Her colleagues followed up by threatening to cut off the official's genitals and mail them to his mother.

Finally, on January 3, 1949, Ademola resigned. Her activism had gained support from other parts of Nigerian society, including the *Oro*-wielding society of Ogboni. Ademola went into exile.

Funmilayo was instantly recognized as a hero. Nicknamed the "Lioness of Lisabi," she was seen as the second coming of Madam Tinubu, a powerful businesswoman who'd led Nigeria a generation before. While some remained critical, calling the activists "storm troopers" and accusing her campaign of being a personal vendetta, she refuted their claims:

> What people are saying is that I attacked Ademola. I didn't really attack Ademola. I attacked imperialism. Those Europeans were using him against his people. . . . I was attacking Europeans indirectly and they know it.

Unfortunately, the victory was short-lived. Within a year, Ademola came back from exile and made himself a thorn in Funmilayo's side. He replaced the women's tax with a new water tax and arrested Funmilayo when she protested. Uncowed, she expanded her activism from local areas (around her hometown of Abeokuta) to all of Nigeria. She got involved with writing a new constitution, ran for an assembly seat, and pushed hard for women's suffrage. She was busier than ever.

Which made it all the more devastating when her husband died.

Diagnosed with prostate cancer in 1952, Dotun had been getting sicker, just as Funmilayo was less able to spend time with him. He died in 1955, and she went to pieces. Gone was the boy she'd spent years pining away for. Gone was the man who'd supported her every step down her arduous path. Gone was the husband with whom she'd raised four children to adulthood. Gone was her rock.

She began to shift her focus to education, the interest that had bonded Funmilayo to her husband. Partly this was due to Nigeria falling into a political morass: although it had held elections in 1954 (she was the only female candidate!), it quickly devolved into regional infighting. Women were allowed to vote in some places, and not in others. Where she'd previously united women of all ethnicities and religions against Ademola and for suffrage, they no longer all had a common goal. When she went abroad to help other countries,[*] her

---

[*] Notably, she'd spent some time in China, where she met Mao. This led to suspicions she was a Communist—she wasn't, although she admired their political ethos. The government refused to grant her a passport after that.

countrymen began viewing her with suspicion, as not truly Nigerian. By 1959, she'd fallen out of favor.

She kept busy with running the newly established Reverend Kuti Memorial Grammar School, even as the nation fell into chaos. A military coup, followed by a bloody civil war, nearly tore Nigeria apart. The school fell on hard times, with unpaid teachers and rioting students. But when the government stepped in to assume control of it and all other schools, Funmilayo came back to activism full-time. Closing the school down rather than handing it over, she hit the protest trail again—this time accompanied by her musician son, Fela.

Of all her children, Fela was, on paper, the one least like her. Internationally famous for his pan-African music as well as his hedonism, Fela had spent his adolescence borrowing Funmilayo's car to go clubbing.* He'd married but had an affair with a Black Panther (who described Funmilayo thusly: "Fela's mama didn't take no sh*t!"). He would go on to marry 27 women at once—all of whom were part of his band.† Although Funmilayo didn't approve of almost any of this, Fela was still, according to all her children, her favorite.

But Fela had inherited his mother's stubbornness and, more importantly, her political fervor. His music was inherently political, criticizing soldiers of the military regime as "zombies"—a critique that repeatedly got him arrested. He forsook the European surname Ransome for a Yoruba one, Anikulapo (which Funmilayo would also adopt). He lived at a compound (the Kalakuta Republic) he'd founded that he declared independent from the Nigerian government. He was both his own person and his mother's son.

In early 1978, the government, outraged at Fela's defiance, sent 1,000 soldiers to destroy his home. In the ensuing chaos, they threw Funmilayo out of a second-story window. Shortly thereafter she slipped into a coma. She died eight weeks later, surrounded by her children.

In death, she became a symbol. On the anniversary of her death, her children marched through the streets seeking justice for her and the destruction of the Kalakuta Republic. Her son Koye went into politics and became Nigeria's Minister of Health. Fela also grew more political, running for president the next year (he didn't win) and spending the 1980s releasing music critical of the government. He was soon joined by his brother Beko, who became a traditional activist after his mother's death. It's a measure of how much trouble he was that the government tried kidnapping him and bombs were thrown at his house.

But perhaps nowhere is Funmilayo's influence more felt than among the women of Africa. Today, Nigerian girls grow up hearing of a woman who toppled a dictator, who taught activists across the entire continent. They look up to a hero who lived not long ago: their "Lioness of Lisabi," the "Mother of Africa," Funmilayo Ransome-Kuti.

---

* She had been the first woman in Nigeria to drive a car!

† This wasn't as lurid as it sounds—although he was involved with many of them, his stated goal was to offer them protection, as they were unmarried and unable to find employment outside of his work.

# Cut Nyak Dhien

### (1848–1908, INDONESIA [ACEH])

## The Mother of Indonesian Revolution

The Dutch had gone too far.

They'd been a problem in Aceh for centuries. As far back as the 1500s, the Acehnese had been fighting their incursion. For a time, treaties had kept them out. But they'd come back. And they'd burned down one of Aceh's most important mosques.*

Which is when Cut Nyak Dhien got involved.

Up to this point, Cut Nyak Dhien had led a pretty good life. The daughter of district chiefs (*uleebalang*), she was wealthy and beautiful, with a well-to-do husband and a young son. But everything changed when the Dutch invaded. She and her family fled, and within five years, her husband was dead, double-crossed by an Acehnese native. She was 30.

She began to obsess over getting vengeance on the Dutch invaders. Pledging to marry any man who would assist in avenging her late husband, she sought not a new husband, but a comrade. She found that in the leader of a band of guerrilla fighters, a man named Teuku Umar.† Although Umar already had two wives, both nobles, Cut Nyak Dhien quickly established herself at the top of the pecking order—as evidenced by the fact that she, not the others, convinced him to quit smoking opium. This was obvious even to a Dutch observer, who wrote that the acting chief of the area was Teuku Umar, "or rather his wife, who makes him do what she likes." Together they had a daughter, Cut Gambang.

For a time, with Dhien advising and Umar executing, their guerrilla warfare was successful, but it did not last. As the Dutch began applying more pressure, Cut Nyak Dhien and her family had to repeatedly flee, eventually to a neighboring district. Finally, in late 1893, to the shock of everyone, Teuku Umar and 30 of his men surrendered to the Dutch. They pledged fealty to their hated foes, and in return, the Dutch made Umar a commander.

However, it was all a ruse. After spending six months learning Dutch military tactics

---

\* This was the Baiturrahman Grand Mosque. The Dutch apparently felt bad enough about its destruction that they began rebuilding it only a few years later.

† Cut Nyak Dhien and Teuku Umar were first cousins. And she was twelve when she was engaged to her first husband, Teuku Cek Ibrahim Lamnga. Different times!

and being accused of being a traitor, Teuku Umar went out on a military expedition for the Dutch . . . and never came back. He'd been a double agent the entire time. Taking with him a ludicrous amount of Dutch money and weaponry, Umar drove the Dutch insane with rage due to his plot—a plot that Cut Nyak Dhien quite likely helped put together.

The Dutch response was brutal. Troops chased them across Aceh on horseback, burning down their houses wherever they stayed. Within three years, the Dutch killed Teuku Umar, after an Acehnese double agent betrayed him (double agents, as you can tell, were a real problem on both sides).

However, Umar's death did not stop the revolutionaries: Cut Nyak Dhien simply took the reins. As despondent as she was at the death of her second husband, she was yet more determined. As legend has it, when her daughter, Cut Gambang, began to weep at the news of her father's death, Dhien slapped her and said, "As Acehnese women, we should not shed tears for martyrs." From there, the two women gathered their belongings and returned to their comrades in the jungle to continue their lonely war against the Dutch.

The ensuing years of jungle warfare took their toll. Although she sold all her valuables to finance the fight, Dhien soon was destitute and starving. With the Dutch looking for her, she could not so much as approach towns, and would often go many days without even a grain of rice. Even after the sultan of Aceh surrendered to the Dutch, she fought on. Even as she developed arthritis and began going blind, she fought on. Even as her comrades insisted she surrender and get medical treatment, she fought on.

One day in late 1904, the Dutch finally found her. As her comrades and daughter fled, Dhien realized she was surrounded, and put up her hands to resist. Just then, she heard the voice of her commander, Pang Laot Ali, telling her that they wouldn't hurt her. Realizing that he'd given her up to the Dutch so that she could see a doctor, she cursed his name. "Don't you touch me, you traitor," she is said to have snarled. "It would have been better for you to show me your nobility by stabbing me."

She was exiled to the island of Sumedang, 2,000 miles away from her home—the only female political prisoner ever sent there. By now nearly fully blind, she gained a reputation as "Ibu Perbu" (The Queen) for her deep knowledge of Islam. She died there a few years later, at age 58. Cut Gambang continued fighting, and it is thought she died a few years later in battle. The fate of Dhien's son is seemingly unknown.

Dhien is remembered in modern Indonesia as a national hero. As with so many heroes worldwide, her portrayal has been molded to fit that narrative. Her face adorns Indonesian currency: a painting of her bearing aristocratic jewelry and a demure head scarf, a notable departure from the only surviving photo of her, which shows her captured, in rags, and sobbing in rage. While some versions of her story attribute direct quotations to her, none of her writing survives, and so she cannot speak for herself.

The Aceh of today is ferociously rebellious, religiously conservative to the point of fundamentalism. This Cut Nyak Dhien fits it well, in the same way that a divinely inspired **Joan of Arc** fit 14th-century France. But the historical Joan of Arc was, like everyone in this book, more complex than the wartime image of her. It is worth remembering that, in all likelihood, so was Cut Nyak Dhien.

## · ART NOTES AND TRIVIA ·

Cut Nyak Dhien is seen here as a scout for her raiding party—comprised of her husband Teuku Umar and her two children. Her portrayal is a mix of the modern, put-together depiction seen on Indonesian currency, and the disheveled, jewlery-bereft image seen in historical record.

# Isabel Godin des Odonais

## (1728–1792, ECUADOR [VICEROYALTY OF PERU])

## The Mother Who Walked Through Hell

**I**sabel wanted to go to France.

She'd spent virtually her entire childhood dreaming about it. As the daughter of a wealthy colonial governor, she grew up with every luxury available to 1700s Ecuador*—but in her young mind, it was nothing compared to the magic of France.

In her teens, her dream began to come into focus. A dashing young Frenchman, Jean Godin des Odonais, came to town on a scientific expedition. Isabel took to him immediately, and by all accounts, Jean was equally smitten by her: until his dying day, he would write at length of his love and admiration for her. They married within a year.

Years later, with Jean's work wrapped up, they made plans to move to France. Jean went ahead to arrange passports and travel across the Atlantic. He was to return for Isabel and their unborn child—the only one of four who'd live past childhood. He thought he'd be gone two years.

He was gone for 20.

Because Spain and Portugal ran South America (and neither were getting along with France), they wouldn't let Jean make the return trip. He couldn't even get letters to Isabel—he could barely get them to Europe. And when his letters begging for passage *did* make it to Spain and Portugal, they were mired in bureaucracy. He tried everything he could think of to reunite with Isabel, getting so desperate that he tried instigating war between France and Portugal. His efforts were unsuccessful; he spent two long decades almost going crazy trying to get to her, and she had no idea.

Still, Isabel waited. Even as neighbors said Jean wasn't coming back. Even as her daughter grew into a woman. Even as her family fell on hard times. She waited and waited and waited—until her daughter died of smallpox. She had been 19 and never got to meet her father. So Isabel stopped waiting, and based on the merest rumor that Jean was still alive, left to find him.[†]

---

\* Which was, at the time, the Viceroyalty of Peru.

† The rumor actually did originate with Jean. He'd finally gotten his passport, and was trying to send word back to Isabel that a boat was waiting for her on the Oyapock River, near Brazil. He didn't go himself, because he'd

Joining together a group of 42 people, she set off to reunite with her husband on an incredibly dangerous journey. The group included her two brothers, her nephew, her servant, Joaquim, some maids, a doctor, and several native porters.\* The 3,000-mile route, which wound around an active volcano, across ramshackle wooden bridges, and through the heart of the Amazon jungle, had only been done by a handful of groups before. They estimated it would take six months.

The group started dwindling when they found an abandoned village. It had been ravaged by smallpox and burned to the ground. The porters fled immediately. The group continued in a canoe down a flooding river, although none of them knew how to canoe or swim. Isabel nearly drowned, and they lost many of their supplies. They soon ended up at a sandbar, where they split up. The doctor's small group took the boat and continued, promising to send back help.

But after two weeks with no rescue in sight,† Isabel, her brothers, and her nephew built a raft and set off downriver. The raft sank almost immediately, taking their supplies with it. They continued on foot, with Isabel finally switching from frilly dresses to her brother's spare trousers. They walked into thick jungle without food, direction, or sunlight. There they became a playground for wasps, scorpions, fire ants, and many things worse.

The carpets of flies refused them sleep. The jungle refused them food. Four weeks, they walked. And they began to die. First her nephew. Then her brother. Then her other brother.

Until Isabel was the only one left.

Isabel had lost everything. Her children, her home, her family. Twenty long years of heartbreak, weighing her down. And so, she lay down on the jungle floor, curled up next to her brother, and waited to die.

But try as she might, she could not die. Even as she began to slip away, a voice called out

---

been secretly fomenting war with Portugal for so long that he was convinced the boat captain—a Portuguese man—was going to kill him. Twenty years in bureaucratic hell had done a number on Jean.

\* Her brothers and nephew joined for a variety of reasons. Partly they wanted to look after her, but they had their own reasons for going to France—her brother wanted the nephew to have a European education. The family had fallen on hard times after her mother's death and they were hoping to make a new start. The doctor was an acquaintance who just wanted to get to the east coast. Her servant, Joaquim, seemingly went willingly, as he was going to be freed after they finished the journey (more on that later).

† The group who'd gone ahead—the doctor, his companion, and Joaquim—did eventually return to the sandbar. However, they only found the corpses of the servants they'd left behind. From this, the doctor assumed Isabel had died, and spread the word around town. He also sold her belongings that she'd sent with him. The doctor was kind of a jerk.

to her, a voice that would not let her go to sleep, that talked of tasks unfinished and duties undone.

It was the voice of her dear Jean.

He said, "Get up, Isabel."

And slowly, she began to crawl forward.

After eight days alone, she stumbled across some native hunters, and immediately collapsed. Over the next month, they nursed her back to health, ridding her of botflies and other parasites. Her hair had turned permanently gray. Her hand was crippled. But she was alive. She gave them two gold necklaces,* and set about freeing her servant, Joaquim, from jail, as he'd been suspected of murdering her (a charge which the eyewitnesses could have, but didn't, clear up).

Six months later, for the first time in 21 years, on a boat on the Oyapock River, Isabel Godin saw her husband.

They sailed to Europe three years later, and in her beloved French countryside, she lived a quiet, long, happy life.†

## · ART NOTES AND TRIVIA ·

Isabel's outfit in the image is very deliberate and true to her story: she is wearing the two gold chains she gave to her saviors. She is wearing her brother's pants, which she switched to when they entered the jungle. Moreover, she's wearing sandals that she carved from her brother's boots once he died. Her dress had gotten so tattered by the end that she was mostly using a scarf as a shirt.

---

* This was some of the only adornment to survive her journey. The gift was an incredible act of generosity, enough to provide for them for possibly years to come. Unfortunately, the priests who were running the mission where she was staying promptly confiscated the gold necklaces and gave her saviors 3–4 yards of cotton instead. She, being a devout woman, felt she could not talk back to the clergy, even though they had just proven themselves colossal douchebags.

† Afterward, they had a relatively uneventful life. Jean was promoted in the science world, and Isabel lived to the age of 65. She seemingly had some severe PTSD, and never talked of the experience much—the story survives from Jean's testimonials to his beloved wife. Jean's relatives would relate that in her later years, Isabel would sometimes take out sandals and a cotton dress—the only remnants of her clothing from the expedition—from an ebony box and look at them.

# Isabella of France

(C. 1295–1358, FRANCE/ENGLAND)

## The Mother Who Conquered England

She grew up on tales of gallant knights and wicked witches, of maidens fair and loves true. Each promised the same social contract: be a dutiful wife and your husband will be faithful to you.

She kept by the contract. Suitors measured her like a horse, checking her mother to see how she'd turn out. She passed their tests. By the age of seven, she was betrothed to Edward II, heir to the English throne. He was powerful, handsome, popular. She'd won. She'd married well.

Except life isn't a fairy tale—and neither he, nor she, would fit the roles assigned to them.

To say the marriage started off on the wrong foot is putting it mildly. Edward II, it became clear, was infatuated with his lover,* Piers Gaveston. To be fair, Isabella was only 12 at the time they married, but regardless, Edward showed astonishing disrespect. He sat with Gaveston at his wedding; at his coronation, he put up tapestries of Gaveston's arms instead of Isabella's; he sent France's marriage gifts to Gaveston;† he let Gaveston upstage her at her own coronation.

Isabella was hardly the only person Gaveston disrespected. Mocking his peers and flaunting his status, Gaveston infuriated the nobility to the point of civil war. He'd come up with insulting nicknames for them: "Burstbelly," "Churl," "old Hog," "the Player," "the Fiddler," "the Black Dog of Arden." It was such a problem that Edward exiled Gaveston for a spell, but it wasn't long before he was back.

Regardless, Isabella and Edward gave their marriage a real try. Seeing him embroiled in a hopeless war with Scotland, Isabella helped arrange the backing of France, stepping up as a political ally and confidant. They would have four children, conceiving Edward III during Lent (when they weren't supposed to sleep together). When their living quarters caught fire, he carried her to safety. And all their lives, even when their relationship was bad—and it got *very* bad, as you'll see—they referred to each other with titles like "my very sweet heart."

---

\* There's like one person out there who's still arguing they weren't lovers, inserting the word "allegedly" into her Wikipedia entry over and over. Give it up, dude, they were totally doing it.

† There's a recurrent myth that he gifted them to Gaveston, and that Gaveston put on Isabella's jewelry and paraded them around in front of her. There's no evidence for that, but the myth gets repeated endlessly. Even got me, in the first draft of this chapter!

But Gaveston had Edward's love, albeit not for long.

After months of insults, Gaveston pushed his luck too far. The nobles threatened to rebel, and Edward II, overwhelmed by their unrest and a costly Scottish war, could not protect his lover. Gaveston had grown so unpopular that not only was he kidnapped and stabbed to death (against the orders of the king), but the local churches refused to perform burial rites.

With Gaveston dead, Isabella became Edward's closest ally, and they had many good years together. She helped him regain standing with the nobles (it helped that his chief antagonist, the Earl of Lancaster, was her uncle). She negotiated with his enemies. She sat in on council meetings. She traveled with him to France. With French backing, Edward's lieutenant Roger Mortimer drove back the Scots, putting Edward's reign finally on solid footing.

But in time, the cycle began again. Edward, ever a mercurial and difficult man, again overplayed his hand and lost a catastrophic battle with Scotland. Worse still, in his defeat, he began to cozy up to a new lover:[*] Hugh Despenser the Younger. Despenser was much worse than Gaveston. He stole from strangers, friends, and family; he had women tortured into insanity; he jailed people without charge. Despenser quickly solidified a real grasp on Edward: when some nobles banished Despenser,[†] Edward had him brought back. Worse still, Despenser started to turn Edward against Isabella.

Still, Isabella tried to make the marriage work. When Edward began a brutal crackdown on errant nobles, she risked her neck to provoke them into making the first move. Approaching a political enemy's castle, she demanded to be let in until the castle archers opened fire on her, killing six of her men. She retaliated shortly thereafter and overran the castle. It was the beginning of extensive political purges that affected hundreds, and killed Isabella's uncle, the Earl of Lancaster.

It wasn't enough. Despite putting her life on the line for him, and aiding in her uncle's death, Isabella had lost both Edward's ear and his protection. He left her to fend for herself as he and Despenser retreated—she had to flee south, evading enemy armies and navies.[‡] As Edward became simultaneously embroiled in a war with France (seriously, he was fighting *everyone*), he took it out on Isabella. He stripped her of her possessions, her riches, and her income. And in a final insult, he sent her to France to negotiate a peace. This would prove to be what historians refer to as "a huge mistake."

---

[*] There's less textual evidence that these two were romantically involved than there is for Edward and Gaveston, but Edward was definitely infatuated with Despenser.

[†] He became a pirate immediately. This did not earn him new admirers.

[‡] Some accounts list this as the second time he did this, the first being a decade earlier, while she was pregnant; but it's more likely that was a historian getting dates confused. Historians: they're people too!

Once away from Edward, in her own homeland, she renounced the social contract. She had married well. She'd been a dutiful wife. But there was to be no happily ever after.

She began consolidating power. First, she convinced her husband to send their son, Edward III, to France as an additional proxy. Once he arrived, Isabella refused to let him leave. She married her son to Philippa of Hainault, receiving an army as dowry. Isabella made a secret nonaggression pact with the Scots in advance of her eventual return. When a furious Edward II demanded she come back, Isabella declined, saying that "someone has come between my husband and myself trying to break [their marriage]; I protest that I will not return until this intruder [Despenser] is removed."

And to firmly put an end to the marriage, she took a lover of her own. This was Roger Mortimer, the man who'd driven back the Scots for Edward II all those years ago. Targeted by Edward II in the purges, he'd also escaped* to France. Away from his wife and their 12 children, his involvement with Isabella was cheating on his end as well. Their relationship became a massive scandal, losing Isabella many of her supporters: most of her retinue left in disgust. She'd gone beyond the pale.

But their affair was just a warmup. She and Mortimer landed in England with 700 troops and spread word she was to oust the king. Clad in funeral attire, she began marching, gathering supporters along the way. By the time she arrived in Bristol, they had over 2,000 troops. By contrast, Edward had to beg his 12 archers not to desert him.

So great was public ire toward the king that Isabella arranged to have him deposed. This had never been done before, and there was no protocol for it. She gave all major social organizations a vote, and convinced many clergy to speak out against him. In the end, they stripped him of his crown.

She had conquered England, the first outsider to do so in centuries. She had done so with virtually no bloodshed, with the notable exception of Hugh Despenser, whose unbelievably violent demise practically evened the whole thing out.†

Edward II was jailed, but after several months of incarceration, he was abruptly pronounced dead. Many at the time (and even today) believed that Mortimer and Isabella ordered Edward's murder, although evidence is thin. Some believe that he escaped and became an itinerant wanderer, going by "William the Welshman."

With Edward III still a minor, Isabella and Mortimer ruled in his stead. They ended the hopeless Scottish wars. Isabella continued seeing Mortimer in semisecret. She'd written her

---

\* The first person in 200 years to escape the Tower of London!

† After a gauntlet of public humiliation that involved him getting tattooed all over with Bible verses, he was stripped naked, half-hanged, and had his genitalia cut off—which were then thrown into a fire. He was hung over the fire and died howling for forgiveness. Afterward, his executioners split his belly open, removed his organs, and tossed them in the fire. His decapitated head was sent to London, while his body was sawn into quarters, each sent to the four next largest English cities. He was, suffice to say, not a popular man.

own rules. Now in her thirties and a mother of four, she was no longer that spotless young ingenue that suitors had checked for blemishes. She'd suffered years of humiliation from a world with no regard for imperfect women. She would show it no regard in return.

She wasn't a good ruler. Isabella and Mortimer spent lavishly, practically bankrupting the realm—and when they ran low, they seized funds from nobles. They granted Scotland outrageously generous peace terms that proved unpopular both in England and in Scotland. Mortimer abused his position, much as Despenser and Gaveston had. Nothing had changed.

Within a scant three years, their enemies began closing in. Sensing their end was at hand, Isabella and Mortimer fortified themselves in a tower—only for soldiers to infiltrate in the middle of the night. After a violent clash,* Mortimer was detained, although Isabella put up no fight. Once the situation had settled and the two had been arrested, the ringleader of the assault revealed himself: Edward III, newly 18 years old.

After a brief trial, Roger Mortimer was hanged. Edward III assumed the throne. He pardoned Isabella, painting her as Mortimer's pawn, and let her retire to the north, where she grew old, spending her days in quiet contemplation.

One of her frequent visitors was her daughter-in-law, Philippa. Philippa had been betrothed young, much like Isabella, but hers was a partnership that proved one of the greatest in English history. Edward III and Philippa ended the ceaseless infighting and led England to stunning victories against France (helped, in part, by **Jeanne de Clisson**, covered elsewhere in this book). Somehow, the marriage Isabella made to continue England's civil war instead ended it.†

Isabella spent her final decades trying to better herself. She spent time with her family. She joined a religious order. She resolved disputes. When she died, she was buried with Edward II's heart, clothed in her wedding cloak—she'd preserved the garment for 50 years.

In the centuries after, most portrayals cast her as a femme fatale or a neglected wife.‡ Historians cast her as a morality tale, a feminist icon, an avenging lover. But she doesn't fit neatly into any such role, same as she never lived up to the fairy-tale social contracts thrust upon her. Like so many of us, she was neither gallant knight nor wicked witch, and yet somehow a tangled mix of both.

---

* Roger stabbed a guy to death before he was taken down. Another guy who was in the tower with them was caught while trying to escape down the privy chute. Bad way to go.

† And, to be fair, replaced it with the Hundred Year War, which Edward III was basically winning throughout his entire life. Part of the grounds for the war was actually Isabella's claim to French titles, so in a way, she started it.

‡ Save *Braveheart*, possibly the most historically inaccurate movie of all time: it portrayed her hooking up with William Wallace, a man who died when she was 10.

# Sacajawea

## (1788–1812, UNITED STATES)

### The Mom Who Mapped America

She's one of the most celebrated women in American history, one of a select few to ever show up on American currency. But nobody knows much about Sacajawea.[*] Sure, every middle schooler gets the basic outline: Lewis and Clark, walking across half of North America, Native American guide. If you had a decent teacher, you probably heard that she did the entire trek with a baby strapped to her back. But her husband's name? Where she died? When she died? These finer details are usually left out of her story, which is a shame, because hers is a life worth exploring.

First off: she had a childhood so rough that it's a minor miracle Lewis and Clark would describe her as "cheerful." Abducted from her native Shoshone tribe in her early teens, Sacajawea was raised by an enemy tribe until she was 16—at which point she was either wooed, traded, or gambled away.[†] In any event, she ended up as the second wife of a real piece of ~~crap~~ work: French-Canadian frontiersman Toussaint Charbonneau.[‡]

Regardless, she was a ray of sunshine throughout Lewis and Clark's government-backed

---

[*] And here we come to our first point of contention: the spelling (and pronunciation!) of her name. While her name is usually written as Sacagawea, the Hidatsa (the tribe that had abducted her) tend toward "Sakakawea," which mirrors the Hidatsa pronunciation of her name. However, that is itself a corruption of her Shoshone name, which uses a soft *j* sound in place of a hard *k* sound—hence "Sacajawea." The "Sacagawea" spelling is an apparent compromise between the two pronunciations, but this author has opted to go with the spelling closest to the original intent.

[†] The facts and even timeline of this are impossible to untangle. In many versions, she was kept as a second-class citizen (if not outright slave) with the Hidatsa, and all but given away to Charbonneau. Others dispute this, pointing out that the Hidatsa did not engage in slavery, and that they likely would have made Charbonneau pay a dowry.

[‡] A brief digression on Toussaint, because some historians have recently made the argument he wasn't *so* bad (looking at you, Susan Colby). He beat Sacajawea so badly that Lewis and Clark had to stop him. Yes, spousal abuse was more common then, but that's hardly an excuse. In addition, he purportedly sold women into slavery (this one's a bit harder to source), and he got straight-out stabbed for raping a woman in 1795 (nobody's disputing this one). Put aside, if you can, the facts that he was "perhaps the most timid waterman in the world" (Lewis and Clark's words); that he almost doomed the whole trip by capsizing its boats (Sacajawea salvaged the goods of this incident); that he was a polygamist who wed a minimum of five wives; that all his wives were 16 years old or younger; and that the last wife he took was 14 when he was 70. Even putting aside all that, he was hardly a paragon of his gender, to put it mildly. To put it harshly: nuts to this abusive rapist.

7,000-mile trip to map a route to the West Coast*—despite having *just* given birth, and carrying the newborn on her back the entire way. It is a testament to her temperament that Lewis and Clark considered her a good investment, regardless of the prima donna tendencies of her husband.†

On April 7, 1805, Sacajawea, Toussaint, their child Jean-Baptiste, and the 30 men of the Corps of Discovery set out westward. Jean-Baptiste, soon nicknamed Pomp,‡ proved one of the trip's MVPs: by presenting a nursing mother with an infant child, most Native American tribes accepted that the party was out on peaceful business. Who would bring a baby to war? Furthermore, he kept everyone's spirits high with his campfire dancing. Clark, in particular, took a liking to him.

Sacajawea was no less important. Having been raised in the Shoshone tradition—that is, having to forage, cook, clean, and do almost everything non-horse-related (which was the men's duty)—she proved invaluable to the trip's survival. Furthermore, her impressive recall helped tremendously. She recognized traditional Shoshone hunting grounds, down to the exact spot where she'd been abducted as a young girl. She encountered this tragic spot stone-faced and without emotion.

She was, however, overcome with feeling when she guided the expedition to the home of the Lemhi Shoshone, her childhood tribe. Wailing openly, she finally heard news of her friends and family for the first time in many years. She reunited with another girl who'd been abducted and escaped, and with her brother, who'd grown up to become a chief. She even came face-to-face with the man to whom she'd been betrothed in her infancy. The man looked Charbonneau up and down, then rescinded his marital claim.

After two weeks, the trip continued its journey west, leaving the warm confines of Sacajawea's tribe. It is here that the group reached its nadir, almost starving a scant month after leaving the Shoshone.§ Nevertheless, they survived, navigating unknown tribes—Pomp

---

* Lewis and Clark had been tasked with several things. Part of it was to map the continent (Thomas Jefferson and company were very interested if there was a major east-west river they could use), but in part they were to keep an eye out for ancient creatures. The theory of extinction was not well-accepted at this point, and Jefferson held out hope that they would come across living mastodons in their travels.

† Toussaint initially did not want to do anything other than interpret—he was fluent in Hidatsa and French, and Sacajawea in Shoshone and Hidatsa—and he balked at the idea that he'd be asked to participate in other activities.

‡ It remains unclear whether this name was a joke based on his juvenile dancing, or whether he was nicknamed after the Roman general Pompey.

§ There's a myth that's persisted that they were so hungry that they ate candle tallow to survive. This isn't true— at their hungriest, on September 20, 1805, they ate bear fat, which truthfully isn't that far off from the tallow they had. It's likely true that Lewis and Clark contemplated eating tallow, as they were practical sorts, but they never resorted to it.

and mom again proving excellent ambassadors—and eventually achieved their goal: they made it to the West Coast. Sacajawea got to see the ocean for the first time in her life.*

The trip back took a turn when baby Pomp became deathly ill. Virtually the entire group took this personally, as Pomp had charmed all of these rough-and-tumble adventurers. Lewis and Clark stayed up all night looking after him, administering poultices and tartar cream. After several weeks, Pomp made it through. He was saved, in the words of modern-day doctor E. G. Chuinard, by "good doctoring, good mother's care, and good luck."

Almost a year to the day after they had departed the Hidatsa village where Lewis and Clark had met Sacajawea, the group returned. Here they split ways, with Lewis and Clark paying out Charbonneau's contract (Sacajawea didn't get anything). The parting was especially difficult on Clark, who'd grown so fond of Pomp that he wanted to adopt him. At the very least, he urged Toussaint and Sacajawea, they should come visit him in St. Louis.

Three years later they did so, but city life was not for Toussaint and Sacajawea. After spending over a year there, they decided to move back. Sacajawea was pregnant with a second child and sick besides. She wanted to be among familiar faces. But realizing that an educated life would open doors for their child, they relented and put Pomp in Clark's care.

Unfortunately, Sacajawea would not last the year. She died in late 1812, probably of complications relating to the birth of her daughter, Lizette. Toussaint gave Lizette too to Clark, and went back to his life in the wilderness. While Lizette apparently died in childhood, Pomp went on to become a flamboyant "gentleman adventurer," crisscrossing the world as a jack of all trades.

The last mention Sacajawea gets in Lewis and Clark's journals sums her up well: "She has borne with a patience truly admirable the fatigues of so long of route, encumbered with the charge of an infant, who is even now only 19 months old. She was very observant. She had a good memory, remembering locations not seen since her childhood. In trouble she was full of resources, plucky and determined. With her helpless infant she rode with the man, guiding us unerringly through mountain passes and lonely places. Intelligent, cheerful, resourceful, tireless, faithful, she inspired us all."

---

* She almost didn't get to, though! She was tasked with setting up the camp and foraging for food, and told to stay put for several weeks. It was not until they caught wind (possibly literally) of a beached whale that she requested to go and finally see the ocean. Lewis and Clark gave the go-ahead.

## · ART NOTES AND TRIVIA ·

This picture depicts the expedition finally making it to the Pacific Ocean. Sacajawea enjoys the cool sea breeze with Pomp on her back, while in the background, the corps inspects a beached whale. Toussaint is seen tripping and falling down the cliff, because this author is not about to depict that jerkwad in a positive light.

## The Other Sacajawea

In the early 1900s, a historian named Grace Hebard made a startling claim: Sacajawea had not died in 1812, but instead lived until 1884, and died on the Wind River reservation in Wyoming. This theory had a huge number of problems from the get-go. For one thing, there was plenty of documentation, and oral histories, of Sacajawea's 1812 death. For another, the reservation in question belonged to Eastern Shoshone, and Sacajawea was Lemhi, or Northern Shoshone.

In 2008, after a thorough investigation, anthropologist Thomas H. Johnson concluded that the woman buried at Wind River was really a Comanche leader named Paraivo, or Chief Woman. A combination of wishful thinking and misremembered histories contributed to a case of mistaken identity that persists even to current day, with numerous monuments and memorials of the Wind River Sacajawea.

# Mandukhai Khatun

(1448–1510, MONGOLIA)

## The Mother Who United the Mongol Tribes

Everyone has a moment that defines their life. The Mongol queen Mandukhai had that moment after her first husband died. Young, unsupported, and faced by rival clans rushing to claim the throne, she wanted to go it alone, but she asked her advisors for a second opinion. One counseled her to accept the marriage proposal of the local warlord Une-Bolod—a traditional, smart course of action. After some consideration, she replied, "You disagree with me just because Une-Bolod is a man and I am only a widow." Moreover, she charged the advisor, it was only because Mandukhai was a woman that "you really think you have the right to speak to me this way."

She concluded by flinging a bowl of hot tea at the advisor's head. And went on to become the most important woman in Mongolian history.

Mandukhai was always the sort of woman to march to her own drummer.

Born over 200 years after the death of Genghis Khan, Mandukhai was brought up in a world of feuding clans. The feared Mongol Empire had long since collapsed, driven back to its homelands and reduced to tribal infighting. Mandukhai was meant to be only a bargaining chip in this endless feud: an aristocrat's daughter traded off as another wife. True, she'd been wed to the latest Great Khan, a man 25 years older named Manduul, but the Great Khan was a far less respected title than in the time of Genghis. Besides, Great Khans in those days had a nasty habit of coming down with a bad case of knife-in-the-gut.

The first years of her reign grew complicated quickly. What little of Manduul's attention she commanded was immediately taken up by the Great Khan's shiny new toy: his young nephew, the only known male heir to Genghis Khan.[*] However, after a few short years of peacocking, this Golden Prince overplayed his hand, and Manduul had him exiled and killed. Soon, Manduul himself died, as did his primary wife. With the Golden Prince dead, Manduul had no male heir—Mandukhai had only given him two girls.

---

[*] This was Bayan Mongke, the Golden Prince. While Genghis Khan was incalculably fruitful, the ensuing centuries had seen virtually every legitimate claimant to his legacy systematically assassinated. A ton of people likely still carried his genetics, but in terms of royal descendants? It was down to Bayan Mongke.

Which left Mandukhai, at 23, suddenly alone on the throne, and at the aforementioned crossroads.

One of the reasons she might have struck out on her own at that point was that she had a secret weapon. Unbeknownst to most, the Golden Prince had borne a son who'd survived the turmoil—although he'd been malnourished, crippled, and raised in poverty. Mandukhai found him, administered the best medical care available, and installed him as the Great Khan. She gave him the name Dayan Khan: "Khan of the Whole," which was a clever stroke. Besides obviously signaling the intention to unite the warring clans, "Dayan Khan" had the added benefit of sounding like "Great Yuan" to neighboring Chinese ears. This title carried with it the connotation of a claim to the Chinese throne as well, which is some master-level shade throwing. He sat on the throne, but according to Mongol tradition, Mandukhai, now his queen, was in charge until he came of age.[*]

Mandukhai knew she was still in a remarkably weak position. She was a young woman without many allies, married to a child who could barely walk. The Mongols respected strength, and she needed to show some, fast.

She displayed just that—as well as smarts—with her next move. Managing to win over her old warlord suitor Une-Bolod to her side (by making him next in line should the sickly Dayan Khan die), she declared war against the Oirat Mongols to the west. She did so carefully. She spent time organizing her army (forethought a rare trait for Mongol leaders) and chose a specific battleground that would be advantageous to her. Once satisfied, she donned armor, strapped Dayan Khan to a camel, and rode into battle. She was determined to demonstrate that she was unlike prior generations of pampered Mongol rulers, and willing to rough it among the troops, just as Genghis had.

In the words of *The Secret History of the Mongols*,[†] she "destroyed them entirely, and annihilated them." For the first time in over 70 years, Mongols of east and west were united under the same banner.

She was not done, but she was on pause—as she solidified her power over her new holdings, others began to make moves. The southern Mongols, wanting to show their strength against Mandukhai, expanded their raids farther south into Chinese territory. In response,

---

[*] Mongol tradition was for the successor to a Great Khan to marry his predecessor's wife, and so the two did marry at this point, although it was obviously platonic (the kid was seven!). But generally, the Mongols of Genghis Khan's era had remarkably few hang-ups when it came to marital fidelity within the family—virtually everyone's spouses could, and did, sleep with whomever, within the same family.

[†] The most significant Mongolian historical document of this period. Notably, it had several sections related to the feats of Mongolian women, specifically Genghis Khan's daughters, ripped out.

the understandably spooked Chinese drove the southern Mongols back,* cut trade with their northern neighbors, and extended the Great Wall, at Great Expense.†

With the southern Mongols chastened by the Chinese, Mandukhai saw her chance. She sent Dayan Khan, now 15 and much tougher, to conquer them and prove himself to everyone. He made short work of them, and followed up with a campaign to conquer the last major holdout Mongol tribe: that of his father's killer. He conquered them with shocking ease, and in so doing, rescued his birth mother, who'd been taken by his father's killer. To his dismay, she had grown accustomed to her new life, and wanted nothing to do with this son she'd barely seen since his birth.

Mandukhai and Dayan Khan found common ground over this. Both scarcely had any living family, having both been sent away when young. Perhaps it was this sense of having no family, combined with a hefty dose of political savvy, that led the two to cement their marital relationship, and start a family. Yes, she was 33, and he was 17. Yes, she'd basically raised him. Yes, it's kind of weird. But hey, history's full of stuff like this. And they actually seemed to genuinely like each other, which is more than you can say for most of these sorts of marriages.

For the next several decades, Mandukhai and Dayan Khan continued to wage small battles, bringing tribes under their banner—even when Mandukhai was pregnant. Famously, at age 40, eight months pregnant, she rode into battle and suffered a nasty fall from her horse. Immediately, four warriors formed a wall around her. All of them were of tribes unrelated to her, which shows the level of respect she commanded, even at her most vulnerable. She survived the battle and gave birth to her third set of twins a month later.

By 1490, with virtually all the Mongols united for the first time in centuries, Mandukhai and Dayan Khan turned their attention to solidifying their legacy. Genghis's empire had fallen apart for a variety of reasons, not the least of which was his questionable parenting: his children had grown up greedy and spoiled, and they bickered endlessly after his death. Mandukhai had carefully nurtured Dayan Khan into a great leader, and she did the same with their children (10 in all). Mandukhai's brood took posts across the edges of the Mongol empire and kept the peace for generations. Even after the Mongols were conquered by the Qing over a century later, Mandukhai's descendants stayed in power, and would until the 1940s.

While the exploits of many other Mongol queens were minimized, censored, or forgotten, the Mongols never forgot the deeds of their greatest queen, the "reincarnation of Genghis Khan": Mandukhai the Wise.

---

\* This was the work of comically underappreciated virtuoso Commander Wang, whose surviving diaries mostly consist of him complaining about being underfunded.

† The debate over the wall is funny in how shockingly modern it is. They debated costs endlessly, until one official did a thorough cost-benefit analysis. The honest-to-god thinking was that the Mongols would suffer shock and despair when they beheld the wall, and join the obviously superior Chinese. This was wishful thinking.

# Ida Laura Pfeiffer

(1797–1857, AUSTRIA)

## The Mom Who Saw the World

Ida Pfeiffer's dad probably didn't intend for his strictness to lead to his daughter hanging out with Indonesian cannibals. But it did. It just took a while.

The seeds for Ida Pfeiffer's late-life globetrotting exploits—which were so infamous as to earn her a cameo in Henry David Thoreau's *Walden*—lay in her childhood. Although her father was fine with her dressing as a boy and playing as a soldier,* his permissiveness ended there. He was noted for randomly refusing even the most benign requests his children made, to "steel them for disappointment." Her posthumous biography tiptoes around this bizarre parenting style in the most hilariously euphemistic way, describing it as "eccentric," and saying it "would hardly find a defender at a time like the present"—said "present" being Austria in 1861, not exactly famous as history's most liberal child-rearing paradise.

Between the two, her parents covered all the bases: her dad provided physical discomfort, while her mom slathered on the emotional anguish. Although Ida hated all things girly—she'd cut and burn her own fingers to prevent having to play piano—she gave that all up for a chance to marry her tutor. She fell deeply for him, began wearing skirts and practicing embroidery, everything she thought would make her a fine lady. Her mother already thought of the tutor as a son, and had him stay with them frequently. Truly, there could be no better match. Which is why her mother refused to let them marry, tossed the tutor out of the house, and set Ida up with a random lawyer.† Steel yourself for disappointment, indeed!

After that, Ida had a quiet life for around 20 years.‡ She had kids who grew up and left

---

* She was a total warmonger as a kid. When Napoleon invaded Austria and some French soldiers crashed at her house, she told them, "If I myself could murder Napoleon, I should not hesitate one instant to do so." She then turned her back on Napoleon himself during a victory parade. She was only 12 but clearly had the fully developed chutzpah of an 80-year-old senior who'd long since stopped giving a hoot.

† Her first words upon meeting her husband: "You should know I'm in love with someone else." His reply: "I think we all are." He was a pretty cool guy and they got along, even if they were never in love.

‡ At least, according to her biography. Who knows, maybe she fought off an alien invasion and forgot to mention it.

the house, her mom died, and eventually so did her husband. Finally, she was 45, and had nothing holding her back anymore. It was time to go buck wild. She was going to travel, and she was going to do it alone.

The first problem she ran into was that she had no money. Her late husband's financial woes had sunk her funds to where she could just barely make ends meet at home, let alone travel. Other women of the time who'd gone on extensive travels had all been wealthy. But here Ida's lifetime of disappointment training kicked in: she could sleep on a bed of nails, while on fire, with a snake biting her all night, and she'd be fine. This gave her options. Not great options, but options.

The second problem was the social stigma around traveling, which she circumvented through flagrantly lying to everyone around her. She said she was just going on a little religious pilgrimage to Jerusalem,* but took, shall we say, the scenic route—through most of the Middle East, and on to Constantinople. She was gone for nine months.

Soon after she got back, she recouped most of her costs by publishing her travel diary, although she had to be coerced into it: it was "repugnant to her modesty." Still, the anonymously credited journal was a smash hit, owing in no small part to her blunt honesty (more on that later), and it was reprinted four times. It financed a six-month journey to Scandinavia (for which she learned English and Danish), and planted the seeds of her first around-the-world trip.

Again, she told her children she was just stepping out for tea—in Brazil. This time she was gone for two and a half years, during which time she was attacked by highwaymen at knifepoint, met the rebel queen Pōmare IV of Tahiti,† went on tiger hunts in India, and engaged in dangerously exhaustive desert journeys through the Fertile Crescent on camel. When she showed up at Tebris, the English consul didn't believe a woman could have done it. She celebrated her 50th birthday like this.

And then she did it again! After lying low for three years (and writing a bestselling travelogue), she went on another around-the-world trip, this one even more dangerous. It's on this four-year sojourn that she met the headhunting Dayak people of Borneo, and cannibalistic Batak people of Indonesia—whom she joked with, saying she was too old and tough to make good eating.

---

\* Which was quite the vacation destination at the time! It had opened up considerably after Muhammad Ali had made Egypt safer for travelers. No, not that Muhammad Ali, a different one. Although it's a lot of fun to picture the presumably time-displaced boxer punching his way through Bedouin territory. Maybe on a future episode of *Doctor Who*.

† Queen Pōmare IV, a woman who warred against French colonialism for five years and was known as the "eye eater," for reasons that are self-explanatory. She would have still been at war with France when Ida met her. They presumably commiserated on their hatred of the French.

The most astonishing thing about Ida Pfeiffer was her open-mindedness. While European travelogues of the time were awash with pearl-clutching descriptions of brutal savagery, Pfeiffer didn't buy into it. Her first visit to the Middle East praised the oft-maligned Turks for their social responsibility and tolerance of other religions, while snarking at European travelers for being gossipy, loud, and rude.* She praised the Bedouins for being hospitable and welcoming while everyone decried them as thieves and murderers.

Which isn't to say she was a scion of enlightened social wisdom—she was absolutely a mixed bag. She referred to men as the "superior" sex and called Arabs lazy for not having terraformed Jerusalem into a flowering paradise. She called harem women ignorant and uneducated, but said they were probably happier than European women. Upon seeing the decapitated heads displayed by the Dayak people, she described them sympathetically as trophies of bygone years—much like "the tattered flags that we hang up in our public buildings are to us." She then went on to call the Dayak people stupid and ugly, and say that they had a weird way of walking. But then asked herself, aren't Europeans "not really just as bad or worse than these despised savages? Is not every page of our history filled with horrid deeds of treachery and murder?"

Hey, she was trying! It was pretty revolutionary for the time.

Ida only became more open-minded as years went on. By the time she encountered the cannibalistic Batak, whom she'd been repeatedly warned would try to kill and eat her, she so firmly believed that they weren't as bad as people say, she became the first European to ever meet them. And she was right! She found that they had a good legal system (usually eating only the most depraved criminals), were trustworthy and literate—and yes, cannibals. She went on to describe, at length, the dishes they'd cook people into, as if she were writing for Jeffrey Dahmer's Lonely Planet. She was a curious one.

She kept thinking of retiring, but never could quite seem to sit still. After her second world journey, she decided to visit Madagascar. This was a mistake. In short order, she was taken in by a handful of European expats, who were plotting a coup d'etat against the cruel ruler of the time: **Ranavalona I**, covered elsewhere in this book. Although Pfeiffer had no axe to grind, she was in the wrong place at the wrong time, and was caught in Ranavalona's web. Ranavalona marched the now-61-year-old Ida through malaria-infested swamps for months, which soon thereafter (possibly in conjunction with cancer) proved to be the death of Ida.

In the end, Ida had traveled over 150,000 miles of sea and 20,000 of land, in an era before airplanes or comfortable trains. She brought a huge amount of geographic, botanic, and ethnographic knowledge to Europe—and although she was not a trained scientist, her contributions merited a gold medal from the king of Prussia and an honorary membership

---

* A trait that Americans have famously elevated to an art form. The student has become the master.

in the Berlin Geographical Society. Austria, for its part, seemingly didn't care much about anything she did (it's okay, she was well-prepared for disappointment).

In her posthumous biography, attached to her last travel journal, her life is summed up with a final quote: "She had what, in common life, we emphatically term *character.*"

### · ART NOTES AND TRIVIA ·

This one's pretty simple—Ida is spinning a globe (who knows where it'll stop next!), surrounded by people in her life. From right to left, we have:

- Her husband!

- A woman from a harem, and the sultan who held the harem.

- A Batak warrior! They have some pretty crazy outfits.

- A Dayak woman!

- Ranavalona I, who's mean muggin'.

# Mother Jones (Mary Harris Jones)

(1837–1930, UNITED STATES)

## The Most Dangerous Mother in America

You don't understand how bad the strikes were. You can't—there's simply no modern comparison that captures the scale. Imagine: hundreds of thousands of people walking off the job and into the street; one-fifth of the entire US labor force striking within a single year; the entire city of Seattle shutting down under a general strike; the army coming after workers by dropping bombs and installing snipers; Appalachian mines turning into war zones between workers and hired mercenaries.

But it happened. It gets censored from history books and scrubbed from holidays meant to commemorate it,* but it happened.

And at the center of it all, blazing from city to city like a general marshaling troops, was the grand dame of the labor movement, the "most dangerous woman in America": Mary Harris Jones, better known as Mother Jones.

She was unassuming, which is what made her effective. She wore clothes that were old-fashioned when her grandmother was a child. She talked constantly of her old age and impending demise. She drank with the boys and told filthy jokes. She was your cool grandmother.

But as soon as you opened your ears, she had you. She'd start with a story, usually with her at some coal mine. There would be a boss, and he'd be the vilest, most ridiculous, awful caricature of a human being ever. They'd argue, he'd bluster, but—and here's the important part—she'd win. She'd then draw parallels from that story to the conditions wherever she happened to be, always with plenty of humor and profanity. She'd speak with such knowledge, conviction, and maternal care that you could be sure you were next on the chopping block. Then, she'd present the one and only way to survive: together, in the union. She'd cap it off with her oft-repeated battle cry: "Pray for the dead, and fight like hell for the living!"

And here's the thing: she wasn't wrong! US working conditions were a blighted hellscape. Things we take for granted, like minimum wage, worker's comp, and the weekend? Didn't

---

* What did you think Labor Day was about? Why do you think International Working Women's Day got the "working" part removed? They didn't become perfunctory, toothless Hallmark holidays out of nowhere.

exist. You could die on the job—many did—and few would bat an eye. If you complained, you were out on the street, replaced with someone else. And that was a good-case scenario! In mining towns, where the company owned everything, it was even worse: you had to shop at their stores and pay their markup; you had to weigh your coal with their rigged scales, and accept the reduced pay they'd give you. It was easy for many to accept it as their lot in life, but Mother Jones made the argument that a better world was possible.

Her argument worked. Various unions—especially the United Mine Workers—sent Mother Jones in as an elite strike force to the most far-flung, intransigent work forces. It wasn't uncommon for her to hike over mountains or walk miles uphill in a muddy creek bed to reach some distant mine. Often, there wasn't any other way, since the companies owned the very roads leading to the mine.

When her rallying cries didn't achieve the desired effect, she resorted to a classic maternal tactic: guilt trips. She'd organize the workers' wives into a "mop-and-broom" brigade, promising more (and better) home time with the union. Clad in aprons and clanging kitchenware, they would shame their husbands off the job and onto the strike lines. It wasn't the only way she'd use this tactic: to try to end child labor, she marched on Teddy Roosevelt's home with legions of kids who were missing fingers or had other disabilities.

By 1900, the United Mine Workers boasted over 300,000 members.

Big business used every trick in the book against her. Corporations leveraged private detectives to drum up false charges and get her (and other labor leaders) arrested. Formal accusations of libel, slander, sedition, and terrorism weren't uncommon. The court systems were similarly rigged: after the Ludlow Massacre, where the Colorado National Guard killed over 50 strikers,[*] all the National Guardsmen were acquitted, save one who got a light reprimand. The investigation didn't interview any of the strikers, only the officers. The investigators blamed the strikers for the massacre, and called them "ignorant, lawless, and savage South-European peasants" who did not understand the concept of American liberty.

Which highlights another dividing tactic on the part of the corporations: race. They'd pay different ethnicities at different scales, and stoke tensions so they resented each other instead of rallying together. Mother Jones proved excellent at breaking through this, having lived a childhood as one of the era's more despised minorities (Irish Catholics). She would march unafraid from ethnicity to ethnicity,[†] and when she hit language barriers, she found

---

[*] Around a dozen were women and children, who suffocated and burned to death in a tent. This chapter started with "you don't understand how bad the strikes were" for a reason.

[†] Unfortunately, save the Chinese. She said some awful, racist crap about the Chinese. She also was against giving women the vote (she thought the system was rigged, so why bother) and said some nasty stuff about Margaret Sanger. All your faves are problematic.

common ground through gesturing, broken English, and the "French Classics" (profanity).

One of the corporations' last, and most powerful, tools was the press, which savaged Mother Jones endlessly. In a move that certainly has no parallels to today, they'd label her Communist, Socialist, and Fascist, despite those labels being at odds with one another. One reporter wrote breathlessly that she had been a brothel madam (she almost certainly hadn't). Every time she staged a protest or a strike, she was viciously mocked as a whining nag who hadn't stated her goals clearly enough for the press's liking. This was not an achievable goal: she stated her goals often and eloquently, but the press would purposely ignore, obfuscate, and misrepresent her words to paint her as an unreasonable shrew.

(The press would go on to do this for every protest movement of the past hundred years. See also: Occupy Wall Street, the Tea Party, Black Lives Matter. This is why we can't have nice things.)

As the labor movement grew more powerful, the opposition became more dangerous. It started with implicit threats: a gun-toting spectator at a rally, or a fire started in the hotel room neighboring hers. It quickly grew beyond that. All over the country, mine guards would bomb the houses of activists, shoot strikers, tap phones, install machine guns at mines. States would declare martial law and send in the National Guard, who were never on the side of the workers. In the face of this, Mother Jones became more militant in her advice: "We are law-abiding citizens, we will destroy no property, we will take no life, but if a fellow comes to my home and outrages my wife, by the Eternal he will pay the penalty. I will send him to his God in the repair shop."

Mother Jones was arrested numerous times, and not in the flippant, in-and-out-of-jail way. She was once arrested under martial law for conspiracy to commit murder, and sentenced to 20 years in prison (she was held for three months). On another occasion, she was held under house arrest for nine weeks, guarded by 150 cavalrymen. When 1,000 women and children in their Sunday best marched in protest, 100 of the cavalry rushed them in response, badly injuring six of the protestors.

All because they asked for fair wages and a seat at the table.

But after the bloodiest uprising since the Civil War,[*] as popular opinion began to support the labor movement, big business brought out their very oiliest snake: John D. Rockefeller. He switched up the game plan. Instead of attacking workers head on, he made a big show of changing his values, when all he changed was his image. He gave *just* enough to workers to splinter

---

[*] This was the 1921 Battle of Blair Mountain, where 10,000 armed coal miners fought 3,000 lawmen. Mother Jones pleaded with workers not to march in, fearing a slaughter. They accused her of losing her nerve. Around 1 million rounds were fired and upward of 100 people killed. Private planes flew overhead and dropped bombs. After a week, the president sent in the army to break it up. The miners had just wanted to start a union.

them into factions, and no more. With the more hard-line workers already in prison, many of the strikers, battered and depleted, gave in. He'd bought peace and prevented lawmakers from mandating actual change—and he'd done it cheaply. The labor wars were over. Modern-day PR was born.

Rockefeller even charmed Mother Jones, as he saw through her persona and struck at her weak points. And it *was* a persona: in reality, she was seven years younger than she professed. Most of her anecdotes, while getting at a larger truth, were hyperbolic, if not outright fiction. She hadn't been at half the early labor events she claimed to have attended. Her autobiography was more propaganda than fact.

The truth was that the "grandmother of all agitators" was a woman who'd long been running from herself. An Irish immigrant named Mary Harris Jones (née Mary Harris), she lived a normal, if difficult life for her first 40 years. She'd been married to an iron molder who was in a union, but neither was much involved. The turning point was when an outbreak of yellow fever killed her husband and her four children. She never got over it. She turned her energies to "mothering" other people, joined activism circles, and became Mother Jones. She hadn't been able to save her birth children, but she'd save her adopted ones.

And so, when Rockefeller approached her, he cleverly did so as a supplicant child, flattering her wisdom and years of experience. She fell for it hook, line, and sinker.

She died at age 93, shortly after celebrating her 100th birthday. Her obituaries blunted the memory of her as a radical, characterizing her as a sweet grandmotherly sort who'd opposed Socialism (she hadn't, although she'd opposed specific Socialists). Her bitter enemies professed to love her, and systematically reworked her image into that of a toothless lion.

But she was not forgotten. Legends and folk songs about her still pepper the Appalachian countryside. An all-woman miner strike in the 1980s called themselves "the Daughters of Mother Jones." She became the namesake of *Mother Jones* magazine, one of the world's largest radical magazines. And in the most fitting piece of immortality, her words live on, shouted by activists upward of a century after she'd uttered them: "Pray for the dead, and fight like hell for the living."

## · ART NOTES AND TRIVIA ·

Mother Jones is dressed in the dowdy black attire that was her uniform. It's covered in mud from her long hike up a creek bed. She's wearing handcuffs from the time, as she was often arrested. The environment and outfits are taken from photos from the Battle of Blair Mountain. Every single one of the signs in the background is an actual protest sign from the era, painstakingly traced—they had some great typography. And yes, the "God Bless Mother Jones" sign is real.

# Savitribai Phule

## (1831–1897, INDIA)

## *The Mother Who Fought the Caste System*

he carried two saris.

It was necessary: every time she walked to the girls' school, she'd get pelted by rocks, mud, and feces. But she couldn't walk into class like that, covered in stains. The students needed to see her overcome the hate. They needed to see that they could too. That would be the first lesson she taught, and maybe the most important.

Her name was Savitribai Phule. She was the first woman to teach girls in India. It was just one of many taboos she would trample.

To understand what she faced, we first need to take a step back and explore the Hindu caste system. At the bottom were the "untouchable" Dalits,* so reviled that, at the time, they were forced to carry pots to catch their spit and branches to sweep away their footprints. Sitting at the top of the caste system were the Brahmins who monopolized education, political posts, and were the only accountants and moneylenders, which gave them secular power as well.

Savitribai and her husband, Jyotirao, took exception to this. Married young—he was 13, and she was nine—the two had a happy marriage, filled with a shared drive to improve India. With Jyotirao's tutelage, Savitribai learned to read and write in both Sanskrit and English. While neither were Christian themselves, both enjoyed the relatively egalitarian teachings of the missionaries,† a fact that would lead their detractors to decry them as "tainted" by foreign teachings.‡

Come 1848, when Savitribai was only 17, she and Jyotirao started India's first native-run school for girls. They had visited a missionary-run girls' school and come away convinced that the future lay in educating India's women. Initially they only had eight students, but

---

* "Dalit" is the modern-day term for the lowest castes, meaning "oppressed" in Sanskrit. Lest you think this is over-and-done-with history, it's not. **Phoolan Devi**, who died in 2003, was a Dalit vigilante who spent years avenging abuse suffered by the lower castes, before landing in jail and then becoming a politician. The ideas that oppressed and eventually killed her are still deeply ingrained in Indian society.

† Yes, the situation was so bad that they looked at mid-1800s English attitudes toward class and race and decided, "let's do *that*."

‡ Obsession with purity: rarely a sign of quality in a person.

they expanded rapidly. By 1851, they were teaching 150 girls (and several adults) across three schools—including Dalits. They gave stipends to prevent students from dropping out, and conducted parent-teacher conferences to explain the importance of education to the parents.

They didn't focus just on the lower castes: they worked just as hard to better the lot of upper-caste widows. Restricted from remarrying, the widows would often suffer domestic abuse. Tonsuring (shaving the head) was standard and rape was common. These women would be disowned once pregnant, and, bereft of options, they often resorted to suicide or infanticide. The Phules opened an organization to help these women, personally housing them and keeping their identities secret. Savitribai went further by canvassing against the killing of "illegitimate" children and organizing city barbers to stop shaving widows' heads.

They faced intense backlash. Savitribai was pelted with so many rocks, balls of mud, and feces that she eventually had to have an escort. Jyotirao was disowned by his family—partly for his heretical outlook, and partly because he refused to take on a second wife to have a child. Without his family's backing, he and Savitribai fell on hard times, moving into a Dalit neighborhood and taking on jobs to fund the schools and food centers.

Savitribai would fearlessly put herself at risk to help the community. In one of her few surviving pieces of writing, she writes to tell her husband of a local Romeo-and-Juliet Brahmin/Dalit couple. When the girl's pregnancy was discovered, a mob chased them down with the intent of killing them. "I came to know about their murderous plan," she wrote. "I rushed to the spot and scared them away, pointing out the grave consequences of killing the lovers under the British law. They changed their mind after listening to me."

Danger and reduced circumstances did not slow the Phules' charity. In 1868, during a dry spell, they opened their well to Dalits, who were banned from most other wells. In 1877, during a severe drought, they collected funds from neighboring villages and fed over a thousand people each day. It was well known that anyone who came to their house would not leave empty-handed: Savitribai was famous for giving away saris to those who needed them. And in 1873, nearly 20 years after being cut off for not having children, they would adopt a pregnant widow's son, Yashwantarao.

Even in her family life, Savitribai was extraordinary. When Jyotirao died in 1890, his family would not let the adopted Yashwantarao do the funeral rites, and began squabbling over who would carry the *titve* (funeral mud pot). Savitribai herself took it and led the procession—a task reserved for men even to present day. When her son married, she conducted the wedding herself, without priests, dowry, or significant expense.

Savitribai's death could not be more typical of her character. In 1897, her son, Yashwantarao, now a doctor, set up a clinic to treat a pandemic of Bubonic plague. Savitribai personally took people to the clinic to ensure their care, even though it was six miles away. When a

10-year-old boy fell so sick that he could not walk, she carried him the entire distance to her son's clinic. The boy survived. Savitribai did not.

Although her work was long unrecognized next to that of her more-famous husband, time has brought Savitribai posterity. An upsurge in academic research accompanied by public recognition has led to her story becoming more well known, inspiring the creation of plays and the naming of buildings. Sushama Deshpande, a playwright who created a play about Savitribai's life that consistently performed to packed houses, summed it up thusly: "Every Indian woman who is educated today owes Savitribai a debt of gratitude. . . . She epitomises the aspirations of women even 150 years after she burst on the scene."

## · ART NOTES AND TRIVIA ·

A beleaguered Savitribai, sari caked in dung, walks to a hospital with a child on her back—the very act that resulted in her death. In the background, Brahmins issuing forth from a temple chuck rocks at her, while Jyotirao attempts to stop them. To the right, a variety of people gather around a well, a reference to the well that Savitribai and Jyotirao opened to the Dalits.

# Soraya Tarzi

## (1899–1968, AFGHANISTAN)

## The Mother of an Afghanistan That Wasn't

Afghanistan in the 1920s was not what you'd think. It was a rapidly modernizing haven for liberal ideals, where women played an increasingly large role, no one more so than the wife, confidant, and political ally of King Amanullah Khan:* Queen Soraya Tarzi.

Their rise and fall was a tragedy that would echo throughout the world for decades.

Soraya was a figure unlike any in Afghan history. The daughter of one of Afghanistan's greatest intellectuals,† she grew up in exile in Ottoman-controlled Syria (which was pretty nice at the time. Soraya went to school, got exposure to all manner of cultures, and found her voice.

Amanullah was an equally novel figure: a king who, as legend has it, would roam marketplaces disguised as a commoner. Sick of Afghanistan being treated like a pawn in a game of chess between Russia and Britain, he declared Afghan independence from Britain as his first act. The ensuing war was brief but intense, but in the end, Britain acquiesced.‡ Afghanistan was free, and Amanullah was a hero.

The new government soon issued a slew of reforms with Amanullah's "Book of Order": slavery was abolished; torture was forbidden; child marriage and polygamy were banned; *burqas* were made optional; "bride prices" were functionally outlawed; all religions were welcome. The laws were established on secular grounds, but Amanullah, being a religious scholar, could argue an Islamic basis for all of them.§

And heading up the novel mandate to educate girls was the new Minister of Education: Soraya.

This was unheard of for Afghan consorts. Queens didn't so much as publicly appear

---

\* He technically wasn't king at first; he took the throne in 1919 as amir, then became king.

† Mahmud Tarzi, father of Afghan journalism.

‡ They won a military victory but lost the political one; the League of Nations had just formed, and pressure to end colonialism was mounting, so they let Afghanistan go.

§ For example, he argued polygamy was only acceptable if you treated all your wives equally, which was impossible for mere mortals. He put his money where his mouth was—he was pretty strictly monogamous with Soraya, an extreme rarity for kings.

with kings. Or found progressive magazines for women. Or encourage women to enter politics. But Soraya did all this and more. She even created a special court to hear women who'd been abused and wanted a divorce. And to enforce the law? She formed an all-female secret service who'd make unannounced house calls to monitor abusive men and check in on women.

The reaction to the reforms was . . . mixed. The cities welcomed change, but the conservative rural areas broke into open revolt. Amanullah quelled it in short order, and to commemorate his victory, commissioned an obelisk. He dubbed it the Minaret of Triumph of Knowledge over Ignorance. His celebration was to prove premature.

The two continued at breakneck speed, achieving their goals rapidly: new power plants; paved roads; a telephone system for women's suffrage; guaranteed rights to women and minorities; a ban on revenge killings; a new emphasis on journalism and science. They spent outrageous sums to push the country forward as fast as possible, but it was working. They just had to secure more, so they hit the road to line up international allies.

As they toured Europe, Soraya continually made an impression. At a British arms factory, she wowed everyone with her marksmanship. In Russia, she ferreted out a spy by making a ridiculous statement in a language he shouldn't have been able to understand and watching for the shock on his face.

Determined to not be a pawn anymore, the two coyly played Russia and Britain off each other, dropping hints that they were going to sign a treaty with one or the other. This drove the Russians nuts—they were so convinced that the couple was carrying a British treaty that they ransacked all their belongings. They became convinced it was in the one piece of luggage they hadn't checked: Soraya's personal bag. When they finally managed to separate her from it long enough to investigate it, all they found was a case full of lingerie.

However, their tour enraged rural Afghans. Pictures spread throughout the region that depicted Soraya lewdly.* Rumors began to spread: they were secret Christians; they were going to line up the elderly on death panels and kill them to sell their body parts. Who circulated the (possibly altered) photos and planted the fake news remains unclear. To this day, many Afghans suspect Britain.†

It didn't help that the king immediately mandated radical new laws when he returned:

---

\* The exact pictures are seemingly lost to history. Some accounts describe her as merely unveiled with bare shoulders. Others describe her head superimposed on the body of a naked dancer.

† Britain stridently denies this, and has declassified diplomatic cables to show their internal confusion over it. However, given that they would overthrow the democratically elected leader of Iran in a secret operation just 25 years later (look up Operation Ajax!), few people in modern Afghanistan believe them.

compulsory coed education; increase of taxes; separation of church and state; mandatory Western dress code in Kabul; outlawing burqas in public parks; one year of required civil service.

And as a kicker to all of what was already a shocking press conference: the queen publicly whipped off her veil.

The two had pushed too far, too fast. Their work had spread unevenly, and many hadn't reaped the benefits. While Kabul was enjoying new sound-equipped movie theaters, rural Afghans were learning that the government was going to tax their goats. The rural conservatives broke into open revolt, and from their ranks rose an illiterate populist bandit, who vowed to make Afghanistan great again. His name was Bacha-i-Saqao: "the water carrier."

He struck at just the right moment. Amanullah's army was off quashing another rebellion and Kabul was relatively undefended. His reinforcements were stopped at the Afghan border by the British. To the shock of everyone, the monarchy fell.

Soraya, heavily pregnant with their ninth child—the pair would have 10 children together—braved her fear of flying to escape, while Amanullah stayed and fought. After a brief period where he humiliated himself to try to appease the hard-line theocracy of Saqao, he too fled.

Saqao immediately undid everything Soraya and Amanullah had done. All schools were closed; Islam was mandated as the state religion; women weren't allowed to vote; the veil was again mandatory; taxes were abolished; Western clothing was banned; the dissenting press was shut down. He expelled all foreign diplomats—all diplomats except, weirdly enough, the British*—and later instituted a travel ban.

Soraya and Amanullah helplessly witnessed this from exile. They watched as the bandit, paranoid and ignorant on how to run a country, turned on his dwindling allies. Within nine months, he was overthrown, becoming a mere footnote in Afghan history.

The military established control and Soraya and Amanullah stayed in exile. Amanullah died in Italy, a poor furniture maker at the end of his days. Soraya lived long enough to see Afghanistan, in the 1960s, readopt the positions she'd championed 40 years earlier. At the time she died in 1968, Kabul was a hub of fashion, with unveiled women walking the streets in skirts.†

Upon Soraya's death, her body was returned for burial in Afghanistan. Her coffin was

---

* As you can imagine, there's a lot of conspiracy theories around this: supposed eyewitness accounts of direct English support for Saqao, T. E. Lawrence (Lawrence of Arabia) being in the area for unexplained reasons, etc. However, most modern academics seem to affirm that Britian wasn't directly behind it, although they didn't help. It wasn't in their interests to have a destabilized Afghanistan. Nevertheless, newspapers in France, Italy, Russia, and even England assumed Britain was behind it.

† Then the United States and Russia got involved, and things got real depressing again.

met by a crowd of the tribes who'd exiled her, regretful for their past actions. At her funeral service, a group of older women, all veiled head to toe, approached her grave.

They'd come to pray in memory of the woman who'd fought so hard to improve their lives.

## · ART NOTES AND TRIVIA ·

Soraya is seen here defending the students of Masturat, the school for girls she'd helped found (the name is written on the chalkboard in both French and Arabic). She'd sent 15 young women abroad for education in Turkey. Amanullah is to her left, and a veiled teacher—many women chose to keep the veil; Soraya just wanted to give them a choice—is to her right. She is wearing a sleeveless outfit from her trip to Europe, possibly the one in the pictures that circulated of her.

# Jeanne de Clisson

(1300–1359, FRANCE)

## The Mother Who Became a Pirate

In the 14th century, France had a homemade boogeyman. Someone who stalked the English Channel, massacring French nobles and turning coast towns to ash. A pirate who'd been betrayed by the king, and turned on their homeland.

Her name was Jeanne de Clisson. She was known as the Lioness of Brittany.*

It was not always so. For most of her life, Jeanne was a loyal, well-to-do French noble. She lived peacefully with her husband Olivier, tending to their lands and their four children. Olivier was similarly loyal: when war with England broke out, he went to fight for France. There he was defeated and captured by the English, although he was later freed in a prisoner exchange.

Not everyone was thrilled to see him return. The French king, Philip VI, suspecting Olivier had lost on purpose and was working with the English, set a trap. He insisted Olivier come to Paris for a tournament to celebrate France's new truce with England, but once Olivier arrived, the king had him executed, to the shock of everyone. The king publicly strung up Olivier's body in Paris, and sent his head to Nantes, to be displayed on a pike.

Jeanne vowed revenge.

Shortly after Olivier's execution, Jeanne visited a fort that Olivier had once controlled. Recognizing the bereaved widow standing before him, the commander ordered her let in. However, as soon as the gate opened, she sounded a horn. Suddenly, several hundred hidden soldiers under Jeanne's employ emerged, rushing the gates and murdering everyone inside. By the time Philip VI retook the castle, she and her men had disappeared, leaving one soul alive to tell the tale.

Her reputation only grew from there. In short order, Jeanne sold her belongings, forsook her lands, and took her war against France to the sea. She'd attack from the fog without warning, killing merchants and nobles but always leaving one survivor to spread the word.† Before long, much of France was too scared to set sail.

---

* French sources call her La Tigresse Bretagne—somehow she got switched from a tiger to a lion in the translation to English. Maybe England just likes lions more?

† This is an area where sources differ. It's generally agreed that she sold her belongings and used the proceeds—and her contacts with other nobles discontented with Philip VI—to mobilize against France. Most agree she started on land and took to the sea. Whether she started with three ships that she'd purchased independent of England, or whether she had one ship that was scuttled in early fights with France, is unclear.

Philip VI's retaliation was merciless. He raided her ship, killing her soldiers and forcing her to escape with three of her children in a rowboat.[*] For five days and five nights, she rowed. Even as her youngest sickened and died, she continued rowing. On the sixth day, they landed in England. Impressed by the terrifying sight before him, the English king gave her three ships.[†] They were painted black and given red sails. Jeanne named the flagship *My Vengeance,* left her children onshore, and set out again.

Nobody can say how long she haunted France, leaving corpses and cinders in her wake. Some say months, some years, some decades. Regardless, she was not soon forgotten.

Eventually, Jeanne stopped. Why, again, is unknown. She left no explanation, no declaration that she'd achieved her goals, no signs that she'd grown weary of war. She simply put down her arms, remarried, and faded from the stage of history. Her legend grew throughout the centuries, becoming a cautionary tale to all: there is nothing deadlier than a woman wronged.

## The War of the Four Jeannes

The war in question was the War of Breton Succession. In it, England and France were in each other's faces over who got to rule Brittany/Bretagne—part of the Hundred Years' War. England backed the claim of John de Montfort, half brother of the previous ruler—and Jeanne de Clisson's short-lived second husband! (It was quickly annulled; the first had died quite young. Olivier was her third husband.)

France's candidate to the throne was Jeanne number two: Jeanne de Penthièvre, full sister of the previous ruler. This put Clisson and Penthièvre at odds, but they weren't the only Jeannes! There was also Jeanne La Flamme, who was Montfort's wife and also a pirate in her own right! (Clearly Montfort had a type.)

Lastly, almost a century after the start of these wars, a fourth Jeanne would emerge to end it: Jeanne d'Arc, better known as **Joan of Arc.**

---

[*] This part differs from telling to telling. In some, her ship sank because of a storm. In others, it was because of the French, and she escaped with help of the storm.

[†] This was Edward III, son of **Isabella of France**, by now an old man. Again, various tellings have Jeanne starting out with the three ships instead of getting them from England, although given the expense involved, English backing seems more likely.

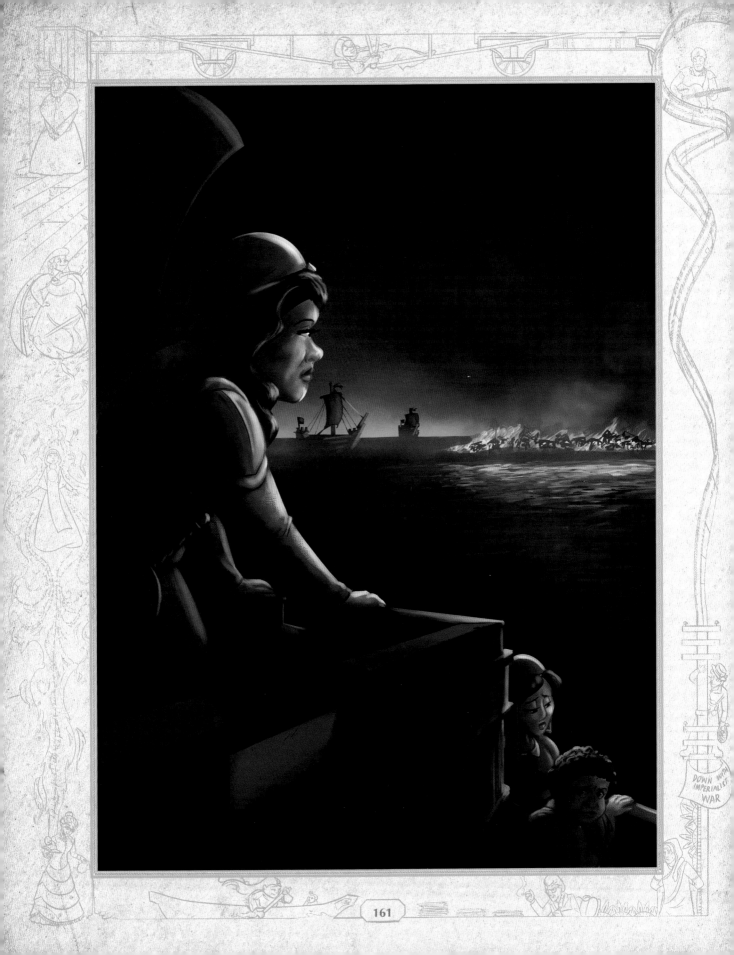

# Olympias of Macedon

### (C. 375–316 BCE, GREECE)

## *The Mom Who Made Alexander Great*

here's an easy way to measure the power of a historical woman: find out how outrageous the rumors were about her. **Elisabeth Báthory** was said to have killed hundreds of servants and bathed in their blood—and was a powerful countess, richer than the emperor. **Arawelo** of Somalia supposedly castrated every man in the country—and was running the place better than them, to boot. And Olympias, the mother of Alexander the Great? She slept with snake gods.

Now, of course she didn't. Báthory wasn't a blood-bather and Arawelo wasn't the world's most prolific circumciser. At most, Olympias did some religious rites involving snakes.* But it's a sign of just how much influence she wielded—and how much it unnerved southern Greeks—that such legends about her would spring up.

It makes sense that she freaked out southern Greece. Olympias† hailed from Molossia in the north, and was thus, compared to southern women, terrifyingly independent. She could own property. She could talk to men not related to her. She could even *leave the house on her own*! And not only could she do all that, but she also had the ear of the most powerful man on the planet: her doting son, Alexander the Great.

She had spent many years securing Alexander's future. Married to the notoriously polygamous Philip II, Olympias spent years throwing elbows among the other five wives, jockeying for higher status. It helped that her family was well-regarded (word had it they were descended from Achilles himself), and helped more that she bore him a son. When Philip's only other male heir proved unfit for ruling,‡ he sided with Olympias and made Alexander his heir.

But although she stayed on top of the game for many years, trouble erupted when Philip brought on a seventh wife. The new wife's father, at a feast, publicly insulted Alexander and

---

\* She was part of some Dionysean cults that involved snakes, drinking, drugs, and dancing your face off as a kind of pressure-relief valve, like a really, really old-school Burning Man.

† Who likely started life named Polyxena, then changed it to Myrtale, then Olympias, and finally Stratonice in the last years of her life. She was kind of the Puff Daddy of ancient Greece.

‡ This was poor Philip Arrhidaeus, who had an apparently somewhat severe learning disability—which the historian Plutarch blamed on Olympias drugging him (she got blamed for a lot of things). He was a recurrent pawn throughout this story's endless backstabbing.

Olympias, saying, "At least now there will be legitimate heirs." Alexander took grave offense, throwing a cup at him, only for Philip to not come to Alexander's defense. In some versions, he even drew a sword on Alexander, his own son and heir. In anger, both Alexander and Olympias left town, threatening to raise an army against Philip, until he capitulated and made amends.*

In celebration of said amends, though, Philip was assassinated, and many thought Olympias was behind it. Was she? Probably not, but it wouldn't have been surprising. She had the motive, there were just better ways of doing it. The way Philip was taken out—stabbed in public by a wronged lover†—was about the least subtle and most dangerous plan she could have concocted, and Olympias was no idiot.

Alexander ascended to the throne, and quickly set about bloodily consolidating power. Olympias joined in the purges, killing her to-date most dangerous political enemy: Philip's most recent wife (and her baby). Violent? Yes. Inhumane? By today's standards, totally. Bog-standard for the time? You bet. (Admit it, if this was about Genghis Khan, you wouldn't have blinked.)

Over the next 13 years, as Alexander swept his conquering armies across Asia, Olympias became possibly the most powerful woman in the world. She ran the international diplomacy and handled much of the domestic policy, but she did not do so alone. Throughout his empire, Alexander placed competing figures at odds with one another, and northern Greece was no exception. Here Olympias butted heads with the official head of state, Alexander's general Antipater, vying for power in private as he reigned in public.

Alexander died suddenly in 323 BCE, and things fell apart. There wasn't a clear heir to the throne, and so everyone settled into warring factions. Olympias again jockeyed for power, joining with her newly widowed daughter, Cleopatra, to stymie Antipater's attempts to secure alliances. Although she was not greatly successful in this, her immediate problems were solved in 319, when Antipater died of old age.

However, her troubles didn't go away, they just changed form. By this point, there were two competing claimants to the throne: Philip's previously mentioned unfit-for-ruling son, Philip Arrhidaeus, and Alexander's infant son, who'd not been born when he died: Alexander IV. Hellbent on solidifying a dynasty for her family, Olympias took custody of her grandson.

---

* The amends were to marry Olympias's brother, Alexander of Molossia, to Olympias and Philip's daughter, Cleopatra (not *that* Cleopatra). While this uncle-niece marriage sounds a bit incestuous, because it is, it basically gave Olympias's family more status and power within Philip's household. It does not, however, stop it from being kinda gross.

† A male lover. Oh, didn't I mention? Philip was bisexual. All the men in this story were, including Alexander. *Especially* Alexander. Welcome to Ancient Greece!

She began backing his claim, which put her into conflict with another woman: the teenage Adea Eurydice, wife of the disabled Philip Arrhidaeus.

The 50-year-old mother and the teen bride came head-to-head on the battlefield in what is one of history's first recorded wars between two women. Olympias won handily: according to Greek historian Diodorus, upon catching sight of Olympias, Adea Eurydice's men just up and defected. Olympias was predictably brutal in victory, first bricking up the losers in a wall and then, when that proved surprisingly unpopular, stabbing them to death.

Unfortunately, Olympias's military victories didn't last long. Her next opponent, Antipater's son Cassander, proved a better general than Olympias's general (Olympias wasn't allowed to lead armies directly, being a woman and all). Cassander was heavily motivated to kill Olympias. In the many brutal purges that had followed Alexander's death, she'd killed his brother and 100 of his supporters. Not that he was blameless in this: his men had burned 500 of her allies to death. To be honest, everyone was going buck wild at this point. Another general trampled upward of 300 people to death with elephants. Life was crazy.

Without any better allies available to help lead her armies, Olympias was defeated and sentenced to death. The specifics of her death are a bit murky, but it's generally agreed that, prior to her execution, Cassander tried tricking her into publicly defying the court, to turn public opinion against her. She didn't fall for it, and the many loyalists around grew uneasy at the prospect of killing her—in one version, 200 soldiers marched to her quarters and couldn't bring themselves to do the deed. In the end, the families of those she'd had killed were brought in to stone her to death. After her death, Cassander refused to let her body be buried.

Olympias's legacy thereafter was hopelessly entangled by political PR. Each historian was allied with a different faction and had a vastly different take. The pro-Olympias writers trumpeted her as a quasimythical figure, linking her to Achilles and adding in a dream about her womb being sanctified by Zeus's lightning before giving birth. Her detractors said that if Zeus came to her, it was in the form of a snake that she was sleeping with, and that seeing her do so unsettled Philip II. The pro-Olympias camp portrayed her as wise and virtuous. The others, a wanton sexpot.

In the end, Olympias was an ambitious woman in a charged political climate who took her lumps like anyone else. She failed in her larger goals, but so did pretty much everyone else of the era. Her dynasty may not have borne out, but her name, and that of her son, are remembered even today, and what more could you expect? In the words of historian Elizabeth Carney, "One doubts that any royal woman in such parlous times could have done better."

# Trinidad Tecson

## (1848–1928, PHILIPPINES)

## The Mother of the Philippine Red Cross

**Y**ou could start talking about most women in this book by saying how unlikely it was for them to become who they'd turn into. Not the case with Trinidad Tecson: she'd have easily won a "most likely to lead a rebel army" award if there were such a thing.

As the daughter of an affluent couple—so affluent they could afford to raise 16 kids!—Trinidad got quite the education. Not only did she learn to read and write (not a foregone conclusion in those days), but she learned to fence from a renowned master, to protect herself from a local bandit. She put the lessons to good use. As a child, when she and her brothers were alone on a remote farm, a young intruder broke into the house, only for her to whack him in the head with a bolo knife. After that, he quite understandably ran off.

But her burgeoning reputation wasn't yet formed enough to scare off a spurned suitor. Seeking revenge for being turned down, the suitor convinced some civil guards to raid her house, looking for smuggled tobacco. She would not let them do so, and decided to put the situation to rest with her trusty bolo knife (hey, it worked last time). After a brief fight, the guards ran away. Her suitor filed a lawsuit against her father, but after three months, the judge sided with Trinidad. Her father was so amused that he nicknamed her *babing lalaki* ("female man").*

She did not stay single forever. She married at age 19, and had two children: Sinforoso and Desiderio. She spent a long life with her husband, working with him to earn a living selling cattle, seafood, and salt.

Although she lived a quiet life for many decades, it never dampened her fiery nature. At 47 years old, when much of the Philippines was beginning to organize for freedom from Spain, Trinidad joined the revolutionaries (Katipunan). She is the only woman on record to engage in the ancient tradition of *sanduguan*, where one spills their blood to proclaim their affiliation. But that was the sort of woman she was.

In the ensuing years, she put herself in more and more danger as part of the Katipunan. She twice stole weapons from the Spanish, once from a courthouse and once from a jail.

---

* Which ostensibly was meant as a compliment, but it's sure not much of one. A far better name for her would come later: Henerala Ninging, which translates to something along the lines of "General Sparkle."

Betrayed soon thereafter by an accomplice, she ran from the authorities—only to pick right back up by stealing provisions. At one point while securing food, she and others were found by some soldiers. She threw herself on the ground, pretending to be hit by gunfire, and then escaped into tall grass when the soldiers turned their backs. On another occasion, she was caught when trying to hide some firearms. She was interrogated for five days, but gave up no information.

Once the war officially broke out, she took up arms herself. Between 1896 and 1899, she fought in 12 battles, at one point getting wounded in her right thigh. Her greatest hour came at Biak-na-Bato, the headquarters of the revolution. When the Spaniards unexpectedly found the revolutionaries' cave hideout, Trinidad, along with her husband and two servants, held them off. She sounded her bugle to fool the attackers into thinking she had more men on the way, and stalled them until reinforcements arrived. For her efforts, she was given the rank of brigadier general.

In addition to her efforts on the battlefield, she also spent much of her time looking after the sick and wounded. She organized other women in this regard, and when the rebel government had to relocate, it was she who led them over mountains and through forests. For this, she was given the titles Mother of Biak-na-Bato and Mother of the Philippine Red Cross (she had a lot of titles).

In 1899, the Spanish did finally give up their claim to the Philippines—but not to the Filipinos themselves. Instead, they handed the land over to the Americans, who'd defeated Spain on another front (the Spanish-American War). The Filipinos, who hadn't been consulted, reacted poorly to this turn of events and refused to cooperate. What ensued, few Americans learn about, but it was horrific. American troops massacred entire villages, and upwards of 250,000 civilians died.* This early foray into American imperialism so disgusted Mark Twain that he suggested replacing the US flag with a skull and crossbones. By 1902, the war was over and the Philippines were an American colony. Trinidad, exhausted and starving, surrendered.

After the war, she continued selling meat and seafood with her husband and children—but would outlive all three. When her first husband died, she remarried, and when her second died, she did so again. She outlived her third husband too, but continued looking after others well into her final years.

Trinidad died in 1928, at 80 years old. Although she did not live long enough to see her nation become independent, she did see the United States, in 1916, legally commit to grant-

---

* That's the most common estimate. Filipino historian E. San Juan Jr. claimed the death toll was closer to 1.4 million, or one-sixth of the entire population.

ing independence—which happened after World War II. She was buried in the Plot of the Veterans of the Revolution in the Cementerio del Norte. Her memory was lionized across the country to present day, and she has become the namesake of many streets, schools, and memorials.

## · ART NOTES AND TRIVIA ·

This is one of the actual caves in Biak-na-Bato that the Katipunan used to stage their campaigns. This illustration hearkens to an event where the Spanish unexpectedly ambushed them while the Katipunan numbers were at their lowest. Trinidad stayed at the cave entrance to hold them off, while others circled around. Using a bugle and the echoing of the cave, she made enough noise to convince the Spanish that there were more fighters than there actually were. They tarried long enough that the second group managed to flood a stream and force the Spaniards into the cave, where the Katipunan surprised and disarmed them. It was only then that the Spaniards learned that they lost to a handful of men, and a woman with a bugle.

Trinidad is seen here wearing the traditional Katipunan outfit and hat, and is standing in front of a load of supplies, as reference to her theft of supplies and ammunition.

# Tamar of Georgia

(1160–1213, GEORGIA)

## The Mom Who Vanquished Her Ex

"One knows a lion by its claws and Tamar by her actions."

Although it may not seem so, this charming 12th-century turn of phrase cuts to the heart of Georgia's greatest monarch, Tamar. While most of Tamar's biographies emphasize her warlike tendencies—she *did* conquer massive swaths of land and curb stomped her terrible ex-husband's armies (twice!)—truth be told, she was remarkably nonviolent, especially given what the era warranted.

(Just to be clear: we're talking about Georgia the country, not Georgia the land of peaches.)

As you might imagine, life in the 12th century was not a high-water mark for human civility. Tamar's father, George III, was, it's fair to say, downright impolite. When Demna, the rightful heir to the throne, put in his claim to rule, George III responded by blinding, castrating, and imprisoning him. George III was equally unneighborly to the Georgian nobles, keeping their political scheming in check by instituting a new national sport: getting your kneecaps broken.

(Just to be clear: This is the Georgian George III, not the Georgian *Era* George III, who was English. Well, also technically Georgian. It, uh, yeah. Let's just move on before this turns into an Abbott and Costello sketch.)

When Tamar became king,* it was after co-ruling with George III for six years. She had the relevant experience and the official say-so of the departing king, so you'd think the Georgians would be okay with it. But they weren't, because—you guessed it, vagina. Critics got to critiquin', schemers got to schemin', and rebels got to rebellin'. While the time-honored response from her father's regime would have involved copious bloodletting, Tamar proved herself more gentle. She instead quietly strengthened her power base while outwardly negotiating compromises—most notably, her marriage to Rus Prince Yuri, jerkwad extraordinaire.

---

\* Tamar took the throne as "king" instead of "queen." There wasn't much of a linguistic distinction in the word that Georgians used at the time. This wasn't uncommon: also happened with **Hatshepsut, Wu Zetian,** and Jadwiga of Poland, among others. Tamar was the first female sovereign of Georgia.

Yuri's marriage to Tamar was a noxious cocktail of slave-shtupping, prostitute-frequenting, and heavy drinking, peppered with public insults toward Tamar for not bearing him a child. All this and more* was brought to light during their divorce proceedings.

Yes, that's right, Tamar divorced him. In the 12th century. In a fervently Christian nation. At a time when the church expressly forbid it. This was not a mere separation—Tamar convinced the bishops to officially dissolve their marital bonds and allow her to remarry. Which she promptly did, keeping the throne for herself (her new hubby was titled king consort), kicking Yuri out of the country, and having two kids. Her gentility went beyond allowing Yuri to live—she actually sent him away loaded down with riches. It was as amicable a parting as one could hope for.

However, Yuri wasn't about to let things go. He ganged up with some malcontent Georgian nobles and led two different insurrections against her. She and her new husband (who, it should be mentioned, was himself a champion butt-kicker—this being one of the reasons she chose him) soundly trounced both uprisings. In a marked departure from the policies of kings past, after his defeat, she didn't castrate Yuri *even a little*.

After that began her infamous policy of expansionism—a policy, historian Antonia Fraser argues, that was largely enacted to give the Georgian nobles' idle hands something to do. It was enormously successful: the nobles fell under her banner, Georgian borders ballooned outward, and the country entered its golden age.

An amusing anecdote from this time: one of Tamar's warring neighbors was the Sultan of Rum, Suleiman II. In his declaration of war on Georgia, he sent her a letter that began with the zinger "every woman is feeble of mind," and ended with the demand that she become his Muslim wife or Christian concubine. She *crushed him*.

While the nobles busied themselves with warfare, Tamar devoted much of her attention to Georgian culture. Under her reign, the country began to find its own national identity, a unique blend of east and west. Her life served as the inspiration for the epic poem *The Knight in the Panther's Skin*, which is to this day widely considered Georgia's greatest piece of literature.

Her legend only grew after her death.† She was canonized by the East Orthodox Church

---

* Notably, he was also accused of sodomy. Not making a judgment call on sodomy—but Georgia, being very religious at the time, was not okay with it. The court records are silent as to whether this had any relation to their childlessness.

† Although not always in laudatory fashion. In Mikhail Lermontov's 1800s poem "The Demon," he characterizes Tamar as a lusty tyrant, sleeping with dudes and then tossing them off a cliff the next day. Which is pretty much the opposite of what she did with Yuri, whom she let walk free repeatedly. Fraser also supposes that the villainous Tamora in Shakespeare's *Titus Andronicus* was based on Tamar, although others think it more likely he took her name from **Tomyris**, the Scythian queen who purportedly killed Cyrus the Great.

as the Holy Righteous King Tamar, and got her own feast day (May 14). Some legends had her conceiving her son by a sunbeam, or controlling the weather. To this day, Tamar remains one of the most popular names in Georgia. Not bad!

## · ART NOTES AND TRIVIA ·

This is the traditional outfit in which she's always pictured. Her dominant right hand is indicating mercy, while her other hand, holding a sword, is ready to bring the pain. The backdrop is the cave town at Vardzia, which she used as a staging ground for her troops when attacking Suleiman II. According to legend, she walked with the soldiers bare-foot, and then addressed them from a church balcony. On the left is Shota Rustaveli, writing down her exploits in poem form. Obscured and pouting at right is her crappy husband Yuri.

# Marsha P. Johnson

## (1944–1992, UNITED STATES)

### The Godmother of the Trans Civil Rights Movement

Y ou wouldn't expect Marsha to be cheery.

After all, she'd been through hell: an abusive childhood, years of living on the streets, decades of persecution, hundreds of arrests, at least eight mental breakdowns—she'd even been shot. But here she was, emerging every morning adorned in flowers, a living, breathing, smiling defiance of the odds.

It's little wonder that the New York City trans community she defended so vigorously took to calling her "Saint Marsha": patron of the downtrodden.

Marsha P. Johnson's* charity was legendary. Although she, like so many in the 1970s and 1980s transgender and transvestite communities, had no roof to call home, she gave as much as she could. She'd beg for money, but when she got some, she'd buy food and share it far and wide. People who spoke of her would almost always mention how she'd use the last of her money to either bring sweets to the hungry or buy flowers—which she'd also give out.

Her kindness was sorely needed to balance out the cruelty the trans community experienced. Virtually everyone had run away from brutal home situations, like having scalding water thrown on them by their parents. Unable to get jobs or hold down apartments, most resorted to sex work to make ends meet—and the johns were usually abusive too (that's how Marsha got shot). The law made dressing in the "wrong" gender's clothes illegal, and the cops took full advantage of that to terrorize them constantly. They couldn't even find support with the gay community they were lumped into:† many gay men referred to Marsha as "it."

But when pushed to it, Marsha would fight back. In 1969, the cops raided one of the few LGBT bars in New York City: the Stonewall Inn. As was standard procedure, anyone who

---

* The P stood for "Pay It No Mind!" (said while snapping in the air). When she once informed a judge of that, he laughed and said, "That's exactly what I'm going to do," then let her go.

† At this point in history, the idea of a trans community separate from the gay community was in its nascent stages. In the absence of modern terminology, Marsha referred to herself with female pronouns and either called herself a "gay man" or, more often, refused to identify as a man or a woman. The term "transgender" barely existed at this point.

did not have three pieces of male attire was going to be arrested. But that night, the trans community refused to go quietly. In the words of trans luminary Sylvia Rivera, later speaking to a crowd of gay men, "*You* all had rights. We had nothing to lose."

It's said that Marsha started the riots. As legend has it, she threw a shot glass into a mirror—"the shot glass heard around the world," as others quickly dubbed it. While that may not have actually happened,* she *did* fight the cops. As a crowd of hundreds gathered and spontaneously began to fight back against the police brutality, Marsha climbed a lamp post and tossed a bag onto a police car, shattering its windshield.

The Stonewall Riots became the starting point for her activism. Sylvia Rivera inducted her into the Street Transvestite Activist Revolutionaries (STAR), a group that Rivera had started. They established a shelter for homeless trans youth called STAR House. It wasn't ideal—it operated out of a slum run by mobsters, and you had to climb over a pile of garbage to even enter. But for its members, it was revolutionary. Marsha played the role of den mother, babysitting and feeding trans kids. She even did fundraising and ran bake sales. Sylvia asked her to be the first president of STAR, but Marsha declined: "I tend to go off in other directions."

With a rallying cry to call their own, Sylvia and Marsha began pushing trans visibility even further. When the leaders of the 1978 gay pride parade tried keeping them out (for fear of damaging the gay movement's growing respectability), Marsha and Sylvia ran to the front of the parade. Once it got going, they unfurled their own homemade banner, and refused to take it down. Their efforts paid off: the gay community began to accept trans people, and by 1980, the Gay Pride parade invited them to march upfront.

Upbeat and colorfully dressed, Marsha made a great face for the movement. Her outfits came from thrift shops—she'd creatively repurpose household items for fashion (one of her more famous outfits involved Christmas lights in a wig). It's little surprise that she caught the eye of Andy Warhol, who made her the subject of a photo series. She even joined the LGBT performance group the Hot Peaches, where she sang loudly, strangely, and off-key, winning the adoration of every audience who saw her.

But behind her sunny exterior, she suffered from untreated mental illness. It was rare that she'd lash out, but when she did, it was terrifying. In these episodes, she'd revert to her birth name, Malcolm Michaels, and attack those around her. Her religious tendencies would spiral out of control: while she'd often declare love for Jesus on regular days ("The only man I can really trust!"), during these spells she'd make sacrifices to Poseidon (whom she identified with her father) by tossing her clothes in the river. The police would hospitalize her, she'd get

---

* Most of the eyewitness accounts don't mention this, and it seems to have been a later invention.

some spotty treatment, and would be fine for a while—but she never had access to ongoing care, and she would relapse.

Despite the lack of care provided to her, she cared for everyone around her. When her friend and sometime roommate David Combs contracted HIV, she became his nurse and stayed by his side to the end. This was an era where the understanding of HIV and AIDS was somewhere on the order of "you get it because God hates you," so for her to stay by his side was a rare and powerful thing.

The last time anyone saw Marsha was at the 1992 gay pride parade. She disappeared and her body was found six days later floating in the Hudson River. Although the police ruled it a suicide, eyewitnesses described her getting harassed the night before, and described a wound at the back of her head.

When the trans community held her funeral, hundreds more people attended than they'd planned for—enough that they had to apply for a last-minute permit. The police initially declined, but when they realized it was for Marsha, they gave the go-ahead: "Marsha was a good queen. Give them the street."

## · ART NOTES AND TRIVIA ·

Here Marsha's wearing one of her more-photographed parade outfits, complete with a "Stonewall" sash. The light behind her is giving her a beatific glow, as a callback to her "Saint Martha" reputation, as she hands out cookies to those in need. Behind her, pumping a fist in the air, is Sylvia Rivera, along with a handwritten banner for STAR (based on their actual banner). They are marching through Sheridan Square, where Marsha would often hold court. In the background on the right are two statues established in Sheridan Square to commemorate the Stonewall movement.

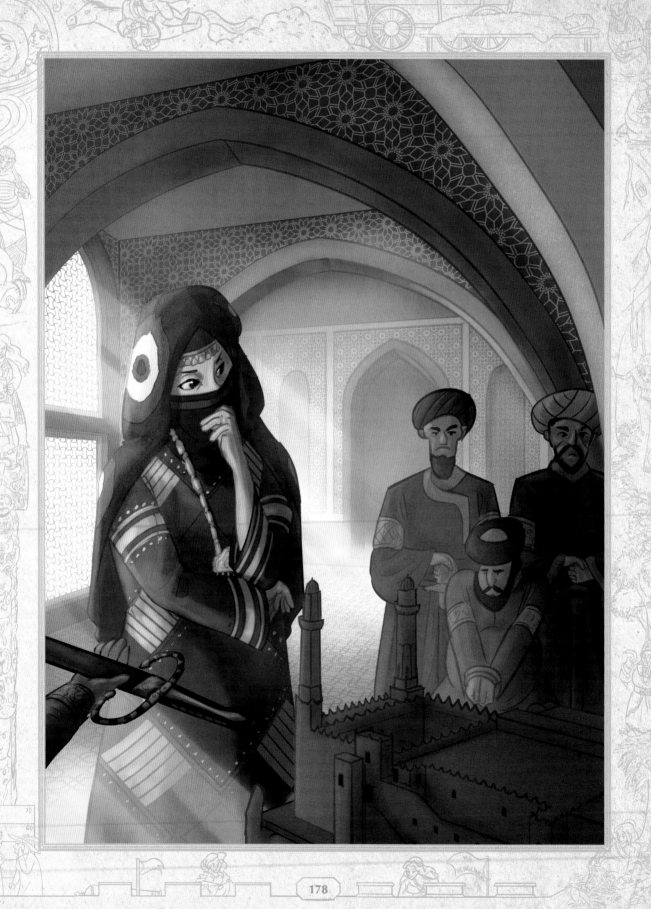

# Arwa al-Sulayhi

## (C. 1048–1138, YEMEN)

### The Mother of Yemen's Golden Age

 rwa al-Sulayhi was in serious trouble.

Rebellions were breaking out everywhere. The sultan had been assassinated, and his killers were still on the loose. The heir to the throne—Arwa's husband—was paraplegic and in no condition to rule. Her children were too young to rule, and her chief advisor, her mother-in-law, had just died. It was down to Arwa to protect her nation and her family. But this was the world of caliphates: women didn't simply take the throne.[*]

Except Arwa did. And held onto it longer than virtually anyone in Yemeni history.

This was a radical departure from the road she'd been set on. Yes, she'd been brought up from childhood to join the ruling class—heck, she'd basically been adopted by the ruling family after her parents died. But her intended wasn't in line to rule, and Arwa wasn't groomed for the throne. Instead, she led a pleasant childhood watching her foster parents work. The sultan, Ali, spent years bringing all of Yemen under one banner and starting a new dynasty. The queen, Asma, helped run affairs of state and tutored promising young heirs—and few were more promising than Arwa.

Arwa's life took an abrupt turn shortly after officially marrying into the ruling family. Within a year, her husband's older brother suddenly died, making her husband next in line—and Arwa queen consort-to-be. The "to-be" part vanished sooner than expected, when the sultan and queen were ambushed. The king was killed instantly, and Asma cruelly imprisoned, with Ali's decapitated head displayed in full view of her cell. She spent a year attempting to get word of her location to her son, until she was finally able to sneak a message out in some bread. Overnight, a huge Yemeni force rode to her rescue, scaring her captor into fleeing.

Unfortunately, more tragedy struck when Arwa's husband finally reunited with his

---

[*] This isn't to say there weren't female rulers, but their taking the throne was neither simple nor common. A generation before Arwa's birth, Sitt al-Mulk ruled the Fatimid Caliphate in lieu of her young nephew. During Arwa's life, the mother of the then-current Fatimid caliph, a woman thought to be named Rasad, did similarly. And over 100 years after Arwa's death, two different women would become sultans: Razia Sultan and **Shajar al-Durr** (who defeated Louis IX in battle, then ransomed him back for 30 percent of France's GDP).

mother, Asma—seeing Asma in that condition triggered such a shock in the man that he was left mostly paralyzed.* The new king was unable to rule.

Asma, who'd had no small amount of experience in statecraft, took the reins, bringing Arwa in as her protégé. The two would be acclaimed in very similar (and rare) fashions. Both would earn the nickname "Little Queen of Sheba"† and both, more importantly, would have their names proclaimed as sovereigns in the *khutbah* (official prayers)—the only women in Islamic history able to make that claim.

But where Asma was brash, Arwa was subtle. Asma would boldly refuse to wear a veil or hold meetings from behind a screen. While Arwa did not accept the screen, she did wear the veil, and kept her son's face, not hers, on the coins. Unlike Asma, she was a new, unproven monarch—she was usually referred to as "al-Musta'li's mother" instead of by her own name or title. She chose her fights carefully, keeping a low profile and quietly directing her focus.

When Asma died, leaving Arwa running the show, she consolidated power quickly.‡ She moved the capital away from Sana'a, where her authority was eroding, to the mountainside fortress of Dhu Jibla. Not only was Dhu Jibla more defendable, it had the added bonus of being nearer to the stronghold of Ali's escaped killers. Within a few years, she decided to confront them, and set a trap. She convinced her allies to spread word that they had abandoned her, to lure the assassins out. They fell for it—in their eyes, who *wouldn't* desert such an unvirtuous woman?—but when the assassins attacked, they were crushed by her forces, who hadn't deserted her after all.

She was brutal in victory. In a cruel piece of symmetry, she imprisoned her enemy's wife and kept the assassin's decapitated head outside her cell. Vicious? Yes. Grotesque? Absolutely. Effective? You bet.

In short order, many of those who'd doubted her abilities as an untested female ruler fell in line. While there would always be holdouts who would not accept a woman in charge, they were in the minority. She was given the title of *hujja*, the highest rank in the Yemeni *da'wa*:§ the first time a woman had ever been given a high title of any kind. She began to be

---

* The details of this are vague in all the records. Some claim his paralysis was the result of battle wounds. Others claim it happened shortly after his mother died.

† The original Queen of Sheba was from Yemen. They're very proud of this. Wouldn't you be?

‡ It's worth noting that one source adds in a scene here where she initially refuses to take the throne, with the totally-not-sexist-at-all excuse that "a woman who is [still] desirable in bed is not suitable for running a 'state.'" Similar episodes of modesty are a dime a dozen with these sorts of stories—it's a trope so that readers don't get out of sorts at the thought that a woman might have a baseline level of ambition, and immediately decide there's something "off" about her. Keep an ear out for them with your local politicians!

§ An institution of the Muslim world based around spreading Islam. She was effectively the head proselytizer, even put in charge of spreading word to western India.

referred to as Sayyida al-Hurra ("the Noble Lady").[*] She even kept hold after her husband and son died, leaving her with a tenuous claim to the throne. She quickly arranged a political marriage with her husband's brother (a marriage she refused to consummate) and went back to work.

She relegated the military expansion (a necessity, to prevent her from appearing weak) to her second husband, while she focused on her personal priorities. She set up charities and expanded education, making sure that teachers were paid well and that all were welcome, regardless of gender or religion. She built roads, commissioned art, and hired architects to make buildings, including a beautiful mosque and a stunningly huge palace. The palace was reputed to have 365 rooms, and she would sleep in a different one each night, so assassins wouldn't be able to find her.[†]

While the fates of most of her children are unknown, she was apparently quite devoted to them, as evidenced by an anecdote about her daughter, Fatima. When Shams al-Maali, Fatima's husband, decided to take another wife—much to Fatima's chargin—Arwa took exception to this. Arwa sent an army and Shams took right off.

But no matter how stable Arwa kept Yemen, she had little sway over the chaotic workings of the international world. In her reign, her branch of Islam[‡] had a schism over succession, and soon after, the Fatimid Caliphate—of which Yemen was a part—had one too. Inevitable assassinations[§] and civil war erupted, she chose sides, and spent the rest of her days consolidating power for the successor she backed.

Arwa died of old age, an unbelievably rare feat in those days. She had outlived two husbands and at least one child. Unfortunately, her passing led to—surprise—yet another schism over succession, and the Sulayhid dynasty (and Yemen's golden age) ended with her.

## · ART NOTES AND TRIVIA ·

As a reference to her dual nature of warrior and builder, Arwa is here mulling over choices: a sword or an architecture mockup (of the actual Queen Arwa mosque). In the background is a defeated foe, whom she may (or may not) show mercy. Her outfit is a traditional Yemeni dress (which are seriously beautiful, and well worth researching).

---

[*] Not to be confused with 16th-century Moroccan pirate queen **Sayyida al-Hurra**, covered in Volume One, whose real name remains unknown.

[†] On leap years, she would presumably spend the additional day having a slumber party in tents in the backyard.

[‡] This would be the Nizari/Musta'li split, which was a schism in Isma'ilism, which came from a schism in Shi'a, which came from a schism over who would succeed the Prophet Muhammad. Caliphates were *terrible* at holding to lines of succession. (Not that Europe was any better—I'm looking at you, Hundred Years' War.)

[§] Worth noting: we're talking the *original* assassins, as in, *al-Hashashin*, the military sect of the aforementioned Nizari, from which the word "assassin" was derived.

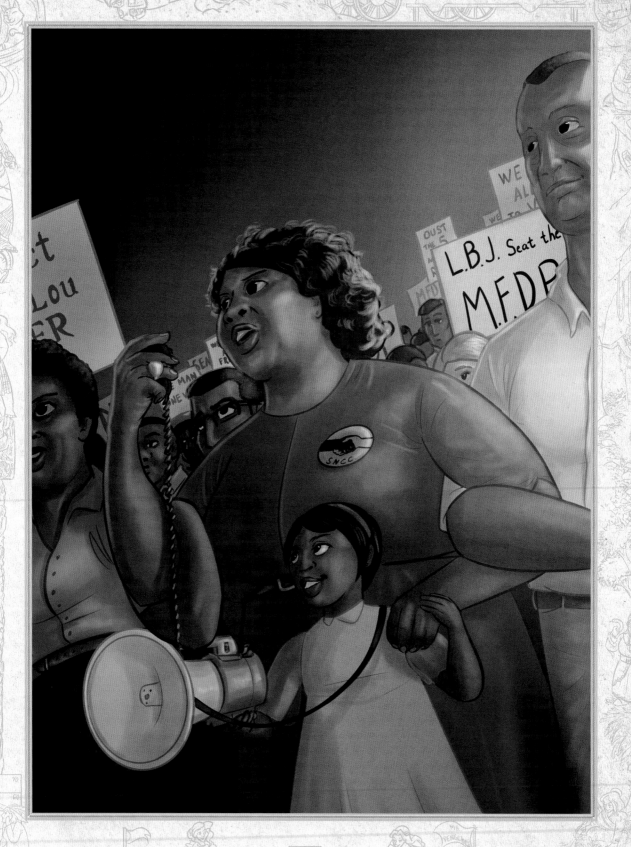

# Fannie Lou Hamer

(1917–1977, UNITED STATES)

## The Mother Who Marched

annie Lou Hamer was 35 when she learned she could vote. Nobody had been in a hurry to tell her. As a poor black woman with two kids, Fannie wasn't exactly the target demographic for Mississippi's politicians. If anything, she was their worst nightmare: since the Civil War, the Deep South had spent decades laying down a web of Jim Crow laws specifically to keep black people from having a voice.

Still, she stepped up. On August 31, 1962, she decided to run the gauntlet, and register to vote. The decision would change her life.

It wasn't like she hadn't suffered enough before then. The 20th of 20 children, she'd grown up with rags on her feet and holes in her clothes. Tricked into working for a sharecropper,* she was picking cotton by age six, and had dropped out of school by age 12 (a shame, because she was a natural intellect, winning spelling bees and effortlessly learning to read). When her family saved up enough to buy some livestock, a white man poisoned the animals because her family was "getting ahead." When Fannie went to a doctor to treat a stomach cyst, she was given a "Mississippi Appendectomy": an involuntary hysterectomy.†

She'd been beaten down at every turn by a system that did not want her to succeed. So she determined to change that system. She was going to register to vote.

It's important not to gloss over what happened next. This section detailing her abuses is long, but her struggle was longer. As you read this, realize that virtually every contemptuous tactic mentioned has a descendant still in use:

- Upon showing up at the courthouse, she was met by a crowd of gun-toting white people.

---

\* He offered food to the hungry Fannie. Not understanding the ramifications, she took it, only to find herself indebted for it. She picked cotton for years to pay off her debt.

† This phrase is attributed to her, although it's a little uncertain who coined it—suffice to say, it wasn't an uncommon experience for poor black women. Her two daughters, Dorothy Jean and Vergie Ree, were adopted before this.

- She had to provide her personal information, which was secretly handed over to the White Citizens Council.*

- She was given a literacy test, which almost nobody could pass: she had to interpret dense legal writing. She failed, but vowed to come back.

- On the way out of town (the nearest registration spot was 30 miles away), police stopped her rented bus because it was the wrong color. The cop gave the driver an outrageous fine, and only lessened it when the entire bus threatened to go to jail over this, and cause a high-profile incident. They pooled their limited resources and paid the fine.

The harassment followed Fannie home. Her boss told her to withdraw her application to vote or she'd lose her job—a job she'd done for 18 years. She didn't, and soon, both she and her husband were unemployed. Within 10 days of her return, she'd been evicted, and white people were engaging in drive-by shootings of her house. She left her family, living as a refugee among friends and distant relatives, to keep her loved ones safe.

All because she'd tried to register to vote.

Most incredibly of all, Fannie went back to register again come December. "Now you can't have me fired," she said, "because I'm not livin' in no white man's house. I'll be here every thirty days until I become a registered voter." She failed her second time, but in January 1963, she passed.

Life got even harder after that. Unable to vote until she'd paid two consecutive years of poll taxes (yet another barrier), Fannie suffered a year and a half of retaliations. Her name was printed in the newspaper as a new voter, which led to potential employers blacklisting her from finding work. Carloads of gun-toting white people circled her home nightly, threatening to shoot her. Elected officials raided her house at four in the morning. She was sent outrageous utility bills, such as one claiming she'd used 6,000 gallons of water (her house had no running water). The unpaid utility bills led to her husband being arrested. Thankfully, they had enough money for lawyers to get the charges dismissed.

Not that they had *much* money. With both husband and wife now blacklisted from most jobs, the Hamers relied on donations from friends and local charities. Fannie did not trust larger organizations like the NAACP, who hadn't advocated for less "respectable" people like

---

* A group that had grown out of the Ku Klux Klan (KKK). In the 1980s it would evolve into the Council of Conservative Citizens, and give inspiration to monsters such as Dylann Roof, who in 2015 murdered a study group at an AME Church—the same predominantly black organization that provided community to figures like **Sojourner Truth** and **Madam C. J. Walker**.

herself. She kept her activism mostly local, working with groups like the SNCC* who reached out to her. She focused on the world she knew.

That world continued to hurt Fannie. When she began attending workshops, she was arrested in Winona, Mississippi, and made to endure torture. The police stripped her and beat her severely. She was blinded in her left eye, her kidneys were permanently damaged, and her polio-afflicted limp was severely exacerbated. She was beaten so badly she was barely recognizable.

Others with her had it just as bad: a 16-year-old girl was beaten so badly the police demanded she wash the evidential blood out of her clothes (she hid her bloodied bra). A male activist tried helping, and was beaten by the KKK, who burned his penis.

They stayed there three days as their jailers, realizing word was leaking of the abuses, tried to cover their backs. Fannie and the others were offered early release, but refused to take it for fear they'd be killed and quietly disposed of (not an uncommon occurrence). Their jailers pressured them by turning the shower temperature up to scalding, but they stayed put. The others later testified that they would have given up but "Fannie Lou wasn't scared cause she just kept right on goin'."

Finally, caving to outside activist pressure, their captors fined them each $100, and forced them, at gunpoint, to sign a statement saying they'd beaten each other and the cops had nothing to do with it. They were free.

Take a step back: all of this, everything written so far, happened because Fannie just wanted to vote. She didn't even try to vote—she just wanted to *register*. That's it. She wanted to do something perfectly legal, and this was the reaction. And these events took place not that long ago: the children of the men who did this to her are still alive. This is not ancient history. This is living memory.

Soon, Fannie became a national celebrity. By 1964, the FBI had her under surveillance. She began running for local office,† registering voters, and organizing charity drives. Before handing anyone donated clothes, she insisted they get registered to vote—and would drive them to do so herself, helping them face the inevitable reprisals. Predictably, Fannie faced many herself: phone harassment, burning crosses, Molotov cocktails, and bomb threats.

All this activism happened outside of traditional political circles. She wasn't working as a Democrat or a Republican, or even engaging closely with the NAACP. She wanted to look after the poor black voter, who'd been ignored by every political actor in the country. And to that end, in 1964, she decided to take on the Democratic Party.

It was an important election year. John F. Kennedy had been assassinated, and Lyndon B. Johnson was running to fully legitimize his time in the White House. He needed ev-

---

* The Student Nonviolent Coordinating Committee, who'd first made Fannie aware of her right to vote.
† Under the Mississippi Freedom Democratic Party, which she started. She never won.

erything to go well—but Fannie, seemingly out of nowhere, threw a wrench into his plans. Arriving almost unannounced, she declared a challenge to Mississippi's representatives (an all-white delegation who'd long worked to suppress blacks). She wanted a seat at the table for people like her.

It plunged the convention into chaos. Many supported the charismatic Hamer, but others tried to keep her from getting too large a presence. When it looked like Hamer would get to speak on live television, Johnson staged an impromptu press conference to prevent the networks from covering her (some aired her later anyway). In the end, Hamer's group didn't get a seat at the convention, which disillusioned her yet further, but it did help to put pressure on Congress: the following year, they'd pass the Voting Rights Act, striking down many of the Jim Crow laws that had so bedeviled her.*

In the years to follow, Fannie only got more radical. Frustrated at the NAACP for being more concerned with its appearance than helping the downtrodden, she returned to local labor organizing. At wit's end trying to work within the system, and sick of seeing those around her brutalized, she flirted with violence as a possible methodology: "I don't believe in killing, but a good whipping behind the bushes wouldn't hurt them."

Her series of losses culminated in the worst of all: that of her 22-year-old adopted daughter, Dorothy. Sick and malnourished throughout her life, Dorothy had often been the subject of Hamer's attention at home. In 1967, Dorothy suffered a cerebal hemorrhage, and Fannie drove her to a nearby hospital—which refused to see Dorothy because she was black. They drove to another, which again refused to admit her. They continued going from hospital to hospital until they came to Memphis, Tennessee, 119 miles away. As Fannie approached the hospital entrance, Dorothy died in her arms.

After that, Hamer turned away from politics. Feeling that the most good she could achieve was through owning land, she started the Freedom Farm, a cooperative that provided crops and housing, and helped the community get down payments on homes: almost the same idea that **Sojourner Truth** had advocated a century earlier. Although the farm would eventually go under, it was, for a time, enormously successful.

Hamer died at 59 of heart failure, after years of failing health. She spent much of her last decade with her young daughter, Vergie, with whom she'd go on tours. She'd start speeches by saying "This is my baby and she's going to sing with me"—which she did, beautifully. Although the public memory of Hamer is of an unstoppable, indomitable woman, Vergie later

---

* This act was significantly defanged in 2013 by a Supreme Court ruling that made one of its key components unenforceable. This component would have prohibited certain jurisdictions from changing their voting laws without first running it by the US Attorney General.

recounted her mother's exhaustion and private breakdowns. She was just as human as any of us, and suffered just as much as you or I would.

Hamer took solace in the fact that she'd left a better world for her daughters. Before her death, she gave an interview where she recalled enrolling Vergie as one of the first black students at a newly desegregated white school. As they approached the entrance, Vergie noticed her mother, famed for her persistence, hesitating. Walking ahead, she implored Hamer to keep moving: "Come on, Mama." Remembering it later with pride in her daughter and shame in herself, Hamer said, "That's hard when it's your child. But she's not afraid."

## · ART NOTES AND TRIVIA ·

This image doesn't depict any specific rally, but is a mishmash of activities ranging from Fannie's initial registration drive (her SNCC pin) to her appearance at the Democratic National Convention (the "L.B.J. Seat the M.F.D.P." sign). To her left, she's locked arms with her husband, Pappy, while her daughter holds her megaphone. All of the signs portrayed here are tracings of actual protest signs.

# Irena Sendler

## (1910–2008, POLAND)

## The Mother of the Children of the Holocaust

I urge you not to make a hero out of me," she said. "That would upset me greatly."

It's a difficult request to follow. After all, this was coming from a nurse who smuggled over 2,500 Jewish children to safety during World War II, at great personal cost. That's practically the dictionary definition of heroism. But what Irena Sendler* meant was to not put her on a pedestal—that anyone could and should act the same.

Irena meant it: she had no special background to make her actions a foregone conclusion. She was a poor Polish Catholic woman who'd had a tough childhood.† Despite this, she took after her doctor father in looking out for those even less fortunate, by becoming a social worker. But even in her youth, she had a strong sense of right and wrong: when her university separated out Jews into separate sections, she would go sit with them in solidarity (she almost didn't graduate because of it). When the Germans attacked Poland, she organized numerous refugee aid stations across Warsaw—numerous because they kept getting destroyed by bombs.

When Warsaw fell, Irene joined a Polish resistance organization named Żegota to provide aid to Jews. This was no simple act: even handing a Jew a glass of water in occupied Warsaw could get you shot. But she and the other members of Żegota did much, much more than that: they gave money, they provided food, and most famously, they secreted thousands of children to safety out of the Warsaw Ghetto.‡

Irena, who went by the codename of Sister Jolanta, headed up many of these efforts. As a nurse, she could (at least in the early days) enter the Ghetto under the pretense of providing medical aid. This left her the unenviable task of convincing mothers to give up their children

---

* "Sendlerowa" in Polish, due to Polish conjugation of some names.

† Her dad died when she was seven, her family was destitute, and she was laid low by this book's most notorious background character, the Spanish Flu epidemic of 1918–1919.

‡ The Warsaw Ghetto was a massively overcrowded neighborhood into which Jews were forced during the German occupation. The population density was roughly that of a clown car, with the economy of a Depression-era prison and the sanitation of a 12th-century toilet. It was, to put it mildly, unpleasant. To put it accurately, it was hell.

so that she could get them to safety—conversations that would haunt her to her dying day.

Once she and Żegota got the go-ahead, they would ferry the Jewish kids out via one of several methods:

- Hiding the child in a box, a courier would drive out on a truck or a tram. Often the child would cry, so the courier developed countermeasures to mask the sound, like bringing an ill-behaved dog, which would bark at the slightest provocation.

- Some buildings in the Ghetto shared a basement wall with buildings outside the Ghetto walls. Once Żegota found a friendly family in one of these buildings, they would tunnel a hole and use that as an escape route.

- Similarly, a law court bordered the Ghetto, and Żegota found some ushers to occasionally open the Ghetto-facing doors to smuggle kids out through the court building.

- Lastly, they'd also help some older kids and adults find their way to safety, often through work groups.

Getting the Jews out was in some ways the easiest step—once out, they'd have to be hidden, fed, supported, and continually shuttled from hiding place to hiding place. In describing this, Irena repeatedly emphasized how many people besides her helped. Not only did the Jews self-organize inside the Ghetto to maximize their small resources, but a massive support network of brave Polish sympathizers took on the long, difficult task of hiding and often raising these refugees. Irena estimated that every Jew saved required a safety net of 10 sympathetic Poles. She was merely one of the more central nodes of this network of helpers.

Eventually Germany turned its attention to the Ghetto. In mid-1942, they began exporting and killing 6,000 to 7,000 Jews a day from the Ghetto, as well as from nearby nurseries and orphanages. When the remaining Jews staged an armed resistance, the Germans dropped bombs on the Ghetto, leaving the handful of survivors to live in rubble. They murdered over 300,000 people in all.

And eventually they trained their sights on Irena.

The Gestapo raided her home early one morning, flooding her house with gun-wielding soldiers. She was the most important target of the entire organization: she was the only one who knew the original identities of the Jewish children. She'd kept their old and new identities on a secret list for years. If that list were to fall into German hands, it would be catastrophic. Not only would the children be killed, but so would the vast web of sympathetic Poles. Tens of thousands of lives, ended in a mass pogrom.

But Irena had long trained for this moment. She kept the names on scraps of paper in a jar, which was often buried in the backyard. She'd practiced tossing the jar out the window into the bushes. She had contingency plan after contingency plan lined up. In the end, she didn't even need them: although the jar was not buried when she was raided, one of her couriers happened to be visiting the house, and smuggled it out in her armpit. Irena took the few scraps that weren't found in the jar, quickly shredding and tossing them out the window of the police car, as the Germans, exhausted by the late-night raid, dozed off.

As it turned out, the Germans didn't even know she was high up in the organization.

They brought her to Pawiak prison, where they tortured and interrogated her for months. She refused to reveal anything, and after three months, they informed her she was to be shot and killed. At the last minute, as she and other prisoners were being marched to the execution grounds, she was diverted aside and abruptly shoved outside. Żegota had bribed a guard to help her escape. She was free.

Irena spent the rest of the war in hiding, using a fake name. Although it was too risky to stay at her own apartment, she stayed nearby and looked after her ailing mother during the day. When her mother died, she could not even attend the funeral, for fear of being caught by the Germans—who'd discovered her escape and sent the bribed guard to a labor camp. After the funeral, she spent her days treating ill refugees. Even in hiding, she looked after others.

At last, the war ended, and Irena was part of the vanguard trying to get life back to normal. Warsaw was barely standing—the Germans had razed as much as they could on the way out. Nevertheless, she stayed there, working at a hospital-turned-orphanage and lending aid to everyone she could: traumatized children who needed to be rocked to sleep; senior citizens who'd been left without families; homeless "rubble girls" who'd resorted to prostitution.

Unfortunately, postwar life was not kind to Irena. Under the ensuing Communist regime, she became persona non grata. Anti-Semitism, stoked to a raging fire under the Germans, didn't go away overnight, and accordingly, people viewed Irena, with her Jewish sympathies, suspiciously. Many informed on her, and she was repeatedly brought in for interrogation, causing the premature birth of a son, who died after 11 days. She was forced into retirement in 1967, and not allowed to travel abroad until 1983.

The rough treatment extended to her surviving children too. Both had their names struck off the rolls of universities they'd entered, just for being her children. This upset her daughter Janina so much that she asked, "Mother, what was it in your life that you did wrong?"

Compounding her children's difficulties was the fact that the all-too-human Irena spent most of her time absorbed in social work. Her children recounted times where they wished they lived at the orphanage so they'd see her more often. "I sometimes think I was a bad daughter, a bad mother, and not a good wife," she once said. "I had two failed marriages. I was frequently absent from home. My deep involvement in professional and social work had a decidedly negative impact on my family life."

But a strange thing happened in her later years.

In 1999, three teen girls in rural Kansas took on a history class project. Their teacher handed them a clipping from a magazine that had come out after the film release of *Schindler's List*,* profiling other similarly heroic figures in brief, including Irena.† The trio spent a year researching her life, eventually producing a short play called *Life in a Jar*. The play proved so popular they were called upon to perform it repeatedly all over the United States and eventually the world.

And after 50 years of cruel anonymity, the world celebrated Irena Sendler. Three girls an ocean away had rescued the rescuer.‡

The final years of Irena's life were marked by an endless series of awards, interviews, and celebration. Throughout this, she consistently declined to accept the mantle of heroism, knowing all too well her failings and limits. After the release of a book chronicling her story, she began work on two others, telling the same stories from the viewpoints of the Jewish children and the Jewish mothers, giving them back their agency. She died at age 98, still trying to give back.

## · ART NOTES AND TRIVIA ·

This image depicts the moment that Irena was captured, although it takes a bit of artistic license. In reality, she was cornered inside her house, not outside in the garden. Not only was there just one buried bottle instead of a plethora of them, the bottle was not buried at the time of her actual capture. In the background is the Warsaw Ghetto, although the depiction doesn't fit the exact geography of Warsaw.

---

* Which, if you haven't seen it (Really? You clearly never went to Hebrew school), is about Oskar Schindler, a German businessman who similarly saved around 1,100 adult Polish Jews from the Nazis. It won a ton of awards. It's on TV all the time. How have you not heard of this?

† When they brought it up to their teacher, he initially thought the figure of 2,000-plus children was an error, with an extra zero on the end: How could he have not heard of such an absurdly brave woman?

‡ This point cannot be hammered home hard enough: the passion of people like these girls is the only reason we know many of the stories in this book and others. Figures like **Madam C. J. Walker** or **Sutematsu Ōyama** only had their stories told at length because normal people like you or me (or Irena Sendler) took it upon themselves to do so.

# Benazir Bhutto

(1953–2007, PAKISTAN)

## The Mother of Pakistan

er story read like a fairy tale: exiled daughter of a deposed ruler, at last returned to confront her father's killer. She'd weathered untold hardships, suffered brutal prisons, yet here she was, running for election, pregnant. When she won, it was as if she'd fulfilled a prophecy: the first woman ever elected to lead a Muslim country. Native-born and foreign-educated, she could be a bridge between worlds, a new start for Pakistan. She gave people hope.

But fairy tales are not real, and her public image turned out to be just that: an image. Benazir, whose name means "without flaw," was anything but.

It's true that she was practically destined to run the country. The Bhutto family was almost indescribably rich: they owned so much land, it would take days to appraise all of it. Her father had served as president (and then prime minister) of Pakistan, and she'd learned much from him. In her teens, she joined him on trips to the United Nations and fielded calls from diplomats like Henry Kissinger and George H. W. Bush.

One of the greatest lessons she'd gleaned from her father was the importance of foreign alliances—and of securing them through PR. Nowhere is this more evident than in her not-subtly-titled autobiography, *Daughter of Destiny.*[*] Aiming to convince Western readers that she was a trailblazer worthy of support, she wrote that her mother had been forced into *purdah*[†] (she hadn't); that Benazir was the first Bhutto to cast off the *burqa* (she wasn't); that her father had named her his political heir (he almost certainly hadn't). The book was heavy on fictitious anecdotes and suspiciously light on policy.

Which is a shame, because her actual story was more than powerful enough. In 1977, her father was overthrown in a coup by the head of the military, Muhammad Zia-ul-Haq. The new regime instituted fundamentalist laws, a radical change for Pakistan: unions and political parties were outlawed; criticizing the army was made illegal; five-times-a-day prayer became mandatory; theft was now punished with amputation; sports stadiums began holding public floggings. The then-24-year-old Benazir spent the next 11 years being a thorn in Zia's side.

---

[*] In England, it was released as *Daughter of the East,* in a shrewd appeal to orientalism.

[†] A tradition in some Islamic societies of isolating women in other rooms or behind curtains, out of the sight of men; **Arwa al-Sulayhi** also fought with this.

They were horrible, desperate years for the Bhutto family. As the Bhuttos filed legal appeals for their father, they continued protesting—and were often beaten by the police for it. Benazir and her mother were constantly under house arrest. After Zia executed their father, two of Benazir's brothers, in desperation, founded a terrorist group.* After they hijacked a plane, Benazir, who had nothing to do with it, was arrested.

Prison was hard. She was incarcerated for five months, usually in solitary confinement. Temperatures in her cell regularly broke 120 degrees F, and her health began to fail. Her hair fell out in clumps, and she began to lose her eyesight and hearing. On top of that, she developed a gynecological disorder and anorexia, before finally being released for medical treatment.

But she was not done for. Zia, also realizing the importance of PR in courting foreign support, had lightened up on Benazir, who was becoming more and more visible on the world stage. Taking advantage of this opening, Benazir escaped to London, where she continued her resistance from afar. It was increasingly evident that the real war was one of opinion: America's. With US/Russian tensions rising over Afghanistan,† President Reagan was ready to fund—and effectively king—anyone who'd prove a good ally. While Benazir was popular, Reagan thought she was too radical to trust.

She began making savvy moves. She returned to Pakistan, to a crowd of 3 million people. She spent year after year in the headlines of American papers, the populist leader rallying against a regime that repeatedly imprisoned her. She made herself more palatable to the Pakistani electorate by marrying, but, characteristically, her husband was little more than a plus-one (notably, she kept her name). She wrote her autobiography. She molded her image to appeal perfectly to the American savior complex.

Not to be outdone, in 1988 Zia made his own appeal to the West by calling for elections—right before Benazir was due to give birth. Although she was heavily pregnant and it was the height of the summer, she went on a PR blitz across Pakistan. In the end, she won, due in no small part to an unexpected stroke of luck:‡ Zia's plane crashed, killing him.

Suddenly, Benazir was prime minister.

But almost immediately, the limits of foreign support became evident. Although she'd won, the elections had nevertheless been rigged, and her party had been cheated out of a majority. She wanted to fight it, but a US diplomat stopped her. The ears of the world were wait-

---

* Named al-Zulfikar, after their father, Zulfikar Bhutto.

† In a reprise of the "Great Game" described in the chapter on **Soraya Tarzi**, Russia and the United States were waging a proxy war in Afghanistan. Reagan wanted Pakistan to help.

‡ Read: sabotage. Who did it is still unknown. The main suspect seems to be one of Zia's generals, Mahmud Ali Durrani.

ing to hear from her, he said, so "instead of complaining about how you've been robbed, why don't you tell them you won?" She didn't contest the results. This would prove to be a mistake.

Now that she was in charge, the world watched to see what sort of leader she'd be. Her first moves inspired confidence: she released political prisoners, reinstated union rights, and opened a dialog with India.

But she was stymied soon thereafter. Without a majority in the National Assembly, Benazir couldn't get anything done. The USSR had collapsed, and America's interest in Pakistan (and Afghanistan) with it. She began cozying up to fundamentalists, just to have a chance at getting anything done, and lost her core supporters in the process. She declared herself as being against abortion. She began wearing a hijab. She was doing anything she could to get something done.

It didn't work. Tensions rose as the government deadlocked. Part of this can be laid at Benazir's feet—she was a campaigner, she'd never had to actually govern. But it was not a winnable situation: 70 percent of the federal budget was devoted to paying off foreign debt, and virtually all of the rest went to the military. In the words of fellow politician Abida Hussain, "If Benazir Bhutto had a perfect head, perfect heart, and a perfect soul, she'd probably still fail."

It is not surprising, then, that the situation broke her.

By her second term in 1992, Benazir gave up hope of bettering her country's situation and busied herself with bettering her own. She and her husband pocketed billions as the poverty rate skyrocketed. She began supplying nuclear technology to North Korea, in exchange for missile technology to use against India. She ousted her own mother from her political party.

The biggest turning point was the murder of her brother. Since forming a terrorist group, he'd been living abroad, but when he returned, he was arrested for the plane hijacking. Once he got out, he began campaigning against Benazir, with cutting insight: "She's talked a lot about democracy, but she's become a little dictator." At the height of his protests, a group of men surrounded his house and shot him to death. His death remains unsolved, but many blamed Benazir.*

In short order, her fortunes reversed. Drubbed out of office by rivals and into exile by tax agents, she spent years in Dubai, caring for her sick mother. Her husband, who'd been in and out of jail for corruption, moved to New York—the two were effectively divorced. She was at her lowest.

Into this void stepped, once again, the United States. They wanted someone that could keep Pakistan predictable, if not stable, and Benazir's successor wasn't it. In exchange for her stepping back up to the plate, George W. Bush's administration would get the corruption

---

* In reality, it was more likely her husband, who wanted to stay in power, who orchestrated it.

charges—foreign and domestic—dropped against her.* She agreed, and went back on the campaign trail, where she died.

Benazir had wanted to appear invulnerable. As her armored car rolled through the streets, she stood out of its sunroof, waving at the crowd. This allowed a young boy named Bilal to approach her and fire three shots, before detonating a suicide bomb. She died 10 days before elections. Nobody ever determined who ordered her assassination. She left behind a son and two daughters.

Benazir's legacy has been a mix of good and bad, and a Pakistan that has regularly fallen prey to fundamentalists. However, one area where she lives on, unambiguously doing the good she may have always desired, is in the minds of Pakistan's girls, who see someone who, despite her flaws, beat the odds.

In 2013, Pakistani teen Malala Yousafzai addressed the United Nations. Shot by the Taliban for her activism, Malala was appearing for the first time publicly since the incident. She spoke of education, she spoke of rights, she spoke of a path forward. And as she did so, she wore the white shawl of her childhood hero: Benazir Bhutto.

## · ART NOTES AND TRIVIA ·

Benazir is seen here in the outfit and car where she'd die. Behind her is the Pakistani flag, and on her lapels are the flags of the United States and North Korea, both alliances that she played to her own advantage. She is seen in the light, getting the attention, but in the dark, her husband counts the money he'd embezzled. In the background, her enemy Zia-ul-Haq approaches on motorcyle.

---

* Except in Switzerland. Switzerland don't play that way.

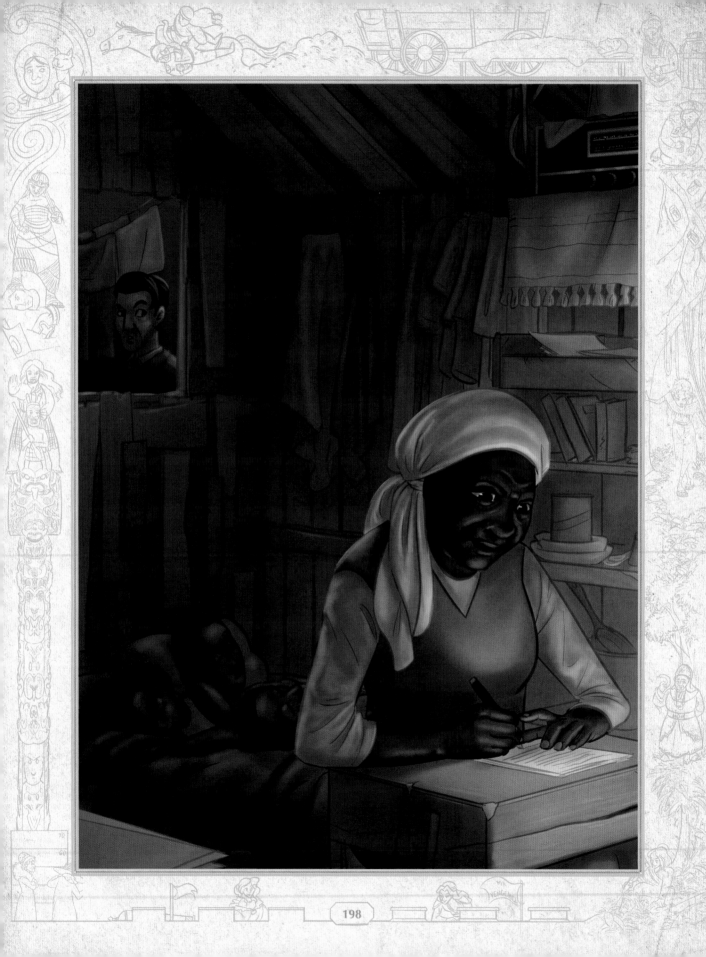

# Carolina Maria de Jesus

## (1914–1977, BRAZIL)

## *The Mother Who Wrote Her Way out of Poverty*

**B**razil didn't know what to do with Carolina Maria de Jesus.

She was brash. She was black. She was funny and harsh and difficult. And she was astonishingly poor—a resident of one of the *favelas* (slums) around São Paolo. But in the early 1960s, she became Brazil's biggest author.

It was an unlikely series of events. Carolina was one of the few literate favela residents, with all of two years of proper education. Hardly an auspicious beginning for an aspiring writer. To provide for her three children, she'd taken to collecting paper and scraps to sell, a soul-crushing task that would net her the equivalent of 25 cents on a good day. She saved some of the paper for herself, though, and used it to write fairy tales and novels, and to keep a diary.

In late 1958, when she was breaking up a favela fight (as she often did), she threatened the two fighting by yelling that she would put their names in her book. This intrigued passing journalist Audalio Dantas, who approached her after overhearing the peculiar threat. She showed him her work, and in it he saw a unique voice he'd soon amplify.

Her first book, *Quarto de Despejo* (*The Garbage Place*) was, for many Brazilians, the first look they'd ever had into the world of the impoverished. It wasn't pretty. The book, a collection of Carolina's diaries, was shockingly blunt in talking about alcoholism, violence, and corruption. It used people's real names, called out reformer politicians as frauds, and laid blame for her neighbors' misfortunes on their own poor attitudes.

More than anything, though, it haunted the reader with its simple, devastating language:

- "How horrible it is to see your children eat and then ask: 'Is there more?' This word 'more' bounces inside a mother's head as she searches the cooking pot knowing there isn't any more."

- "I was so nervous about my children that many times I'd vomit, but there was nothing there but bile."

- "When I'm in the favela I have the impression that I'm a useless object, destined to be forever in a garbage dump."

- "Brazil needs to be led by a person who has known hunger. Hunger is also a teacher."

- "I don't have any physical force but my words hurt more than a sword. And the wounds don't heal."

The book illustrated the difficult life Carolina had had to that point. An illegitimate child who wasn't even allowed in the church where she grew up, she left for the big city while she was young. For a while she floated from job to job: she worked in a hospital, cleaned hotel rooms, sold beer, and even performed in a circus (in which she got to sing and wear a feathery costume, which she loved).

She described how she eventually got a job as a maid, but was fired after four months: "I was too independent and didn't like to clean up their messes. Besides I used to slip out of the house at night and make love. After four months they fired me." When she got pregnant, her employers fired her and her baby's father promptly left town—an experience that would repeat with the fathers of her other children.* She could have relied on some of her more trustworthy lovers over the years for support, but she valued her independence more than anything. She wrote repeatedly of favela women trapped in abusive relationships and didn't want to join them.

Her book was shocking. It was colorful. It was extremely judgmental. And it flew off the shelves.

Predictably, with her success came a tidal wave of criticism. First, her neighbors were furious that she looked down on them and made money off it. But soon complaints flooded in from all over: she was an unfit mother; she was too critical; she was poor with money; she liked having sex;† she didn't write the book herself;‡ she thought too much of herself.

But Carolina weathered the storms and made a better life for her kids. With the proceeds from the book, she fulfilled her dream of living in a brick house. She bought nice clothes for her children, and they no longer walked around barefoot. Where previously she'd have to take her kids everywhere to keep them safe, carrying young Vera on her shoulders and keeping João and José Carlos by her sides, now they could play in the backyard.

Their new life was not idyllic. Her new neighbors shunned her and the cops would implicate her in virtually any neighborhood disturbance. Rumors spread that the government was paying for her house, and opinion began to turn. Her publishers took advantage of her

---

* Two sons and a girl—João, José Carlos, and Vera Eunice. She had a fourth, Carolina, who died in childbirth.
† A condition that seems to afflict a great many people.
‡ This was a rumor spread in part by the journalist who got her work noticed.

half-formed literacy, cheating her out of foreign royalties and making her pay to publish her next three books—none of which sold well.* Her son João fell ill and paying for his medical care drained much of her funds.

A late-in-life career revival illustrated the cruel stance the public had taken toward her. When her first book was republished after 15 years, the accompanying newspaper article was captioned "Carolina: Victim or Crazy?" It emphasized her eccentricities, picking over her appearance and her physicality. She didn't subscribe to the ideological orthodoxy of the left or the narrow morality of the right, and enraged them both. The press, upset that the black critic kept criticizing, disparaged her for the few pleasures she took from life, and wrote her off as insane for not knowing her place.

She died, a forgotten figure, at age 63. Her son João died four months later.

The fate of her surviving children is almost a metaphor for the duality of Carolina's life: one thrived and one struggled. Vera Eunice married and became a schoolteacher, living a good life. José Carlos, on the other hand, was ruled by his impulses: an alcoholic, twice divorced, he would argue with anyone around him. But both, interviewed years after Carolina's death, expressed heartfelt thanks for their mother. "Without her we would have died," said José Carlos. "We stuck to her like glue. My mom was father and mother."

"There is no one in the world I admire more than her," said Vera. "All of us have our defects, and she also had hers, I know. She was a difficult person to live with, but who isn't? For a favela dweller, don't you think this was enough, what my mother did?"

## · ART NOTES AND TRIVIA ·

This is as accurate a re-creation of Carolina's favela home as possible from photo reference, down to her desk and radio. Her three children slumber quietly, while Audalio walks by in the background, noticing Carolina is up late writing.

---

* Partly this was due to social backlash. Partly it was due to the 1964 rise of a military dictatorship.

# Juana Azurduy de Padilla

## (1780–1862, BOLIVIA/ARGENTINA)

## *The Mother of Bolivian Independence*

Bolivia should have been named after a woman.

That's not this book's opinion, but that of Bolivia's actual namesake, Simón Bolívar.* He met said woman in late 1825, after she'd fought, and won, a bitter war to kick out Spain. She was a mestiza woman who'd led an army of indigenous men and women into battle, many of whom thought of her as a saint or a goddess. She lost her husband and four children in the conflict, leaving her a pregnant widow in charge of 6,000 soldiers. She fought all the way to the end of the war, giving birth to her last child on the battlefield.

Her name was Juana Azurduy de Padilla. Upon meeting her, Bolívar remarked that the newborn country should really have been called Padilla or Azurduy, since she was the one who fought for it.

As the story goes, she'd been a fighter from birth. Left to her aunt after her parents died, she was sent off to a convent, where she was to receive a "proper" Christian education in addition to her native upbringing. While she enjoyed tales of warrior saints, she fled the convent after only a couple months, and got married not long after to the love of her life: a creole man named Manuel Padilla. By age 28, she'd settled into a comfortable life, raising their four children in peace.

But peace didn't last long. Upper Peru† declared independence from Spain, and a series of insurrections and revolutionary wars began to rock the country. Manuel, never a great fan of Spain, joined up, leaving Juana to look after the kids. The revolution got off to a rocky start, though, as pro-Spanish (royalist) forces immediately identified Manuel as a rebel and confiscated his lands—with Juana and the kids still on them. Manual rescued his family and whisked them away to a mountain hideout, but soon was off again to organize local guerrillas.

As Manuel continued gathering locals to support the revolution, he began involving Juana more and more. She spoke both Quechua and Aymara, and proved a far better recruiter than Manuel, convincing upwards of 10,000 indigenous people to join the war. She approached them with motherly care, sometimes quite literally: she and Manuel practically adopted the illegitimate son of a Spanish governor and Incan royalty named Juan Huallparrimachi.

---

\* Okay, fine, it's this book's opinion too.

† As Bolivia was named at the time.

By 1813, she'd brought her kids—biological and adopted—to the war and put herself on the front lines. Frustrated that the indigenous recruits were not being put to good use, she got in the face of the rebel commander, demanding to know why. When he replied that they lacked battlefield discipline, she borrowed a training manual and got to work drilling them herself. By the next major battle, her "Loyal Battalion," as they were called, stayed fighting longer than any other unit. She'd led them personally.

This so impressed the rebel leaders that the general in command gave Juana his saber. The native soldiers took to calling her Pachamama, the name of their earth goddess.

The next year, Manuel was captured by the royalists, and Juana was left to command their troops—and look after their kids—without his help. It took a toll. Without a solid base of operations, she and her men were forced to hide in swampland. She fought at least five battles against the royalists, winning most of them. But with their supplies dwindling and her attention diverted, she couldn't provide for her biological children. And while she was able to weather these circumstances, her children couldn't. Starvation, disease, and the ravages of war took them all from her by 1815.*

But she would not remain childless for long: she was pregnant. All the work she'd done since Manuel's capture, all the battles she'd fought in his absence, she'd done while carrying a child. In the Battle of Pintatora, she rode in while pregnant, but did not ride out that way. She gave birth in the middle of the battle, only to realize that this indicated weakness to some of her less loyal subordinates.† Sensing a mutiny on her hands, she absconded with the unit's money and regrouped.

The following year, Spain struck back hard. They occupied much of Alto Peru, and put her on the run. Juana left her newborn daughter, Luisa, with some relatives and doubled down on her resistance. According to legend, she organized a group of indigenous women dubbed the Amazons, and fought alongside them in sixteen battles. She captured the silver-mining city of Potosi, and was given the rank of Lieutenant Colonel. Even her enemies admitted a grudging admiration: one wrote, "I will be the first (to admit) my respect for that woman, but I swear that I will castigate her audacity by making her my prisoner."

In early 1816, Juana rescued Manuel from prison and redoubled their efforts—but it was to little avail. By September, Manuel was dead, killed when trying to help her in battle. The royalists were so elated that they put his head on a pike and paraded it around to intimidate

---

* The documentation on her children is scarce and contradictory. It is certain she had three sons from 1800 to 1806, who died in their childhood. She had a daughter, Juliana, who was with her at this point and died in 1814. Some accounts talk about other sons with her in the swamp, but they're not named and there's no documentation for their burials. The previously mentioned Juan Huallparrimachi died in battle in 1814.

† So much for the "Loyal Battalion."

Juana. It didn't work. She mounted a counterattack and rescued his remains, so that she could give him a proper burial later. She endured extreme hunger, horrid living conditions, and the deaths of many commanders to kept fighting.

And then, one day, the war was won. The Spanish withdrew and the Bolivian Republic was born. Suddenly Juana was visited by the man who'd come in late to save the day, Símon Bolívar. He joked with her about naming the country after her, promoted her to general, and left.[*] Life went back to normal. Women were to be subservient again. Juana was to return to the role of widow, living with her young daughter and subsisting off an inconsistent pension.

For 37 years, she lived like this, in increasing poverty, taking care of Luisa and her sister's illegitimate son, Indalecio. In 1862, she died, impoverished and forgotten, buried in a mass grave.

But her story doesn't end there. The new nation needed its own identity—it needed its own heroes. And Juana fit the bill. Although her role was censored or played down in the initial elitist-authored histories, over time, historians came to celebrate her more and more.

As such, a lot of her story is exaggerated. There's no reliable evidence of her staying at a convent or idolizing warrior saints. Some tellings say the Spanish kidnapped her children, and they died when Juana and Manuel attempted to rescue them. Another said Manuel died while trying to protect his pregnant wife, although she'd had the baby over a year earlier. The new nation wanted a hero to call their own, so they whittled off the rough bits, such as any indication she could have been an imperfect mother. They held her up as an almost unachievable ideal: a mix of Bolivian patriot, Pachamama goddess, and the Virgin Mary.

(This happens a lot: Helen Keller was a socialist firebrand, **Ada Lovelace** was addicted to gambling and opiates, Amelia Earhart was a polyamorous libertine, but these parts of their stories don't get repeated. Your heroines were as messy and human as any of us. Love your edges and never let them go, dear reader.)

In 1903, Bolivia changed the name of the city of Pombabamba to Azurduy. In 1917, it created the municipality of Azurduy. In 1980, the bicentennial of her birth, the nation proclaimed it the year of Juana Azurduy and renamed the airport after her.

In 2015, even Argentina, in which she'd spent some time,[†] made her part of that country's identity. An old statue of Christopher Columbus was removed, and in its place was erected a massive 52-foot-monument of Juana Azurduy. In place of a painful reminder of a colonialist past now stands a native-born heroine, leading a diverse crowd onward into the future.

---

[*] Bolívar himself had been successful in large part to another woman, **Manuela Saenz**, a fiery revolutionary who was known for keeping a pet bear and harvesting the moustaches off her fallen enemies. She and Juana struck up a friendship in late 1825, meeting in person and exchanging some letters after. Manuela's story is covered on the Rejected Princesses website.

[†] Much of the rebellion had been led (and reinforced) from Buenos Aires.

# Pailadzo Captanian

## (1882–1968, ARMENIA/UNITED STATES)

## The Mother Who Invented Rice-A-Roni

MATURITY 4

RAPE ABUSE A

R

It was one of the first recipes Lois DeDomenico ever learned to make: a savory pilaf, with bits of vermicelli diced fine as rice. She'd learned it from her San Francisco landlady, an older Armenian woman who rented out her spare room. Years later, after Lois had moved and lost touch with the kindly old woman, she made the dish for her husband, Tom, who worked at his family's macaroni factory. Inspired, the two altered the formula and released it as Rice-A-Roni: The San Francisco Treat.

But that recipe had undergone a long, harrowing journey to get there: for Lois's sweet landlady, Pailadzo Captanian, was a survivor of the Armenian Genocide.[*]

The Turks had come for them in 1915. At that time, Pailadzo was but a music teacher from a good family, who'd rebelled against her parents by marrying a lower-class professor. They'd been married for six years, had two young sons and a third on the way. And suddenly they had orders to relocate to a concentration camp in the Syrian desert. They knew they'd be forced to walk on foot, during summer. They knew they'd likely die.

The first thing they did was find a way to save their children. Hearing of a Greek priest who was arranging to hide Armenian children with Greek families, Pailadzo approached him with her two sons. Unable to tell her sons the truth, she told them that she was going for a drink of water, and that she'd be right back. She wasn't.

Within days of beginning the long walk to Syria, she and her husband were robbed of nearly all their belongings. Turkish and Kurdish raiders targeted the Armenian refugees mercilessly, stealing, killing, and raping with abandon. The Turkish police escorting them let it happen, and often assisted. They took everything, even clothes: many young women were practically naked. Pailadzo was fortunate enough to have rags to protect her feet from the pebbles and thorns.

Two weeks in, Turkish police came for her husband. One of the last things he said to her was: "One idea consoles me; I know that you will die with honor." It was a reference to a

---

[*] A series of massacres born of the dying days of the Ottoman Empire, in which racist Muslim Turks, looking for a scapegoat for their collapsing nation, turned on the Armenians. They murdered upward of 1.5 million Christian Armenians and led the survivors on death marches into Syria. The word "genocide" was first invented to describe these events.

secret dose of poison that she'd hidden. He didn't think she'd be able to make it, and he didn't want her to suffer.

When the Turkish police returned, they did so without Pailadzo's husband. They had, however, taken his clothes.

The Armenians walked 10 to 12 hours a day, for months, with little food or water. Pailadzo was four months pregnant when she began her journey and going forward only got more difficult. As hard as it was, she was again comparatively fortunate. Other mothers had to carry their children. She saw many of them die.

Every night, she thought of her two abandoned sons, whose mother had lied to them for the first time. She hated herself for her cowardice. Alone, she sang herself the lullabies usually reserved for them.

Her comparative fortune again prevailed when the marchers finally got to Syria. In Aleppo she had an uncle who worked for a German company. Because he held a critical role, he wasn't to be deported—and he was able to extend Pailadzo some aid. She was able to give birth in peace. She named her newborn son Tzavak, meaning "pain."

And then, in 1918, she snuck back into Turkey to get her two older sons. Safe and healthy, they greeted her with tears of relief and anger. They angrily accused her of abandoning them, before asking, over and over, "Where is our father?" Again, she could not tell them. But they knew.

She wrote a book detailing her experiences in 1919, in time for a Paris Peace Conference. It was translated into French and distributed with the hope that after all the country's people had suffered, Armenia could at last win its independence from Turkey. But Pailadzo's pleas fell on deaf ears.

Come 1920, she took her children and moved to America. Of the experience, she wrote, "How can I describe my feelings? When the ship landed in New York City and I gazed at the Statue of Liberty I felt an impulse in me to adore the statue that would give me freedom and safety of life."

Working as a single mother of three was not easy. She held many jobs, and sometimes couldn't make ends meet, at one point putting her sons in an orphanage for a short while. But eventually she landed on her feet. She worked mainly as a seamstress, even making draperies for Franklin and Eleanor Roosevelt.

Her children all went on to live long lives. One became a doctor, studying at Columbia. Her son Tzavak, whose name was changed to Gilbert, joined the army in World War II, helping to stop another genocide. After the war, he invited his mother to move to San Francisco, where she lived in peace, cooking up pilaf and baklava for her children, grandchildren, and the occasional tenant in a tiny little kitchen.

# · ART NOTES AND TRIVIA ·

On the foreground wall hangs a portrait of Pailadzo that was attached to her book manuscript. It portrays her in the clothing she wore crossing the Syrian desert, and is re-created as faithfully as possible. Below that are photos of her deceased husband and of Franklin and Eleanor Roosevelt. The frontmost book on the bookshelf is her memoir, while the others include various Armenian works, and a book on Deir-ez-Zor, the Syrian city to which many of the death marches led.

In the kitchen stands Pailadzo in later life, having moved on from the horrors of her youth, cooking for Lois DeDomenico (who's quite enjoying the taste).

# Velu Nachiyar

## (1730–1796, INDIA)

## The Mom Who Made a Bomb

elu was an infuriatingly talented child.

She was just good at everything! Not only was she fluent in seven or eight languages,* but she was also a master at the mellifluously named martial art of *silambam* (stick fighting). As legend has it, her father organized a silambam tournament, and she beat everyone (including her tutor). Moreover, she was an expert equestrian—when her dad presented a horse so strong it could not be tamed, Velu rode it until it tired itself out.

She continued her unbroken streak of superstardom when she married the prince of Sivaganga, a southern Indian state. They had a daughter, Vellachi, but Velu was not content to be a quiet plus-one to her husband. Not only did she help him with strategic planning and kingdom fortification, she saved his life. While they were out on a jungle expedition early in their marriage, a tiger pounced on him—she in turn pounced on the tiger, killing it with her bare hands.

(It's worth taking a moment here to raise an eyebrow at her hyperbolic action hero feats. Yes, likelihood is, they've been exaggerated. That isn't uncommon for national heroes. But it gives you an idea of her personality that, if you believe historians made up her backstory, *this is the one they chose*.)

Velu's life took an abrupt turn when her husband was killed. His assailants were the villainous Nawab family, with the aid of the ever-pesky British.† The standard move for Indian widows in her situation was *sati*: ritual self-immolation, to prove you were more bereaved than the next widow. Well, it may not shock you that the 42-year-old Velu Nachiyar did not choose that option. Instead, she proclaimed, "I will wreak vengeance. The British army shall be routed. I will throw the Nawab to the dogs. I shall do all this with Goddess Rajeshwari's grace." And then, presumably, she flipped a table.

She escaped into the forest with her daughter and her bodyguards, the Marudhu Broth-

---

* Urdu, English, French, Telugu, Malayalam, Kannada, and Tamil. As impressive as that is, it doesn't even begin to cover the entirety of India, which has *22 officially recognized languages*.

† The circumstances of his death are a bit unclear. Some sources say he was praying at Kalaiyar Temple when the Nawab and British forces stabbed him in the back. Others say he went out, guns blazing. Could be both?

ers, and plotted revenge, even as her enemies took her throne. She wrote to the acclaimed leader Hyder Ali asking for help. Receiving no response to her letter, she then approached him in disguise as a man, and spoke to him in high-level Urdu. He was so impressed by her language mastery (seriously, she was good at everything) that he agreed to help her out.

With Ali's support, Velu marshaled her forces. She trained for eight years, organizing an all-women battalion led by her friend Kuili. After cementing alliances with local lords and merchants, she began her campaign. At 50 years old, she became the first Indian queen to rebel against the British. She would not be the last.

She was a terror on the battlefield. She would send out soldiers to engage the enemy forces, and then retreat backward, drawing her foes into range of her hidden cannons. She continually changed her strategies and proved an unpredictable foe, which confounded the British and paved her way to the gates of Sivaganga.

The city was well fortified, and not so easily sacked, so she again switched tactics. Knowing her enemies would not expect women combatants, she had her female soldiers change from armor into *saris*, and infiltrate the town. Kuili led the charge. Once she'd gained entry to the fort, Kuili found her way to the armory. There, she doused herself in lamp oil, set herself ablaze, and entered the weapons depot—destroying the entire thing, and herself in the process.

This is one of the first recorded instances of a suicide bombing in history.

Velu would repeatedly employ this tactic against her technologically superior foe. In one instance, she sent her adopted daughter, Udaiyal,* to do so. In her memory, Velu renamed her all-female force Udaiyal Padal.

Before the end of the year, Velu had won her war, and retaken her kingdom from the British. That's right, she won. Britain actually ran away.

However, her ensuing reign was not smooth. She relegated much of the day-to-day administration to her longtime bodyguard/administrators, the Marudhu Brothers, who let the power go to their heads. She ended up at odds with them, and after much anguish, Velu ousted them and installed her daughter, Vellachi. Unfortunately, her daughter proved not as strong willed as her mother, and died within a few years.

Velu herself died three years later, a week shy of 67. With no clear heir to take the throne, the British reclaimed Sivaganga, executing the Marudhu Brothers and banishing Vellacchi's husband. However, Velu's deeds would serve as inspiration for many other Indian rulers to

---

* The circumstances of Udaiyal's life vary from telling to telling. In some, she is merely an adopted daughter who martyrs herself by becoming a "human bomb." In others, she is a herd girl who refused to inform on Velu for the British, and was killed for it.

rebel. From Velu's death onward, India would prove no end of trouble for the British empire, and the rebellions against the European colonialists only grew. Finally, in 1947, the country won its independence. As part of their national identity, Indians have since celebrated the heroes who helped free them from Britain—and few get more recognition for that than Velu Nachiyar.

## · ART NOTES AND TRIVIA ·

In a classic "cool guys don't look at explosions" pose, Velu strolls away from a massive conflagration. To her right are the Marudhu Brothers, and to her left are the confident Kuili and the uncertain Vellacchi. Velu's outfit is based on a statue of her erected in 2014 at Soorakulam, near Siviganga.

# Kate Leigh

## (1881–1964, AUSTRALIA)

# and Tilly Devine

## (1900–1970, AUSTRALIA)

## The Mothers of the Sydney Underworld

The Great Depression saw the rise of gangsters worldwide: Chicago had Al Capone, Harlem had Stephanie St. Clair, and Sydney had Kate Leigh and Tilly Devine:* two vicious hellions who each ran their own crime syndicate. With 107 and 204 convictions respectively, both were candidates for the title of "Worst Woman in Sydney."

And they *hated* each other.

Kate's empire started when Sydney passed laws prohibiting liquor sales after 6 PM. Kate, however, felt no need to obey said laws. She dealt in "sly grog," betting parlors, brothels, cocaine, and other illicit substances. She eventually ran over 20 establishments, ranging from high-end to working class.

Tilly's futures found root in a legal loophole: in Sydney, no man could run a brothel, but the law said nothing of women. With grit, tenacity, and an unyielding propensity toward violence—she slashed up johns who skipped the bill, soaked crooked cops in petrol and set them on fire—Tilly built a criminal niche and a fearsome reputation.

The two outlasted their male rivals through wits, brutality, bribes, and exploiting sexist ideas. Nobody believed women could actually be kingpins, so they rarely were implicated in crimes. Much remains unknown about the early days of their enterprises, as everyone involved hated talking to the cops. Nobody even knows what exactly started their rivalry, if anything. But it was personal.

A rare eyewitness account from the early days survived via policewoman Maggie Baker. Assigned to gather info, she went on patrol, only to be stopped by a surly Tilly Devine, who blocked Baker's way and began shaking her. Suddenly, off a passing tram came Kate Leigh, sucker-punching Tilly in broad daylight. She sat on her foe and told Baker, "Do what you gotta do, love. I'll be here when you come back." So began Baker's first week on the job.

---

* Kate Leigh was also known as Kate Barker, Kate Lee, and several other names. Tilly's maiden name was Twiss.

Kate trashed Tilly's brothels; Tilly smashed Kate's stores; Kate slashed up Tilly's sex workers; Tilly slashed up Kate's coke dealers; Kate set up rooftop snipers; on and on, back and forth, for years, with upward of 40 men in massive street brawls.

Part of what made this so ugly was that Sydney had severely restricted firearms. So the criminals mostly used straight razors, giving the neighborhood they frequented the colorful nickname of Razorhurst. Kate and Tilly, though, usually kept to fists and bricks when fighting each other. Well, fists and press releases. (More on that in a bit.)

The two had surprisingly similar backgrounds: Each rose to the top from utterly dire circumstances. Kate had been starved and beaten as a child. She ran away from that, ending up with a series of abusive, alcoholic lovers. She spent half her thirties in jail when she perjured herself for one of them. By the Great Depression, she was middle-aged, with an adult daughter, a lifetime of rough experiences, and a surprisingly chipper attitude.

Tilly grew up in London sweatshops, and became a prostitute in her teens.[*] She married an Australian soldier who bragged of his prospects back home, including a family kangaroo farm. But it soon turned out he was both penniless and kangaroo-less. Before long she was on the street in Sydney,[†] this time with her abusive husband as muscle, as she made a terrifying name for herself.

Kate's reputation was a bit more jovial. She'd often attend random court cases to heckle the judges and lawyers, usually while peeling vegetables. When she wasn't there for heckling, she was providing false witness to get random people out of trouble, seemingly just for kicks.

But come 1930, the cops struck back. Awash in colorful criminals, Sydney passed laws increasing police funding and allowing officers to arrest anyone they thought had "bad character." Anyone found carrying a razor was jailed and flogged. The laws were a massive overreach with horrifying side effects, including a brutal crackdown on gay men, but they did serve to debilitate the gangs.

It's worth taking a moment to appreciate the circus of criminals running around Sydney at the time: there was "Monkey" Webb, who ate raw sausages, barked like a dog on the train, and dated Kate at one point; Guido Calletti, a tough guy who once sued a newspaper for libel and won one-fourth of a penny; Frank Green, a violent madman who constantly fought Cal-

---

[*] The exact age is unknown. Most accounts say around 15 or 16, but some claim she was as young as 12. By all accounts, including her own, she entered sex work without coercion. She continued it even when she didn't need to, financially.

[†] Her relationship with Jim Devine was . . . complicated, to say the least. They had a son, Frederick, whom they left with Tilly's folks in England when they moved to Australia. They had little contact with Frederick throughout their lives. They both beat the crap out of each other on a regular basis, and were a textbook abusive relationship. She was known to turn on a dime if Jim—or anyone else—crossed her, and Jim was the same.

letti for the affections of a woman named Nellie Cameron; and Alfred "N****r" Barker, a gay black man with platinum blond hair, whose real name is recorded by virtually no books on the subject. (Unsure why—seriously, it wasn't *that* hard to find.)

The overreaching laws took Tilly and Kate out of the picture for the better part of a year. Tilly went back to England for nine months to "look after her mother." Kate spent 12 months in gaol (jail) for cocaine possession (she pleaded she was innocent—she wasn't). It was a testament to their organizational expertise that both of their empires kept running fine in their absence.

Kate's stay in prison was quite cushy, and she befriended an elderly pensioner who'd been jailed for shooting her alcoholic husband.* In line with Kate's character, she robbed said inmate within a week of her release. Shortly thereafter, Kate shot a guy in the crotch (he neglected to press charges). None of this played well in the press.

Press became important. Because the police lived and died by public opinion, they targeted any "bad characters." All one had to do, Kate and Tilly realized, was *seem* like a bad citizen to get the cops on you. So the two called a truce and began fighting each other in the headlines, by ratting each other out to the papers *constantly*. One of their more amusing ongoing feuds was about Tilly's Pomeranian dogs: Kate claimed to have loaned them to her, and Tilly responded by denying it and insulting Kate's parents.

They also used the press to promote themselves. Kate would do acts of charity, giving out (possibly stolen) presents at Christmas and buying a Shetland pony for the Razorhurst kids. Tilly tended to have more niche causes, like putting on a charity dance to keep an attempted murderer out of prison. While both donated to the Salvation Army, orphanages, and the like, keeping families afloat through the Great Depression, Kate was generally more successful in remaking her image than Tilly.

It didn't help that Tilly was undergoing a violent, prolonged, public divorce. After she'd returned from England, she found her husband, Jim, had taken to openly sleeping with various women, humiliating Tilly in the process. This culminated in their 25th wedding anniversary, when he came in late, having been out drinking with a lover. He loudly proclaimed to everyone at the lavish party that he was going to marry this new woman, then broke a bottle over Tilly's head. She filed for divorce soon after.

The divorce went on for months, in which she had to destroy her public image by publicly detailing how her husband beat her. Even after all that, Tilly could not satisfy the naive divorce judge. He insisted on witness testimony against her vindictive husband, a dangerous

---

* As the story goes, the woman—an alcoholic herself—went to their toolshed at some point. The man thought that she had a secret bottle of booze she wasn't sharing, so he attacked her. She defended herself by slashing him in his hand, but he bled out and died. Kate became close friends with her—although Kate annoyed nearly everyone else in prison by being loud, bossy, and not doing any work—and picked her up in a limo once she got out. Kate then took her to collect the pension check and robbed her.

prospect for anyone who came forward. However, Tilly was so fearsome that she convinced someone to do so. In short order, her divorce was granted. Still, in an indication of how complicated (and unhealthy) their relationship was, they remained friendly after the divorce, visiting each other regularly to the end of their lives (although it never took long for them to start fighting again).

Tilly remarried three years later, and the ensuing party lasted all night. But just as the couple settled into bed the next day (around noon), they had unexpected visitors: five fire engines and an undertaker. A practical joke. By someone who was quite likely Kate Leigh.

By 1948, Kate and Tilly buried the hatchet. Nearly everyone they'd come up with was dead or imprisoned. Almost all they had left was each other. Not that they were ever *good* friends.

Ultimately, they shared a common weakness: taxes. With the liquor and brothel laws changed, their fortunes and incomes vanished. For years, rumors abounded of their secret cash troves hidden around Sydney, but none were ever found.

Both passed away in poverty years later. A vicious hellion to the end, Tilly had a scarce handful of mourners—one of the only ones to speak was the police chief, who said simply, "She was a villain . . . but who am I to judge her?" It was a far cry from Kate's earlier funeral: she'd died beloved, her latter-day deeds remembered over her years of sin. Her greatest eulogy may have come from Maggie Baker, the policewoman whom she'd leapt to assist years earlier: "When Kate died, I felt, well, there's a bit of good old Australian history that's gone."*

## · ART NOTES AND TRIVIA ·

The lighting here mimics the same washed-out flash photography that you see in 1920s photography. Kate is pictured in purple, getting into Tilly's business. Tilly is seen with a ton of rings on her hand, and a scowl on her face, expressing a far more direct threat. They're both wielding straight razors from the period, a favored weapon of the time. Kate, always more jovial and friendly toward Tilly than vice versa, is crowding Tilly and forcing physical contact.

---

* A close second may be from Tilly herself, who said, "God rest the old bitch's soul."

# Ranavalona I

## (1778–1861, MADAGASCAR)

## *The Mad Mother of Madagascar*

The West called her the Female Caligula, but if half of what they said is true, Caligula was more a male Ranavalona. This famously cruel ruler of Madagascar ostensibly killed between 30 and 50 percent of the entire population during her reign via unspeakable means—yet simultaneously, she kept her country independent, repeatedly defeated the combined forces of the English and French, and instigated one of the first industrial revolutions seen outside of Europe.

She, uh, also tried making a giant pair of scissors to chop invaders in half. Unequal parts conqueror, protector, mother, and lunatic, she was, at the very least, not boring.

First, though: this is another one of those "history is written by the victors" deals where most of what's known about her comes courtesy of angry foreign missionaries. Basically, don't take any of the following stories at face value. More on that later.

So, Ranavalona! She came to power when her husband died at 36 (from either alcoholism, syphilis, murder, or some delightful cocktail of all three). His sudden death left the kingdom in a weird state: he'd spent years cozying up to the British in exchange for some of their weaponry (he'd just started the nation's first standing army!), and was starting to turn on the British when he died. The main claimant to the throne (as Ranavalona had no kids with him), however, was looking to maintain cozy ties with the British.

Well, Ranavalona was having precisely none of that, so she assembled a "screw foreigners" posse, and staged a coup. She took control so fast that some of the king's elite bodyguards only found out he was dead when they saw her on the throne. When a handful of them politely raised an objection, she gently replied by having them repeatedly speared in the gut. She went on to execute most of the royal family—in one case summoning a man to the capital, then killing him for abandoning his post.

The first days of her reign brought bizarre proclamations to accompany the brutal violence. To express mourning for her departed husband, she declared that every single person must, for 10 months, keep their heads shaved. Practically the only exceptions were the nation's professional mourners (it's a thing), who were spared only so they would have hair to tear out amid their hysterical sobbing. She kept her husband's body on display for weeks, with round-the-clock legions of slaves tasked with keeping the flies off. During the mourning pe-

riod, she made it illegal to dance, bathe, play music, sleep on a mattress, look in a mirror, or clap your hands. The punishment was she'd sell you into slavery.

This was not an idle threat: under Ranavalona, slavery, recently abolished to appease the British, returned as one of the cornerstones of the economy. Her favorite slave was undoubtedly Jean Laborde, a shipwrecked young Frenchman whose presence drastically transformed the country. Once Ranavalona found out he was an accomplished tradesman, she set him to work with making a massive industrial complex. Within a couple years of his arrival, Madagascar was self-reliant for weaponry, ammunition, and gunpowder—one of the first industrial revolutions (if not *the* first) to occur outside of Europe.

With the country making its own weapons, Ranavalona was able to repel the combined forces of the French and the British, which was no small feat. They repeatedly attempted invasions, which usually went something like this: "We're gonna bombard the crap out of you from our boats! Okay, you're retreating, great, let's head onto land and chase you! Wait, there's ANOTHER ENTIRE BACKUP FORTRESS hidden behind the one we just blew up!? Oh god oh no oh f— (*death gurgle*)" She'd later decorate her fortresses with the decapitated heads of invaders on pikes.

Ranavalona was not content to merely destroy her enemies, though: she was determined to be a full-on D&D Dungeon Master. At one memorable council meeting, Laborde was tasked with making: giant metal shields for each port, that would bounce cannonballs back at European ships; a massive wall that would cover the entire 3,000-mile coastline; and four enormous pairs of scissors to be hidden on the tracks leading to the capital, then used to snip invaders in two.

He never quite got around to making any of those.

Ranavalona's craziest stunt, though, was undoubtedly the buffalo hunt. At one point, she decided to go hunting and brought along her 50,000 closest pals. The only problem was that there weren't any roads going where she wanted to hunt, so she had people go ahead and make a road for her as she went. Moreover, they had to make a new town for her to sleep in every night. This went on for 16 weeks, and 10,000 workers died. No buffalo were shot.

What she was best known for in her time, though, was her hatred of foreign religion, particularly Christianity. While she'd initially been tolerant of missionaries, she quickly came to see them as an invading force when several openly advocated for her overthrow. As a reaction, she delved deeper into traditional religion, particularly a rite called the *tangena* ordeal, which she made practically everyone in Madagascar do (Christians first). In it, you'd swallow poison and three bits of chicken skin. If you barfed up all three pieces, you were innocent, and free to go! If you died from the poison, even if you were innocent, it was chalked up as a divine mystery of the universe. But if you didn't barf up all three pieces of chicken? You were guilty, and that's where the real trouble began.

In this next section, things get increasingly graphic. Seriously, the mood moves from "slasher movie" to "horror porn" to "Cormac McCarthy novel." If you want to avoid this, just skip to the picture of bunnies. If you want to stay in, welcome to the Tangena Challenge: try to make it to the end without barfing (and if you do, at least make sure to yak up three pieces of chicken).

Ranavalona's methods of execution included:

- Strangling.

- Drowning.

- Stoning.

- Crucifixion.

- Burning on a pyre.

- Tossing you from a ceremonial cliff.

- Tossing you from said cliff, catching you, making you think you're safe, then cutting the ropes.

- Making you kiss her feet, except she'd coat them in poison so you'd die horribly afterward.

- Tying you in a giant burlap sack and hanging said sack from a pole until you died.

- Chaining you to four other people and assigning guards to prevent anyone from giving you food. When one of the four died, you'd just have to drag around the corpse until you too died.

- Flaying your skin off while you were still alive.

- Crushing your testicles in a steel vise.

- Sawing you in half (lengthwise, head first).

- Tying you to a wooden stake in a pit, then filling the pit with boiling water, so your body would cook while you were still alive.

Still here? Fine, here's the worst one. At one point, she was to have four people executed, including an incredibly pregnant woman. As the four prayed fervently for help, her guards built a massive fire to toss them in. Soon, though, it started raining, dousing the flames. The guards kept rebuilding the fire until the storm broke, revealing a triple rainbow. Many people took this—as well as the pregnant woman suddenly giving birth—as a sign that the accused were divinely protected, and fled the scene. Undeterred by this, though, the guards threw the newborn in the fire, followed by his mother and the other three.

THAT IS THE WORST THING I HAVE EVER WRITTEN. OH GOD. BUNNIES BUNNIES BUNNIES. HERE ARE SOME BUNNIES.

Ranavalona held on to the throne for decades, foiling multiple coup d'états with the grace of a veteran supervillain. As an example: when her son, the prince,[*] partnered with Laborde and several Europeans (including **Ida Laura Pfeiffer**, a very unfortunate 60-year-old tourist covered elsewhere in this book) to try and oust her, she not only discovered their plot, but toyed with them for months. She would terrify them by having the military spontaneously raid them—only for the soldiers to do random benign tasks, like picking up presents. She would summon the terrified Europeans to do impromptu piano performances and dance recitals, during which she would stand on a balcony overlooking them, completely silent throughout. She held a six-hour-long meeting on how, exactly, she was to execute the treasonous Europeans, only to surprise them the next day by merely banishing them.

Their banishment, however, was a death sentence in everything but name. When the poor conspirators finally left the capital, they did so with a military accompaniment. Said accompaniment repeatedly led them on long detours through malaria-infested jungles and prevented them from contacting any doctors, turning a seven-day journey into a 53-day-long ordeal. She knew she could not have gotten away with outright killing Europeans, so she just made it increasingly likely that they would die of malaria. It worked, killing all but two of them.

Three years later, Ranavalona died peacefully in her sleep. She was 83. Afterward, her son took over and undid virtually all her major decrees within the first month, to the relief of many.

So, in case you couldn't tell, a lot of what you just read was racist imperialist crap:

---

[*] After the king's death, she took many of the generals as her consorts. It is presumed one of them was the father of Rakoto (Radama II), to whom she gave birth 11 months after the death of Radama I.

centuries-old bogeyman stories concocted by missionaries with an agenda to delegitimize her. Problem is, it's *really* difficult separating fact from fiction here—especially for a non-French-speaker, when most of the relevant documents are in French. Some of the stories, like Laborde's extended Madagascar Malaria Tour, probably did happen as described. Others, like the hoary tale about the pregnant woman, were almost undoubtedly made up—you can find parallels to that exact story in other martyr tales.

The truth of the matter is probably somewhere in between. Ranavalona was undoubtedly a despot, and it's indisputable that a great many died under her reign. But she saw herself, not unreasonably, as a sovereign at war, and in that context, she did the impossible: she kept the nation free. By associating herself so strongly with the native beliefs, she legitimized her reign. This enabled her to make the country self-reliant, strengthen her own nation's culture, and repel the team-up invasion efforts of the two most powerful nations in the world—a feat that her successors failed at, to dire consequences.

Oh, what's that? You think that everyone lived happily ever after once she died? HAH! Here's what actually happened:

As mentioned, her son, Rakoto, undid everything in her reign immediately: abolished the tangena ordeal, ended slavery, established freedom of religion, and opened the borders to outsiders. Foreign merchants were allowed to trade without even paying duties, as long as they didn't sell weapons or ammunition.

Fast forward a year: the country was awash in imported alcohol (one contemporary described one out of four buildings being a liquor store, and the townsfolk permanently drunk). The upper class was furious at Rakoto for not enforcing import/export duties and destroying their livelihoods. Rakoto started losing it, and instituted dueling as a method of solving disputes. Finally, the island was simultaneously wracked with a deadly plague and spasm-inducing cholera, which made it appear that people were uncontrollably dancing. Many considered this the ghost of Ranavalona coming back to haunt them.

Within 30 years, the island became a French colony, and stayed that way for over 100 years. Christianity spread like wildfire and became one of the dominant religions. As recently as 2001, people on the street talked matter-of-factly of Ranavalona as one of their country's greatest villains—for her brutal treatment of the people, yes, but often more for the refusal to accept European culture. One person surveyed remarked, "There is no development in Madagascar if there are no Europeans in Madagascar."

That is, of course, one small sample, and should in no way be taken as representative of the whole. But it, and the rest of the study, is indicative of a lack of critical rigor as regards Ranavalona's actual history, even in her native Madagascar.

## · ART NOTES AND TRIVIA ·

Ranavalona is seen here on the second floor of her colossal wooden palace. Designed by Laborde, it was the largest wooden structure ever built at the time, and considered one of the wonders of the world. You can see the conspirators dancing, playing piano, and plotting around blueprints of the giant scissors. Rakoto is, rather unwisely, stationing possible troops in between the shears. The interior is loosely designed on some parts of Versailles. The checkerboard pattern doubles as a metaphor for the chess game Ranavalona was playing with her captives. Note that she has knights stationed a single chess move away from killing any of them. Continuing the chess metaphor, the group leaving in chains is being led by a bishop, and is moving diagonal to the board. The table next to her has three chicken skins and some poison. Her skin tone is supposed to be surprisingly light, since the Malagasy people were of half-Indonesian descent (seriously, it's fascinating—look up the history of Madagascar ethnicities).

# Other Notables

No book about rad historical mothers would be complete without at least mentioning some of these women (all of whom were already covered in Volume One).

**Boudica:** When her daughters were savaged by the Romans, she led a rebellion that killed 80,000 Romans and burned a nascent London to the ground.

**Tin Hinan:** She led the matrilineal Tuareg of Northern Africa to a new land, and was dubbed "the mother of us all" for it.

**"Stagecoach" Mary Fields:** This six-foot-tall, hard-drinking black woman was not just a gun-slinging Wild West postmaster, but also the town babysitter.

**Rani Lakshmibai:** She led a war for independence against the English with a baby strapped to her back.

**Ada Lovelace:** The mother of the computer algorithm, she used her smarts for science, math . . . and gambling.

**Chiyome Mochizuki:** This elderly woman opened an orphanage to take in female war orphans—and secretly trained them into an army of ninja spies.

**Emmy Noether:** One of the most important mathematicians in history, she looked after her students ("Noether's Boys") like a mother bear.

**Grace O'Malley:** This Irish pirate queen gave birth while battling Algerian pirates, then got right back to fighting.

**Wilma Rudolph:** Crippled by polio in the Jim Crow–era South, this poor, unwed teen mother became a three-time Olympic gold-medal winner for track and field.

**Yaa Asantewaa:** Queen Mother of the Asante, she started a war against Britain to keep the soul and identity of her people intact—and kicked serious butt.

# It Doesn't Have to Stop Here!

There is more information available online on almost every entry you've read here: deleted content, making-of videos, concept art, reference imagery—and that's before you get into the new entries that go up regularly for free!

So come with your comments, your criticisms, your corrections, and join us over at

## www.Rejected Princesses.com

Look for the "behind-the-scenes" link to unlock all the additional content!
(Or don't. I'm not going to tell you how to live your life.)

Thanks for reading!

# Acknowledgments

**Helping with absolutely everything:**
Jeremy Porath

**Unwavering moral support during the year from hell:**
Lindsey Carter
Toli Carter
Melody Chang
Nicole Chen
Sandra Daugherty
Nora Hamada
Jonaya Kemper
Connie Lee
Trina Peng
Ryan Rice
Marina Stabile

**Art help:**
Tom Beuerlein

**Getting this dang thing made:**
Carrie Thornton
Sean Newcott
Suet Chong
Alexandra Machinist
Lily Tillers
Doug Johnson

**Research and translation:**
Jon Truitt
Brittany Bayless Fremion
Jeanette Wu
Carlos Hugo Adolfo Zayas Gonzalez
Sun-young Lee

Kina Park
Dina Abou-Karam
Kitty Chandler
Emma Hacker
Nysa Langevin
Florine Pascal
Anna Williams
Rachel Forster
Naomi Kotek
Morgane Gilson
Stereden
Juliette Almira-Bohic

**Chapter suggestions:**
Gina (Man-deok Kim)
Kara Guminski (Bella Abzug)
Larissa Peixoto (Amanirenas)
hinerditscat on Tumblr (Freydís Eiríksdóttir)
Anna Y. Sinclair (Sister Rosetta Tharpe)
Jon Truitt (Angela Jiménez and Carolina Maria de Jesus)
edwahrer on Tumblr (Marie Equi)
Skolastika Lupitawina (Cut Nyak Dhien)
Kelly Barnhill (Isabella of France)
isaac41256 on Tumblr (Mandukhai Khatun)
melinkp on Tumblr (Soraya Tarzi)
y4kay on Tumblr (Olympias of Macedon)
lilixthekitsune on Tumblr (Irena Sendler)
Celina Diaz (Juana Azurduy de Padilla)
Ruwani Weerasinghe (Kate Leigh and Tilly Devine)
Martin Brennand (Ranavalona I)

# Bibliography

## Ada Blackjack

Niven, Jennifer. 2004. *Ada Blackjack: A True Story of Survival in the Arctic*. New York: Hyperion.

## Amanirenas

Bowman, Alan K., Edward Champlin, and Andrew Lintott, eds. 1996. *The Cambridge Ancient History*, vol. 3. Cambridge: Cambridge University Press.

Cassius Dio. 1917. *Roman History*, bk. 54, vol. 6. Loeb Classical Edition.

Duncan, Rick. 2013. *Man, Know Thyself: Volume 1—Corrective Knowledge of Our Notable Ancestors*. Bloomington, IN: Xlibris Corporation.

Francis, David. 2014. "The Meroe Head of Augustus: Statue Decapitation as Political Propaganda." British Museum. https://blog .britishmuseum.org/2014/12/11/the-meroe -head-of-augustus-statue-decapitation-as -political-propaganda.

"Nubian Archers." The University of Chicago. https://oi.uchicago.edu/museum-exhibits/ nubia/nubian-archers.

Strabo. 1903. *Geography*, bk. 17, translated by Horace Leonard Jones. London: George Bell & Sons.

## Angela Jiménez

"Angelina Vasquez Obituary." Tributes.com. http://www.tributes.com/obituary/show/ Angelina-Vasquez-70755099.

Perez, Esther R. 2015. *Those Years of the Revolution: 1910–1920. Authentic Bilingual Life Experiences as Told by Veterans of the Wars*. CreateSpace Independent Publishing Platform.

Robson, Lucia St. Clair. "Connecting the Thoughts." *Lucia St. Clair Robson: Historical Novelist*. https://www.luciastclairrobson.com /blog/connecting-the-thoughts.

## Arwa al-Sulayhi

Al-Haddad, Adel A. 2006. "Queen Arwa's Capital: Wonderful City with Two Rivers." *Yemen Times*, May 8.

Cortese, Delia. 2006. *Women and the Fatimids in the World of Islam*. Edinburgh: Edinburgh University Press.

Daftary, Farhad. 1980. "Sayyida Hurra: The Isma'ili Sulayhid Queen of Yemen." The Institute of Ismaili Studies.

Mernissi, Fatima. 1997. *The Forgotten Queens of Islam*. Minneapolis: University of Minnesota Press.

## Bella Abzug

Levine, Suzanne Braun, and Mary Thom. 2007. *Bella Abzug: How One Tough Broad from the Bronx Fought Jim Crow and Joe McCarthy, Pissed Off Jimmy Carter, Battled for the Rights of Women and Workers, Rallied Against War and for the Planet, and Shook Up Politics Along the Way*. New York: Farrar, Straus and Giroux.

Levy, Alan H. 2013. *The Political Life of Bella Abzug, 1920–1976: Political Passions, Women's Rights, and Congressional Battles*. Lanham, MD: Lexington Books.

Levy, Alan H. 2014. *The Political Life of Bella Abzug, 1976–1998: Electoral Failures and the Vagaries of Identity Politics*. Lanham, MD: Lexington Books.

## Benazir Bhutto

Allen, Brooke. 2016. *Benazir Bhutto: Favored Daughter*. Boston: New Harvest Houghton Mifflin Harcourt.

Crossette, Barbara. 1988. "Woman in the Daughter of Determination: Benazir Bhutto." *New York Times*, December 2. http://www .nytimes.com/1988/12/02/world/woman-in -the-news-daughter-of-determination-benazir -bhutto.html?mcubz=0.

Hassan, Adeel. 2016. "Not Forgotten: Benazir Bhutto, the Muslim World's First Female Leader." *New York Times,* June 21.

Nichols, Michelle. 2013. "Pakistan's Malala, Shot by Taliban, Takes Education Plea to U.N." *Reuters,* July 12. https://www.reuters.com/article/us-malala-un-idUSBRE96B0IC20130712.

Schofield, Victoria. 2014. "Getting Away with Murder, Benazir Bhutto's Assassination and the Politics of Pakistan." *The Round Table* 103 (4): 445–47.

Shah, Bina. 2014. "The Legacy of Benazir Bhutto." *New York Times,* December 26.

Weisman, Steven R. 1988. "Pakistan's Avenging Daughter: Time for Anger?" *New York Times,* May 2. http://www.nytimes.com/1986/05/02/world/pakistan-s-avenging-daughter-time-for-anger.html.

### Carolina Maria de Jesus

De Jesus, Carolina Maria. 1962. *Child of the Dark: The Diary of Carolina Maria de Jesus,* translated by David St. Clair. New York: Dutton.

Levine, Robert M. 1992. "The Cautionary Tale of Carolina Maria De Jesus." Working Paper No. 178. Kellogg Institute.

Levine, Robert M., and José Carlos Sebe Bom Meihy. 1997. *The Life and Death of Carolina Maria de Jesus.* Albuquerque: University of New Mexico Press.

### Cut Nyak Dhien

Hasan, Nurdin. 2012. "The Queen of Jihad." *The Aceh Globe,* July 9. http://www.theacehglobe.com/2012/07/queen-of-jihad.html.

Malik, Adam. 1980. *In the Service of the Republic.* Singapore: Gunung Agung.

Orohella, Benny, and Zaynab El-Fatah. 1999. "Tjoet Njak Dien." *Victory News Magazine.* http://www.victorynewsmagazine.com/TjoetNjakDien.htm.

Saragih, Aldi Wahyu. 2015. "Cut Nyak Dhien (Inggris Dan Indonesia)." *Media Saragih.* https://mediasaragih.blogspot.com/2015/05/cut-nyak-dhien-inggris.html.

Sufi, Rusdi. 1994. "Cut Nyak Dhien." In *Wanita utama Nusantara dalam lintasan sejarah: Prominent Women in the Glimpse of History,* edited by Ismail Sofyan, M. Hasan Basry, T. Ibrahim Alfian. Jakarta: Jayakarta Agung Agung Offset.

Siapno, Jacqueline Aquino. 2013. *Gender, Islam, Nationalism and the State in Aceh: The Paradox of Power, Co-optation and Resistance.* Hoboken, NJ: Taylor and Francis.

van Duyl, A. G. C. 1897. "The Dutch in Atjeh." *The Imperial and Asiatic Quarterly Review and Oriental and Colonial Record.* Oriental Institute, January–April.

### Fannie Lou Hamer

Ghansah, Rachel Kaadzi. 2017. "A Most American Terrorist: The Making of Dylann Roof." *GQ,* August 21. https://www.gq.com/story/dylann-roof-making-of-an-american-terrorist.

Hamer, Fannie Lou. 2011. *The Speeches of Fannie Lou Hamer: To Tell It Like It Is.* Edited by Maegan Parker Brooks and Davis W. Houck. Jackson, MS: University Press of Mississippi.

Lee, Chana Kai. 1999. *For Freedom's Sake: The Life of Fannie Lou Hamer.* Urbana, IL: University of Illinois Press.

### Freydís Eiríksdóttir

de Terre Neuve, John. 2012. "Skraeling Warlord and Who Were the Skraelings Anyway?" *Wargaming in 28 mm and Sometimes Smaller,* June. http://fuentesdeonoro.blogspot.com/2012/06/skraeling-warlord-and-who-were-they.html.

*The Saga of the Greenlanders.* 2005. Translated by Haukur Thorgeirsson. https://notendur.hi.is/haukurth/utgafa/greenlanders.html.

*The Saga of Erik the Red.* 1880. Translated by J. Sephton. http://sagadb.org/eiriks_saga_rauda.en.

Wolf, Kirsten. 1996. "Amazons in Vinland." *Journal of English and Germanic Philology* 96 (4, October).

### Funmilayo Ransome-Kuti

Johnson-Odim, Cherl, and Nina Emma Mba. 1997. *For Women and the Nation: Funmilayo Ransome-Kuti of Nigeria*. Urbana, IL: University of Illinois Press.

### Ida Laura Pfeiffer

Michaels, Jennifer. 2013. "An Unusual Traveler: Ida Pfeiffer's Visit to the Holy Land in 1842." *Quest. Issues in Contemporary Jewish History. Journal of Fondazione CDEC* 6 (December).

Pfeiffer, Ida, and H. W. Dulcken. 1861. *The Last Travels of Ida Pfeiffer: Inclusive of a Visit to Madagascar, with an Autobiographical Memoir of the Author*. New York: Harper.

Pfeiffer, Ida, and Jane Sinnett. 1855. *A Lady's Second Journey Round the World: From London to the Cape of Good Hope, Borneo, Java, Sumatra, Celebes, Ceram, the Moluccas, Etc., California, Panama, Peru, Ecuador, and the United States*, vol. 1. London: Longman, Brown, Green and Longmans.

### Ilona Zrínyi

Molnar, Miklos, and Anna Magyar. 2013. *A Concise History of Hungary*. Cambridge: Cambridge University Press.

Sisa, Stephen. 2002. *The Spirit of Hungary: A Panorama of Hungarian History and Culture*. Morristown, NJ: Vista Books.

### Irena Sendler

Mieszkowska, Anna. 2011. *Irena Sendler: Mother of the Children of the Holocaust*. Santa Barbara, CA: Praeger.

Wieler, Joachim. 2006. "The Long Path to Irena Sendler—Mother of the Holocaust Children." *Social Work & Society* 4 (1).

### Isabel Godin des Odonais

Wakefield, Celia. 1994. *Searching for Isabel Godin: A True Story*. Chicago: Chicago Review Press.

Whitaker, Robert. 2004. *The Mapmaker's Wife: A True Tale of Love, Murder, and Survival in the Amazon*. London: Doubleday.

### Isabella of France

Carpenter, David. 2007. "Dead or Alive." *London Review of Books* 29 (15, August 2).

Carpenter, David. 2007. "What happened to Edward II?" *London Review of Books* 29 (11, June 7): 32–34.

Daniell, Christopher. 1999. *Death and Burial in Medieval England, 1066–1550*. London: Routledge.

Warner, Kathryn. 2015. "22 August 1358: Death of Isabella of France, Dowager Queen of England." *Edward II*, August 8. http://edwardthesecond.blogspot.co.uk/2015/08/22-august-1358-death-of-isabella-of.html.

Warner, Kathryn. 2015. "Edward II's Relationship with Hugh Despenser the Younger." *Edward II*, September. http://edwardthesecond.blogspot.com/2015/09/edward-iis-relationship-with-hugh.html.

Warner, Kathryn. 2013. "Isabella of France and Her Relationship with Edward II." *Edward II*, September. http://edwardthesecond.blogspot.co.uk/2013/09/isabella-of-france-and-her-relationship.html.

Warner, Kathryn. 2012. "Did Hugh Despenser the Younger Rape Isabella of France?" *Edward II*, April. http://edwardthesecond.blogspot.com/2012/04/did-hugh-despenser-younger-rape.html.

Warner, Kathryn. 2011. "Demolishing Myths About Edward II, Part 1: Isabella's Jewels and Piers." *Edward II*, November. http://edwardthesecond.blogspot.com/2012/11/demolishing-myths-about-edward-ii-part_27.html.

Weir, Allison. 2011. *Queen Isabella: Treachery, Adultery, and Murder*. New York: Ballantine Books.

### Jeanne de Clisson

Adams, James. 2013. "Jeanne de Belleville, Pirate or Politician?" *James Adams Historic Enterprises*. http://www.jamesadamshistoricenterprises.com/treasuretrove/jeandeclisson.html.

de la Croix, Robert. 1978. *A History of Piracy*. New York: Manor Books.

McNeill, Maggie. 2014. *Jeanne de Clisson*, April 3. https://maggiemcneill.wordpress.com/2014/04/03/jeanne-de-clisson.

Moranville, Henri. 1893. *Chronographia regum Francorum*. Paris: Renouar.

Robbins, Trina. 2004. *Wild Irish Roses: Tales of Brigits, Kathleens, and Warrior Queens*. Boston: Conari Press.

Smedley, Edward. 1836. *The History of France: From the Final Partition of the Empire of Charlemagne, A.D. 843, to the Peace of Cambray, A.D. 1529, Part I*. London: Baldwin and Cradock.

Yolen, Jane. 2010. *Sea Queens: Women Pirates Around the World*. Watertown, MA: Charlesbridge.

## Jigonhsaseh

Childs, John Brown. 2007. "On the Peace Road? Some Reflections on 9/11." February 2. www.cisan.unam.mx/Speaking/Speaking/John%20Brown.pdf.

Hines, Anna Grossnickle. 2011. "Sharing a Heritage: The Great Peace and the Constitution. The Peacemaker and the Great Law: A Legend of the Haudenosaunee." Presentation for Lincoln Land Community College, September.

Mann, Barbara Alice. 2000. *Iroquoian Women: The Gantowisas*. New York: Peter Lang.

Martin, Brandon Jay. 2013. "Haudenosaunee Warfare and Politics: Persistence and Adaptation Through Time." Dissertation, State University of New York at Buffalo, May 6.

## Juana Azurduy de Padilla

Alaniz, Rogelio. 2005. *Hombres y mujeres en tiempos de revolucion: de Vertiz a Rosas*. Santa Fe Univ. Nacional de Litoral.

Alba Carosio. 2010. "Las mujeres en el proceso independentista." *Centro de Estudios de la Mujer*, August 7. http://www.rebelion.org/noticia_pdf.php?id=109320.

Chasteen, John Charles. 2009. *Americanos: Latin America's Struggle for Independence*. New York: Oxford University Press.

Cook, Bernard A. 2006. *Women and War: A Historical Encyclopedia from Antiquity to the Present*, vol. 2. Santa Barbara, CA: ABC-Clio.

Crespo, Luis S. 1928. "Juana Azurduy de Padilla." *El Diario*, March 8. Translated by Bolivian Thoughts in an Emerging World, March 12, 2014. https://bolivianthoughts.com/2014/03/12/bolivia-history-101-juana-azurduy-de-padilla.

de la Torre, Arturo Costa. 1981. *La heroica Juana Azurduy de Padilla*. Bolivia: Casa Municipal de la Cultura.

Gorritti, Juana Manuela. 1995. "Juana Azurduy de Padilla." In *Rereading the Spanish American Essay: Translations of 19th and 20th Century Women's Essays*, translated by Mary G. Berg and edited by Doris Meyer. Austin, TX: University of Texas Press.

Hall, Linda B. 2004. *Mary, Mother, and Warrior: The Virgin in Spain and the Americas*. Austin, TX: University of Texas Press.

Mackenzie, Charlotte. 2015. "Bolivian Independence Statue to Replace Christopher Columbus." *Latin Correspondent*, July. http://latincorrespondent.com/2015/07/bolivian-independence-statue-replace-christopher-columbus.

Marion, Javier F. 1997. "Inkarra Myths and Class Conflict: An Interpretive Study of Juana Azurduy de Padilla's Life as Seen Through Late Colonial Currents." Thesis, Master of Arts History, University of New Mexico.

Smith, Bonnie G., ed. 2008. *The Oxford Encyclopedia of Women in World History*. Oxford: Oxford University Press.

Torres, Norberto Benjamín. 2016. "Juana Asurdui de Padilla (1780–1862)." *La historia detrás de la leyenda*. Sucre: Ciencia Editores.

## Kate Leigh and Tilly Devine

"Bailed Up with Revolver." 1914. *Evening News* (Sydney, NSW), June 10.

"Beer and Whisky Under Floor." 1943. *The Age*, May 25.

"Into Cells Again." 1930. *Truth*, October 12.

"Kate Leigh Again." 1921. *Truth*, June 19.

Morton, James, and Susanna Lobez. 2010. *Gangland Australia*. Carlton: Melbourne University Press.

"Mystery Shooting." 1931. *Newcastle Morning Herald and Miners' Advocate*, December 12.

"Notorious Underworld Figure Does Not Fear for Life." 1930. *Truth*, April 13.

"Says Tilly to Kate." 1930. *Truth*, June 29.

Stanley, Peter. 2010. *Bad Characters: Sex, Crime, Mutiny, Murder, and the Australian Imperial Force*. Sydney: Murdoch Books.

"Tilly Devine 'Leighs' Down the Law to 'Truth.'" 1932. *Truth*, February 7.

Tough Nuts: Tilly Devine. https://www.youtube.com/watch?v=fUbfDS8vs2s.

"Two for Trial Over Shooting." 1960. *Sydney Morning Herald*, October 27.

Writer, Larry. 2011. *Razor*. Sydney: Pan Macmillan Australia.

## Man-deok Kim

Bak Jega. "Poem of Farewell to Mandeok, Returning to Jeju." *Jeongyukak Collection*. Translated by Jeanette Wu. http://ctext.org/library.pl?if=gb&file=154452&page=82.

Chae Jegong. 1824. *Pen-am Collection*. Translated by Jeanette Wu.

Gahwan, Yi. *Select Poems of the Greater Easter*. Translated by Jeanette Wu. http://blog.daum.net/yescheers/8597750.

Hilty, Anne. 2011. "Jeju's Female Icon of the Joseon Era." *The Jeju Weekly*, 24 June. http://www.jejuweekly.com/news/articleView.html?idxno=1691.

"Joseon's First Female CEO, Kim Man-deok." 2010. *KBS World Radio*, September 17. http://world.kbs.co.kr/english/archive/program/program_koreanstory.htm?no=20440.

Nosung, sim. *Biography of Gyeseom*. Translated by Jeanette Wu. http://163.239.1.207:8088/dl_image/IMG/03//000000014295/SERVICE/000000014295_01.PDF.

Sojung, Yoon. 2016. "Meet the Joseon Businesswoman Who Saved Jeju." *Korea.net*, March 14. http://www.korea.net/NewsFocus/Travel/view?articleId=133790.

Yang, Sung-kuk, and Bong-hyun Kim. 2012. "A Study on the Entrepreneurship of Kim Man Deok." *Management History* 27 (2): 235–58. Translated by Kina Park.

*Yeongjo Sillok*. Yeongjo 20 (1796), November 25.

## Marsha P. Johnson

Carter, David. 2013. *Stonewall: The Riots That Sparked the Gay Revolution*. New York: St. Martin's Press.

Cohen, Stephan. 2008. *The Gay Liberation Youth Movement in New York: "An Army of Lovers Cannot Fail."* New York: Routledge.

Kasino, Michael. 2012. "Frameline Voices—Pay It No Mind: The Life and Times of Marsha P. Johnson." https://www.youtube.com/watch?v=Bo0nYv9QIj4.

Rivera, Sylvia. 2007. "Sylvia Rivera's Talk at LGMNY, June 2001 Lesbian and Gay Community Services Center, New York City." *CENTRO Journal* 19 (1).

## Labotsibeni Gwamile LaMdluli

Genge, Manelisi. 1999. "Power and Gender in Southern African History: Power Relations in the Era of Queen Labotsibeni Gwamile Mdluli of Swaziland, ca. 1875–1921: Volume I." Dissertation, Michigan University State.

Ginindza, Thoko. 1997. "Labotsibeni/Gwamile Mdluli: The Power Behind the Swazi Throne, 1875–1925. *Annals of the New York Academy of Sciences*, 810 (1, June): 135–58.

Kanduza, Ackson M. 2003. Introduction to "Queen Regent Labotsibeni: Address to the Resident Commissioner." In *Women Writing Africa: The Southern Region*, edited by M. J. Daymond, Dorothy Driver, Sheila Meintjes, Leloba Molema, Chiedza Musengezi, Margie Orford, and Nobantu, Rasebotsa. New York: Feminist Press at the City University of New York.

Kanduza, Ackson M. 2001. "'You Are Tearing My Skirt': Labotsibeni Gwamile LaMdluli." *Agency and Action in Colonial Africa*, edited by Chris Youé and Tim Stapleton. New York: Palgrave.

LaMdluli, Labotsibeni Gwamile. 1921. "Queen Regent Labotsibeni: Address to the Resident Commissioner," translated by Josiah Vilakati. In *Women Writing Africa: The Southern Region*, edited by M. J. Daymond, Dorothy Driver, Sheila Meintjes, Leloba Molema, Chiedza Musengezi, Margie Orford, and Nobantu, Rasebotsa. New York: Feminist Press at the City University of New York, 2003.

## Madam C. J. Walker (Sarah Breedlove)
Bundles, A'Lelia. 2002. *On Her Own Ground: The Life and Times of Madam C. J. Walker*. New York: Washington Square Press.

Freeman, Tyrone McKinley. 2014. "Gospel of Giving: The Philanthropy of Madam C. J. Walker, 1867–1919." Indiana University Lilly Family School of Philanthropy, October.

## Mandukhai Khatun
Vago, Mike. 2017. "China Expanded the Great Wall to Keep This Female Warrior Out." *AV Club*, July 2. http://www.avclub.com/article /china-expanded-great-wall-keep-female -warrior-out-257450.

Weatherford, Jack. 2011. *The Secret History of the Mongol Queens*. New York: Random House.

## Marie Equi
Abbott, Karen. 2014. "'The Hatpin Peril' Terrorized Men Who Couldn't Handle the 20th-Century Woman." *Smithsonian*, April 24. http://www.smithsonianmag.com/history /hatpin-peril-terrorized-men-who-couldnt -handle-20th-century-woman-180951219.

Helquist, Michael. 2015. *Marie Equi: Radical Politics and Outlaw Passions*. Corvallis, OR: Oregon State University Press.

## Masako Hōjō
Benton, Margaret Fukuzawa. 1991. *Heroic with Grace: Legendary Women of Japan*, edited by Chieko Irie Mulhern. Armonk, NY: M.E. Sharpe.

## The Mirabal Sisters
Goncalvez, Vansan. 2011. "In the Time of the Butterflies: Rewriting Dominican History Through the Demythologization of the Mirabal Sisters." *e-scrita* 2 (6): 88–99.

Robinson, Nancy. 2006. "Women's Political Participation in the Dominican Republic: The Case of the Mirabal Sisters." *Caribbean Quarterly* 52 (2/3): 172–83.

## Molly Craig
Pilkington, Doris. 1996. *Follow the Rabbit-Proof Fence*. New York: Hyperion.

## Mother Lü
*Book of the Later Han—Volume 11: Liu Penzi Biography*. Translated by Jeanette Wu. http:// ctext.org/hou-han-shu/liu-xuan-liu-pen-zi -lie-zhuan.

Hinsch, Bret. 2011. *Women in Early Imperial China*. Lanham, MD: Rowman and Littlefield Publishers.

Rodriguez, Junius P. 2007. *Encyclopedia of Slave Resistance and Rebellion*, vol. 2. Westport, CT: Greenwood Press.

## Mother Jones (Mary Harris Jones)
Gorn, Elliott J. 2002. *Mother Jones: The Most Dangerous Woman in America*. New York: Hill and Wang.

Roberts, Rachel. 2017. "International Women's Day 2017: Five Things You Need to Know." *The Independent*, March 8. http://www. independent.co.uk/news/uk/home-news /international-womens-day-2017-iwd-when -is-it-what-happens-everything-to-know -explained-a7617266.html.

## Naziq al-Abid
Akbik, Azza. 2011. "Naziq al-Abid, The Story of a Female Damascene Campaigner." *eSyria*, November 3.

"Behind the Legends / Naziq al-Abed." 2011. *Syria Today*, April 29. Translated by Nadia Muhanna. https://nadiamuhanna.wordpress .com/2011/04/29/behind-the-legends-naziq -al-abed.

Moubayed, Sami M. 2005. *Steel & Silk : Men & Women Who Shaped Syria 1900–2000*. Seattle: Cune Press.

Thompson, Elizabeth. 2000. *Colonial Citizens: Republican Rights, Paternal Privilege, and Gender in French Syria and Lebanon*. New York: Columbia University Press.

## Olympias of Macedon

Carney, Elizabeth Donnelly. 2001. *Olympias: Mother of Alexander the Great.* Melbourne: Owl Pub.

Heckel, Waldemar. 2009. *Who's Who in the Age of Alexander the Great: Prosopography of Alexander's Empire.* Oxford: Wiley-Blackwell.

Plutarch. *Alexander.* Translated by Bernadotte Perrin. http://www.perseus.tufts.edu/hopper/text?doc=Perseus%3Atext%3A1999.01.0243.

## Pailadzo Captanian

Captanian, Pailadzo. 1919. *Mémoires d'une déportée Arménienne.* Paris: M. Flinikowski.

Nelson, Davia, and Nikki Silva. 2008. "The Birth of Rice-A-Roni: The San Francisco-Italian-Armenian Treat." *The Kitchen Sisters.* http://www.kitchensisters.org/fugitivewaves/episode-20.

Pailadzou Captanian. *Find A Grave.* https://www.findagrave.com/cgi-bin/fg.cgi?page=gr&GRid=92251086.

## Ranavalona I

Campbell, Gwyn. 2012. *David Griffiths and the Missionary "History of Madagascar."* Leiden: Brill.

Kamhi, Alison. 2002. "Perceptions of Ranavalona I: A Malagasy Historic Figure as a Thematic Symbol of Malagasy Attitudes Toward History." *Stanford Undergraduate Research Journal*, May.

Laidler, Keith. 2005. *The Female Caligula: Ranavalona, the Mad Queen of Madagascar.* Hoboken, NJ: John Wiley & Sons.

## Rebecca Lukens

Drachman, Virginia G. 2002. *Enterprising Women: 250 Years of American Business.* Chapel Hill: University of North Carolina Press.

Jepson, Jill Christine. 2009. *Women's Concerns: Twelve Women Entrepreneurs of the Eighteenth and Nineteenth Centuries.* New York: Peter Lang.

Lach, Edward L., Jr. 2000. "Lukens, Rebecca Webb Pennock." *American National Biography Online*, February. http://www.anb.org/articles/10/1001035.html.

Michels, Kat. 2014. "Heroines of History: Rebecca Lukens—An Ironclad Matriarch." *Business Heroine Magazine*, March 14. http://businessheroinemagazine.com/rebecca-lukens.

Scheffer, Judith. 1999. "'. . . There Was Difficulty and Danger on Every Side': The Family and Business Leadership of Rebecca Lukens." *Pennsylvania History: A Journal of Mid-Atlantic Studies* 66 (3).

## Sister Rosetta Tharpe

Freedman, Samuel G. 2012. "Using Gospel Music's Secrets to Confront Black Homophobia." *New York Times*, June 1. http://www.nytimes.com/2012/06/02/us/gospel-music-book-challenges-black-homophobia.html.

Heilbut, Anthony. 2012. *The Fan Who Knew Too Much: Aretha Franklin, the Rise of the Soap Opera, Children of the Gospel Church, and Other Meditations.* New York: Alfred A. Knopf.

Wald, Gayle. 2007. *Shout, Sister, Shout!: The Untold Story of Rock-and-Roll Trailblazer Sister Rosetta Tharpe.* Boston: Beacon Press.

## Sojourner Truth

Accomando, Christina. 2003. "Demanding a Voice Among the Pettifoggers: Sojourner Truth as Legal Actor." *MELUS: Multi-Ethnic Literature of the U.S.* 28 (1): 61–86.

Goldner, Ellen J. 2012. "The Art of Intervention: The Humor of Sojourner Truth and the Antebellum Political Cartoon." *MELUS: Multi-Ethnic Literature of the U.S.* 37 (4): 41–67.

Mandziuk, Roseann M. 2014. "'Grotesque and Ludicrous, but Yet Inspiring': Depictions of Sojourner Truth and Rhetorics of Domination." *Quarterly Journal of Speech* 100 (4): 467–87.

McKissack, Patricia C., and Fredrick McKissack, Jr. 1904. *Sojourner Truth: Ain't I a Woman?* New York: Scholastic.

## Sacajawea

Colby, Susan M. 2009. *Sacagawea's Child: The Life and Times of Jean-Baptiste (Pomp)*

Charbonneau*. Norman, OK: University of Oklahoma Press.

Johnson, Thomas H., and Helen S. Johnson. 2008. *Also Called Sacajawea: Chief Woman's Stolen Identity*. Long Grove, IL: Waveland Press, Inc.

Kehoe, Alice. 2016. "'Revenant' Is Right About Native Free-Born Women." *Indian Country Today*, February 22. https:// indiancountrymedianetwork.com/news /opinions/revenant-is-right-about-native -free-born-women.

Sandon, Robert A. 2003. *Explorations into the World of Lewis and Clark*, vol. 2. Great Falls: Lewis and Clark Trail Heritage Foundation.

Schultz, James Willard. 1918. *Bird Woman: The Guide of Lewis and Clark*. New York: Houghton Mifflin Company.

Shure, Natalie. 2015. "The Mystery of Sacagawea." *BuzzFeed News*, October 11. https://www.buzzfeed.com/natalieshure/how -the-west-was-wrong-the-two-sacagaweas.

Stamm, Henry E. 2012. "A History of Shoshone-Bannock Indian Art: Continuity & Change in the Northern Rockies. *Chief Washakie Foundation*. https://web.archive.org/web/2012 0514044112/http://www.windriverhistory.org /exhibits/ShoshoneArt/index.html.

## Savitribai Phule

Devare, Aparna. 2011. *History & the Making of a Modern Hindu Self*. New Delhi: Routledge.

Jalli, Indira. 2011. "*Krantijyoti* (The Lamp of Revolution) (Mid-1800s)." *Feminist Writings from Ancient Times to the Modern World: A Global Sourcebook and History*, edited by Tiffany K. Wayne. Santa Barbara, CA: Greenwood.

Mani, Braj Ranjan. 2012. "A Life Lived Well, and Lessons Thereof." *Round Table India*, September 5. http://roundtableindia.co .in/index.php?option=com_content&view =article&id=5680:a-life-lived-well-and -lessons-thereof-18500&catid=118:thought &Itemid=131.

Pai, Suchismita. 2013. "India: Savitribai, The Mother of Modern Girls' Education." *Women's Feature Service*, February 25. New Delhi.

Rao, Anupama. 2009. *The Caste Question: Dalits and the Politics of Modern India*. Berkeley, CA: University of California Press.

"Savitribai Phule's 186th Birth Anniversary Commemorated by Google Doodle." 2017. *Firstpost*, January 3. http://www.firstpost .com/tech/news-analysis/savitribai-phules -186th-birth-anniversary-commemorated-by -google-doodle-3695225.html.

Wolf, Thom, and Suzana Andrade. 2011. "Changing Education: A Note on the 'Original and Unusual' Worldvoice, Worldview, and Worldvenue of Jan Comenius and Savitribai Phule." *Journal of Applied Christian Leadership* 5 (2):78–104.

Zubaan and Malvika Asher. "Savitribai Phule." *Google Arts & Culture*. https://www.google .com/culturalinstitute/beta/u/0/exhibit /UwKCW6eHcTWSLg.

## Sor Juana Inés de la Cruz

de la Cruz, Juana Inés. 1997. "Response by the Poet to the Most Illustrious Sister Filotea de la Cruz." *Poems, Protest, and a Dream: Selected Writings*, translated by Margaret Sayers Peden and Ilan Stavans. London: Penguin.

Kirk, Pamela. 1999. *Sor Juana Ines de La Cruz: Religion, Art, and Feminism*. New York: Continuum.

Paz, Octavio. 1988. *Sor Juana*. Cambridge: Harvard University Press.

## Soraya Tarzi

Ahmed-Ghosh, Huma. 2013. "A History of Women in Afghanistan: Lessons Learnt for the Future or Yesterdays and Tomorrow: Women in Afghanistan." *Journal of International Women's Studies* 4 (3): 1–14.

Alikuzai, Hamid. 2013. *A Concise History of Afghanistan—Central Asia and India in 25 Volumes*, vol. 10. Oklahoma: Trafford Publishing.

Ansary, Tamim. 2012. *Games Without Rules: The Often Interrupted History of Afghanistan*. New York: Public Affairs.

Fitzgerald, Paul, and Elizabeth Gould. 2009. *Invisible History: Afghanistan's Untold Story*. San Francisco: City Lights Books.

Ghaus, Abdul Samad. 1988. *The Fall of Afghanistan: An Insider's Account*. Washington: Pergamon-Brassey's.

Gregorian, Vartan. 1969. *The Emergence of Modern Afghanistan: Politics of Reform and Modernization, 1880–1946*. Stanford: Stanford University Press.

"Queen Soraya." 2004. *Mahmud Tarzi*. http://www.mahmudtarzi.com/type1.php?menu_id=43.

Sitara. 2015. "The Unfulfilled Dream of the Afghan Human Rights Queen." *Afghan Women's Writing Project, August*. http://awwproject.org/2015/08/the-unfulfilled-dream-of-the-afghan-human-rights-queen.

Stewart, Rhea Talley. 1973. *Fire in Afghanistan, 1914–1929: Faith, Hope, and the British Empire*. New York: Doubleday.

Tanwir, M. Halim. 2013. *Afghanistan: History, Diplomacy, and Journalism*, vol. 1. Bloomington, IN: Xlibris.

Tomsen, Peter. 2013. *The Wars of Afghanistan: Messianic Terrorism, Tribal Conflicts, and the Failures of Great Powers*. New York: Public Affairs.

Tuck, Christopher. 2016. *British Propaganda and Wars of Empire: Influencing Friend and for 1900–2010*. New York: Routledge.

## Susan La Flesche Picotte

Ewing, Rachel A. 2013. "From India, Japan, and Syria, 19th-Century Women Who Trekked to Philadelphia for Medical School." *Drexel University News Blog*, July 24. https://newsblog.drexel.edu/2013/07/24/from-india-japan-and-syria-19th-century-women-who-trekked-to-philadelphia-for-medical-school.

Gould, Suzanne. 2013. "College Doesn't Make You Infertile: AAUQ's 1885 Research." *American Association of University Women*, May 13. http://www.aauw.org/2013/05/13/college-doesnt-make-you-infertile.

"Picotte Memorial Hospital." 2001. *National Park Service*. https://www.nps.gov/nr/feature/indian/2001/picotte.htm.

Starita, Joe. 2016. *A Warrior of the People: How Susan La Flesche Overcame Racial and Gender Inequality to Become America's First Indian Doctor*. New York: St. Martin's Press.

Vaughan, Carson. 2017. "The Incredible Legacy of Susan La Flesche, the First Native American to Earn a Medical Degree." *Smithsonian*, March 1. http://www.smithsonianmag.com/history/incredible-legacy-susan-la-flesche-first-native-american-earn-medical-degree-180962332.

## Sutematsu Ōyama

"Guide to the Sutematsu Yamakawa Oyama Papers, 1872–1983 (bulk 1882–1919)." *Archives & Special Collections Library, Vassar College*. http://specialcollections.vassar.edu/collections/manuscripts/findingaids/oyama_sutematsu.html.

Nimura, Janice P. 2015. *The Daughters of the Samurai: A Journey from East to West and Back*. New York: W.W. Norton & Company.

## Tamar of Georgia

Eastmond, Antony. 1998. *Royal Imagery in Medieval Georgia*. Pennsylvania: Pennsylvania State University Press.

Fraser, Antonia. 2004. *The Warrior Queens*. New York: Anchor Books.

## Te Ao-Kapurangi

Ballara, Angela. "Te Ao-kapurangi," first published in the *Dictionary of New Zealand Biography*, vol. 1, 1990. *Te Ara—The Encyclopedia of New Zealand*. Accessed August 28, 2017. https://teara.govt.nz/en/biographies/1t25/te-ao-kapurangi.

Ballara, Angela. "Te Wera Hauraki," first published in the *Dictionary of New Zealand Biography*, vol. 1, 1990. *Te Ara—the Encyclopedia of New Zealand*. Accessed August 28, 2017. https://teara.govt.nz/en/biographies/1t83/te-wera-hauraki.

"How Aokapurangi Saved Her People." 1962. *Te Ao Hou* no. 41, December.

Smith, Percy S. 1910. *Maori Wars of the Nineteenth Century*. New York: Cambridge University Press. http://nzetc.victoria.ac.nz/tm/scholarly/tei-SmiMaor-t1-body-d37.html.

## Trinidad Tecson

Boyer, Robert H. 2010. *Sundays in Manila.* Diliman, Quezon City: University of the Philippines Press.

de Guzman, Jovita Varias. 1967. *Women of Distinction: Biographical Essays on Outstanding Filipino Women of the Past and Present.* Manila: Bukang Liwayway.

*Filipinos in History,* vol. 2. 1989. National Historical Institute.

Romulo, Lovely Tecson. 1995. "Trinidad Tecson Y Perez." *Women in the Philippine Revolution,* edited by Rafaelita Hilario Soriano. Quezon City: R.H. Soriano.

Santos, Aida F. 2004. "Do Women Really Hold Up Half the Sky?: Notes on the Women's Movement in the Philippines." *Gender, Culture, & Society: Selected Readings in Women's Studies in the Philippines,* edited by Carolyn I. Sobitchea. Seoul: Ewha Womans University Press.

Shaw, Angel Velasco, and Luis H. Francia. 2002. *Vestiges of War: The Philippine-American War and the Aftermath of an Imperial Dream 1899–1999.* New York: New York University Press.

Yoder, Robert L. 1998. "Philippines Heroines of the Revolution: Maria Clara They Were Not." July 16. Universitat Wien. http://www.univie.ac.at/ksa/apsis/aufi/wstat/heroine.htm.

## Velu Nachiyar

Jayakumar, K. 2013. *Sacrifices and Sufferings of Velu Nachiyar—First Woman Freedom Fighter of India.* Golden Research Thoughts.

*Journeys English Course Book 6.* Mumbai: Pearson Education India.

Rajesh, K. Guru. 2015. *Sarfarosh: A Naadi Exposition of the Lives of Indian Revolutionaries.* Chennai: Notion Press.

"Remembering Queen Velu Nachiyar of Sivagangai, the First Queen to Fight the British." 2017. *The News Minute,* January 3. http://www.thenewsminute.com/article/remembering-queen-velu-nachiyar-sivagangai-first-queen-fight-british-55163.

Venkatarama Ayyar, K. R. 1938. *A Manual of the Pudukkóttai State.* Chennai: Sri Brihadamba State Press, Director of Museums, Government of Tamilnadu, 2002–2004.

## Vera Peters

Belanger, Susan. 2015. "Vera Peters, Quiet Revolutionary." *University of Toronto Faculty of Medicine.* October. http://medicine.utoronto.ca/magazine/article/dr-m-vera-peters.

Catton, J., and P. Catton. 2006. "Vera Peters: Medical Innovator." *Framing Our Past: Constructing Canadian Women's History in the Twentieth Century,* edited by Sharon Anne Cook, Lorna R McLean, and Kate O'Rourke. Montreal: McGill-Queen's University Press.

Cowan, D. H. 2008. "Vera Peters and the Curability of Hodgkin Disease." *Current Oncology* 11 (5).

Davis, Craig. 2010. *Dr. Vera Peters Canadian Medical Hall of Fame Laureate 2010.* https://www.youtube.com/watch?v=zHEa6etcGHQ.

"How Vera Peters Revolutionized Treatments for Hodgkin's, Breast Cancer." 2015. *CBC News,* January 11. http://www.cbc.ca/m/touch/health/story/1.2893406.

Lemar, Barron H. 2003. *The Breast Cancer Wars: Hope, Fear, and the Pursuit of a Cure in Twentieth-Century America.* New York: Oxford University Press.

Peters, Vera. 1973. "Treatment of Primary Breast Cancer: A Radiotherapist's View." *Audio-Digest Surgery* 20 (2).

Reinhard-Reiss, Joan, and Sarah S. Donaldson. 2015. "Homage to M. Vera Peters, MD." *International Journal of Radiation Oncology* 92 (1).

Wells, Karin. 2015. "Vera Peters, MD." *CBC News,* January 8. http://www.cbc.ca/news/vera-peters-md-1.2894072.

## Zelia Nuttall

Adams, Amanda. 2010. *Ladies of the Field: Early Women Archaeologists and Their Search for Adventure.* Berkeley, CA: Greystone Books.

Nuttall, Zelia. "The Island of Sacrificios." *American Anthropologist: New Series* 12 (12): 257–95.

# Index

## A

Abzug, Bella, *22*, 23–27
Afghanistan, 155–58, 194, 196
al-Abid, Naziq, *62*, 63–65
al-Sulayhi, Arwa, *178*, 179–81, 193n
Amanirenas, *28*, 29–31
Ao-Kapurangi, Te, *4*, 5–6
Argentina, 203–5
Armenia, 207–9
Australia, 77–79, 214–18
Austria, 141, 144

## B

Bhutto, Benazir, 193–97, *195*
Blackjack, Ada, 89–95, *91*
Bolivia, 203–5
Borneo, 142
Brazil, 123, 125, 199–201
bullsh*t
    attacks on reputation, 2, 8, 23, 37, 40,
        43–44, 58, 64, 87, 94, 108–9, 146–48,
        151–52, 156, 163–65, 172–73, 184, 196,
        200–201, 217, 219–24
    body-shaming, 60, 175–77, 201
    governments behaving badly, 24–26, 36,
        63–64, 68, 76–79, 97–99, 111, 113–17,
        146–48, 157, 175–76, 183–96
    Jesus Christ just listen to women already,
        11–12, 68, 94, 176, 186, 201, 204,
        217–18
    mediocre dudes to the front of the line,
        10–13, 18–19, 68, 72, 89–94, 131–35,
        165
    racism, 24–26, 57–61, 71 ,76–79, 82–83,
        85–86, 94, 104–5, 107, 146, 151–53,
        183–92, 207–8
    rewriting history, 30, 43–44, 94, 138,
        165, 180, 219–24
    sexism, 11, 20, 23–26, 46, 51–52, 63,
        67, 71–72, 108, 143, 165, 171–72,
        180

## C

Canada, 11–13, 43–44, 89–90
Captanian, Pailadzo, *206*, 207–9
China, 49–50, 138–39
colonialists being jerks, 1–3, 29–30, 71–75,
    85, 89–90, 92–95, 113–23, 125, 142–43,
    155–58, 167–69, 211–12, 219, 221,
    223–24
Craig, Molly, *76*, 77–79
Croatia, 45–46

## D

de Clisson, Jeanne, 130, 159–60, *161*
de Jesus, Carolina Maria, *198*, 199–201
de la Cruz, Sor Juana Inés, 51–55, *53*
de Padilla, Juana Azurduy, *202*, 203–205
des Odonais, Isabel Godin, *122*, 123–25
Devine, Tilly, *214*, 215–18
Dhien, Cut Nyak, *118*, 119–121
disability, 74, 83, 94, 120, 125, 138–39, 146,
    185
    developmental disability, 105, 163–65
divorce, 27, 34, 36, 67, 81, 156, 196, 201
    breakups from hell, 127–30, 171–73,
        217–18
Dominican Republic, 97–99

## E

Ecuador, 123–25
Egypt, 29
Eiríksdóttir, Freydís, *42*, 43–44
endings
    happy, 1–21, 66–75, 100–5, 136–39,
        170–73
    mixed, 22–44, 48–50, 56–65, 80–95,
        106–12, 113–17, 126–30, 150–53,
        159–61, 166–69, 178–81, 193–201,
        206–18
    sad, 45–47, 51–55, 76–79, 96–99, 118–25,
        131–35, 140–49, 154–58, 162–65,
        174–77, 182–92, 202–5, 219–25

England, 1–3, 6, 17, 30, 45, 89–91, 113–17, 127–30, 142, 151–52, 155–57, 159–60, 171, 193, 211–13, 216–17, 219
Equi, Marie, 36, 60, *106*, 107–112
era
  4th century BCE, 162–65
  1st century BCE, 28–31
  1st century CE, 48–50
  10th century CE, 42–44
  11th century CE, 178–81
  12th century CE, 14–17, 38–41, 170–173
  14th century CE, 126–30, 159–61
  15th century CE, 136–39
  17th century CE, 45–47, 51–55
  18th century CE, 7–9, 122–25, 131–35, 202–5, 210–13
  19th century CE, 1–6, 18–21, 56–61, 67–75, 84–87, 107–12, 118–21, 131–35, 140–44, 151–53, 202–5, 219–25
  20th century CE, 10–13, 22–27, 32–37, 62–69, 76–83, 89–117, 145–49, 154–58, 166–69, 174–77, 182–201, 206–9, 214–18

**F**

France, 63–64, 123–25, 127–30, 159–61

**G**

Georgia, 171–73
Greece, 163–65

**H**

Hamer, Fannie Lou, *182*, 183–87
Hōjō, Masako, *38*, 39–41
Hungary, 45–46

**I**

India, 142, 151–53, 210–13
Indonesia, 119–21, 142
Isabella of France, *126*, 127–30, 160n
Israel, 25

**J**

Japan, 85–87
Jigonhsaseh, *14*, 15–17

Jiménez, Angela, *100*, 101–5
Johnson, Marsha P., *174*, 175–77

**K**

Khatun, Mandukhai, *136*, 137–39
Kim, Man-deok, 7–8, *9*
Korea, 7–8, 40
  North Korea, 196–97
Kush, 29–31

**L**

La Flesche Picotte, Susan, *70*, 71–75
LaMdluli, Labotsibeni Gwamile, *xii*, 1–3
Leigh, Kate, *214*, 215–18
LGBT, 23, 51, 80–84, 107–112, 164, 175–77, 216–17
Lukens, Rebecca, *18*, 19–21

**M**

Madagascar, 143, 219–25
mental illness, 16, 90, 175–77
Mexico, 51–55, 67–69, 101–5
Mirabal Sisters, the (Minerva, Patria, Maria Teresa, and Dedé), *96*, 97–99
Mongolia, 40, 137–40
Mother Jones (Mary Harris Jones), 36, 110, 145–49, *147*
Mother Lü, *48*, 49–50, *50*
mothers
  adoptive, 8, 33–37, 67–69, 77–79, 85–87, 99, 101–112, 151–53, 176, 183–87, 203–5, 211–13
  best-ever, ix–x
  biological, 1–3, 11–13, 19–21, 29–41, 43–50, 57–61, 71–79, 85–87, 97–99, 119–21, 131–48, 159–69, 189–205, 214–25
  of countries, 1–3, 7–8, 15–17, 45–46, 63–65, 97–99, 137–41, 171–73, 193–97, 203–5, 219–25
  of inventions, 11–13, 33–37, 211–13
  of movements, 63–69, 81–87, 97–99, 151–53, 175–77, 203–5
  single mothers, 1–3, 18–21, 32–37, 56–61, 66–69, 70–75, 89–95, 104–105, 111–12, 118–21, 123, 137–38, 152–53, 159–61,

164–65, 172, 180–81, 198–201, 204–5, 208–9, 211–13, 215–18, 219–25

## N

Nachiyar, Velu, *210*, 211–13
names the *Eat, Pray, Love* crowd will appropriate, 1–2, 15–17, 29–31, 81, 95, 113, 127, 138, 167, 204, 208, 212
native folk, 5–6, 15–17, 43–44, 71–79, 89–95, 101–102, 105, 107–8, 125, 131–35, 203–5
necessity. *See* mothers: of inventions
Netherlands, 119–21
New Zealand, 5–6
Nigeria, 113–17
Norway, 43–44
Nuttall, Zelia, *66*, 67–69

## O

Olympias of Macedon, *162*, 163–65
Ōyama, Sutematsu, *84*, 85–88, 192n

## P

Pakistan, 193–97
Palestine, 25
Peters, Vera, *10*, 11–13, *13*
Pfeiffer, Ida Laura, *140*, 141–44, 223
Philippines, 167–69
Phule, Savitribai, *150*, 151–53
Poland, 189–92
Portugal, 123
pregnancy, 7, 19, 24, 39, 43–44, 72, 101, 128, 134, 139, 152, 157, 193–94, 200, 203–5, 208, 222–24
professions
  artistic/author, 51–55, 80–83, 142–43, 198–201, 206–9
  criminals, 159–61, 214–18
  education, 84–88, 113–17, 150–58
  entrepreneurs, 7–9, 18–21, 32–37, 80–83, 104–5, 214–18
  explorers, 42–44, 76–79, 84–88, 131–35, 140–44
    survivors, 89–95, 122–25
  medicine, 10–13, 70–75, 105–112, 189–92

revolutionaries/activists, 35–36, 45–50, 56–65, 96–105, 113–21, 145–53, 166–69, 182–92, 202–5, 211–13
royalty/politics, 1–7, 14–17, 28–31, 38–41, 84–88, 126–30, 136–39, 154–58, 162–65, 170–73, 178–81, 193–97, 210–13, 219–25
sex work, 7, 174–78
STEM, 10–13, 66–69
propaganda. *See* bullsh\*t: attacks on reputation

## Q

quotes that would go great on T-shirts, 2, 7, 22, 51–53, 58–59, 64, 111, 113–14, 120, 134

## R

Ranavalona I, 23, *140*, 143–44, 219–25, *220*
Ransome-Kuti, Funmilayo, 113–17, *115*
recursion. *See* recursion
religion
  Buddhism, 15, 40–41
  Catholicism, 97, 146, 189
  Christianity, 1, 29, 33–34, 44, 52–55, 58, 71, 81–83, 90, 93, 97, 125, 146, 151, 156, 172, 176, 184, 189, 203, 207, 219, 221, 224
  Greek gods, 163–65, 176
  Hinduism, 151–53
  Islam, 121–23, 155–58, 172, 179–81, 193, 196, 207
  Judaism, 23–27, 81, 189–92
  native religions, 15–17, 68–69, 71, 90, 114, 202–5, 219–25
  Norse religion, 44
  Quakers, 19–21
  weird snake cults that sound like a super fun time, 163–65
Rome, 29–31
Russia/USSR, 87, 92–93, 155–57, 196

## S

Sacajawea, 131–35, *133*
Scandinavia, 142
Scotland, 45

Sendler, Irena, *188*, 189–92
Sojourner Truth (Isabella Baumfree/"Belle"), *56*, 57–61, 184n, 186
Spain, 123
Spanish Flu, 88, 89, 111, 189
Spot. *See* Spot run; Run, Spot, run
Sudan, 29–31
suffrage, 59, 60, 63, 106, 110, 112, 113, 116, 146, 156–57, 183–86
Swaziland, 1–3
Switzerland, 197
Syria, 63–65, 208

## T

Tahiti, 142
Tamar of Georgia, *170*, 171–73
Tarzi, Soraya, *154*, 155–58, *158*, 194n
Tharpe, Sister Rosetta, *80*, 81–83
Transvaal, 1–3
Trinidad, Tecson, 111n, *166*, 167–69

## U

United States, 15–27, 33–37, 57–61, 63, 81–95, 97, 107–112, 131–35, 145–49, 157, 168–69, 175–77, 183–87, 192, 194–97, 207–8

## V

Venezuela, 97–98

## W

Walker, Madam C. J. (Sarah Breedlove), *32*, 33–37, 184n, 192n

## Y

Yemen, 179–81

## Z

Zrínyi, Ilona, 45–46, *47*

1. Labotsibeni LaMdluli
2. Te Ao-Kapurangi
3. Man-deok Kim
4. Vera Peters
5. Jigonhsaseh

6. Rebecca Lukens
7. Bella Abzug
8. Amanirenas
9. Madam C. J. Walker
10. Masako Hōjō

11. Freydís Eiríksdóttir
12. Ilona Zrínyi
13. Mother Lü
14. Sor Juana Inés de la Cruz
15. Sojourner Truth

16. Na
17. Zel
18. Sus
19. Mol
20. Sis

26. Funmilayo Ransome-Kuti
27. Cut Nyak Dhien
28. Isabel Godin des Odonais
29. Isabella of France
30. Sacajawea

31. Ida Laura Pfeiffer
32. Mandukhai Khatun
33. Mother Jones
34. Savitribai Phule
35. Soraya Tarzi

36. Jeanne de Clisson
37. Olympias of Macedon
38. Trinidad Tecson
39. Tamar of Georgia
40. Marsha P. Johnson

41. An
42. Fa
43. Ire
44. Be
45. Ca